HANSON, HENSON, HINSON, HYNSON

AND ALLIED FAMILY NAMES

VOLUME II
EARLY RECORDS OF THE
SOUTHEAST UNITED STATES

*Alabama, Florida, Georgia
and Mississippi*

COMPILED BY
Ethel Nerim Miner

HERITAGE BOOKS
2013

HERITAGE BOOKS

AN IMPRINT OF HERITAGE BOOKS, INC.

Books, CDs, and more—Worldwide

For our listing of thousands of titles see our website
at
www.HeritageBooks.com

Published 2013 by
HERITAGE BOOKS, INC.
Publishing Division
100 Railroad Ave. #104
Westminster, Maryland 21157

Other Heritage Books by the author:

Hanson, Henson, Hinson, Hynson and Allied Family Names

*Volume I: Early Records of the Midwest and Southwest United States,
including Arkansas, California, Illinois, Indiana, Iowa, Louisiana,
Michigan, Missouri, New Mexico, and Texas*

*Volume II: Early Records of the Southeast United States,
including Alabama, Florida, Georgia and Mississippi*

Volume III: Early Records of the Carolinas

Volume IV: Early Records of Kentucky and Tennessee

*Volume V: Early Records of the Mid-Atlantic States,
including Delaware, District of Columbia,
Maryland, Virginia, and West Virginia*

International Standard Book Numbers
Paperbound: 978-1-55613-828-7
Clothbound: 978-0-7884-6911-4

In Memory of Ethel Henson Nerim, 1897-1957
Who Held Our Family together

Dedicated to my husband, ED, without whose help and advice
this book would not have been possible

PREFACE

The research effort on which this book is based started about 1979 or 1980. *I was looking for an Indian...a Cherokee!* And that's all I knew. At that time I was involved in genealogical research for others and could not devote full time to this effort. However, in 1985 I went to work on the Hxnson line full time.

From my earliest recollections I remember my mother telling us that there was a Cherokee Indian in our family history. She said her father's grandfather was a full blooded Cherokee and he was buried on the reservation in Oklahoma. And that's all she knew. So I started to look. It's been a long time and I still haven't found him, but boy, did I find other Hxnsons. From our family history I knew that our ancestors probably were located in the Southeastern states of Alabama, Georgia, South Carolina and Tennessee. I found two works on Hxnsons. *A Henson Family History 1725 - 1850, by A. L. Henson, Independence, Mo. (now deceased)* and *These Irishmen Called Hanson by Ray Hanson, Bloomington, MN.* During my correspondence with these two gentlemen I was referred to J. J. Schefflin of Texarkana, TX. "JJ" had been researching the Hxnson line for many years and was interested in starting a Hanson Research Association. "JJ" and Harold Hinson of St. Louis, Missouri were able to generate enough interest to hold a meeting on the subject May 30, 31 1987 in St. Louis. At that meeting, which was attended by about 30 or so individuals the HHHH Research Associates was formed. The name HHHH was chosen to represent the Hansons, Hensons, Hinsons, and Hynsons and meant to include any other spelling of the name. During that meeting I agreed to work under my own auspices and as a separate entity apart from HHHH associates to compile any available information into a database. One of the most valuable contributions to my research on the Hxnson line is *Henson Pioneers by Les Henson, St. Cloud, MN.* I've compiled what I've gathered, not only from HHHH Research Associate members, but also from many other contributors into what I think is a useful document of over 23,000 records which may be helpful to those researching the Hxnson or related family names and I thought I ought to share it with you.

Meantime, I'll just keep looking for my Indian.

Ethel Nerim Miner
February 1993

COMPILER'S NOTES

The information listed in this publication was compiled from numerous sources plus contributions from many individuals, including members of the Hanson/Henson/Hinson/Hynson Research Associates. This database contains information from available source documents and family history records, mainly pre-1850, although some records later than that date are included. Much of this information has been gathered by various individuals over more than thirty years of research and I am deeply grateful to them for their contributions. It has taken more than seven years to compile.

Over the years I've worked with many different genealogical research formats and computer programs. The format used here is one I have devised myself to improve researchability of the information. All of the Hxnsons are listed alphabetically by firstname by state and then by eventdate, county/parish, and then city. All of the allied family names are listed in the Index. After working with this format for a number of years now I find that it is simply the best system I have ever worked with. When the information from the various sources is correct, everything dovetails together so completely that the researcher can get an immediate picture of a given family line. Conversely, when the information is incorrect (as is quite often the case) this format quickly reveals the conflict. This format was created to provide as much information to the researcher as possible and still facilitate printing of the information for proofreading and study. Some of the information will also lap across fields in order to provide continuity. For example, the EVENT field could show: birth(b), marriage(m), or death(d) and then contain additional information, which then may be combined with information shown in the SOURCE field. To illustrate, the first of the records shown under Examples indicates that Claud Henson was the son of Francis Marion, married to Fannie Barnes, was born 19 Jan 1885 in Stone County, Missouri, was the heir of Zacharia & Amanda, and died in 1964. The second record in the Examples Table is another example of combining the two fields, and indicates that George Henson was a Private in the Civil War, Co G of the 9th Missouri Infantry and the source was the National Archives Record Service. Although an attempt has been made to keep the entries as simple as possible and self-explanatory, in many cases the researcher may have to use intuition and experience to arrive at a conclusion regarding a specific entry. In cases where the individual's occupation is known and thought to be significant, the occupation will be shown as the first entry in the EVENT field. See the third record in the Examples Table. This record indicates that Jacob De(nnis) (in many cases the middle initial field will contain two letters to give the researcher a hint as to middle name; the same is also true of the FATHER field), Henson was the son of William Pe(rry), his mother's maiden name was Silvers, he was born in 1847 in Taney County Missouri as shown on page 270 of the 1850 Census, and undocumented information from a contributor indicates that he was a Preacher and that he probably relocated to Texas, with no dates known. As a further example of how the fields tie together let's take the last four examples below. Phillip Ol (the Ol in this field indicates this is the oldest person of that name in the file) Hinson was issued 640 Acres of land 02 May 1741 on the N Pee Dee in Bladen Co., NC. This entry appears in Craven Co., SC Bk5 p323. The next entry shows Charles the grandson of Old Phillip was born 21 Jun 1763 in Cheraws SC. The source was Charles Revolutionary War Pension #7014 however, Cheraws was not created until 1769 so we know Charles was actually born in Bladen Co., NC! The next entry for Old Phillip shows his 640 Acres of land was entered 20 May 1772 on the N Pee Dee in Craven Co., SC! The final entry for Old Phillip shows his will dated 21 Jan 1777 at St Davids, Kershaw SC! These examples are intended to give you hints on how to read and interpret the data. It also shows the importance of knowing what counties were in existence during each time period. Once you've worked with this format for awhile I think you will agree with me that all genealogical records should be compiled in this fashion. If you want to show family trees and group sheets the information is easily extracted for use in other programs or for other research purposes.

EXAMPLES
(for illustration only, may not be part of the main text)

LN	FIRSTNAME	IO	FATHER	MOM_SPOUSE	EVENT	EVENTDATE	CITY	COUNTY_PAR	ST	SOURCE
He	Claud		Francis Ma	_Barnes Fannie	b heir of d1964	19 Jan 1885	Cape Fair	Stone	MO	Zacharia&Ai
He	George				War Cvl CoB Pvt	1863			MO	Colemans CA
He	Jacob	De	William Pe	Silvers_Carney Mariah	Preacher b	1847		Taney	MO	TX t 1850C :
Hi	Phillip	Ol			L 640 iss	02 May 1741	N Pee Dee	Bladen	NC	SC Crav Bk5
Hi	Phillip	Ol		_ Mary	b of gs Chas	21 Jun 1763		Cheraws	SC	#7014 Pen of
Hi	Phillip	Ol			L 640 Acr ent	20 May 1772	N Pee Dee	Craven	SC	NC Blad 17'
Hi	Phillip	Ol		_Mary	w	21 Jan 1777	St Davids	Kershaw	SC	Bk A1 p148

There are eleven fields in the database. They are:

1. **LN**. Lastname showing the first two letters of the surname Hanson/Henson/Hinson/Hynson.

2. **FIRSTNAME**. (This is the first index field)

3. **IO** . (Second index field.) Initial only. If a number one (1) appears first in this space it indicates this person was an immigrant to America. If Ol is shown this indicates this person is the Oldest person by that name. In some cases this field will show two letters such as Ja, which means the persons middle name was James.

4. **FATHER**. Where room permits, and if the information is known, part or all of the fathers middle name will be listed.

5. **MOM_SPOUSE**. The maiden name of the mother is shown first. If it is not available, her Christian name is shown. Following the underscore _ the name of this person's spouse appears. A number following the spouse indicates first, second, third, etc. marriage.

6. **EVENT**. This field can contain numerous information and may also be linked with the source field to provide continuity to the information. (See examples)

7. **EVENTDATE**. (Third index field.)

8. **CITY**.

9. **COUNTY_PAR**. (PAR = Parish) (Fifth index field.)

10. **ST**. (State) (Fourth index field.)

11. **SOURCE**. Where the information was obtained. If this space is empty caution should be used in accepting the information as fact. May be combined with information from the event field to provide more meaningful information. If no original source is shown that probably means the information was submitted by a contributor from a family history or similar source. (See examples which show how this field may be combined with the event field.)

ABBREVIATIONS:

@	Altered record		hist	History
Acr	Acre		IGI	International Genealogical Index
AIS	Accelerated Indexing System		Ire	Ireland
Atty	Attorney		imig	Immigrant/Immigrated
acc	Accused		ind	Indian
adj	Adjacent		indx	Index
aka	Also Known As		inf	Infantry
app	Appointed		iss	Issued
b	Born		L	Land
bapt	Baptist		Luth	Lutheran
bro	Brother		lttr	Letter
bur	Buried		Meth	Methodist
C	Census		Mex	Mexican
Cher	Cherokee		m	Married
Chur	Church		merc	Merchant
COD	Cause of Death		mom	Mother
Co#	Company Number,e.g., Company A		mort	Mortality
Conf	Confederate		NARS	National Archive Records Service
c	Christened		neph	Nephew
cath	Catholic		ord	Order
cem	Cemetary		PAR	Parish
cit	Citizen		POW	Prisoner of War
cons	Consent		Preb	Presbyterian
cvl	Civil		Prot	Protestant
d	Died		res	Residence/Resides
dau	Daughter		rev	Revolutionary
dece	Decedent		Skan	Skandanavian
Eng	England		SLA	State Library Archives
Epis	Episcopalian		sched	Schedule
Evan	Evangelical		sis	Sister
ent	Entered		sur	Surname
est	Estate		t	To.
f	From or Female		t?	Means "Probably relocated to:"
fam	Family		unc	Uncle
Germ	German		unm	Unmarried
GS	Genealogical Society		WAC	Whites Among the Cherokees
gd	Grand-daughter		w	Will
gs	Grandson		wid	Widow
guard	Guardian		wit	Witness
HS	Historical Society			

INTRODUCTION

Hxnsons* have played an important role in America's history from its earliest beginnings. Our ancestors came from of England, Ireland, Scotland, Holland, Germany, and Sweden (and indeed, from probably every other European country.)...*and some were already here!* In the Northeast the Abenakis, Algonquins, Mohawks, and Mohicans; the Hurons, Senecas, and Iroquois; and in the Southeast the great nations of the Creek and the Cherokee; and on the Great Plains, the Blackhawk, Pawnee, Shawnee, and Sioux, and in the West the Apache, Cheyennes, Cree, Blackfoot, Crow and Comanche. And all of the other hundreds of Indian tribes that inhabited this great country. Intermarriage between the Indians and the Settlers was a common occurrence, hence many of us can include members of these tribes among our ancestors. *I know I can*, I just haven't made the connection yet.

Hxnsons were in America certainly pre-1700. How much earlier we're not sure. A George Henson was certainly among the first of the clan in this country. The Virginia Land Records show that George was born pre-1672 and that he was of age and a witness to a land transaction in Richmond, Virginia in 1693. The Virginia Land Records show that a George Henson had Indians buried on his land in 1677, *Book D, Part 3, pages 288-289, of the Westmoreland, Virginia Land Records.* The records are full of Hxnsons from that time on. One of the most important early Hxnson's was John Hanson, 1721 - 1783. He was one of the American Revolutionary leaders and is mentioned in *Old Kent, The Eastern Shore of Maryland, (The Most Ancient Records of Kent County, Maryland), originally published in Baltimore, 1876, and republished by Regional Publishing Company, Baltimore, Md, 1967,* "John Hanson was elected to the Continental Congress and presented his Credentials 22nd Feb'y 1781, was elected President of the Congress Nov 5th following which position he filled for one year....General George Washington, upon his return from Philadelphia after the surrender of Lord Cornwallis was received by Congress, and welcomed in a congratulatory address by President Hanson." Encyclopedia Brittanica says of this John Hanson "he was sometimes referred to as the first president of our country...but he never had the sweeping powers of a president elected under the Constitution." Another Hxnson who was infuential in the early history of America was Alexander C., who was editor of the *Georgetown "Federal Register" (Md)* during the War of 1812. There are other early Hxnsons , and while not as famous, perhaps just as interesting. For example, early records show that a "Henson" picked up the body of Jesse James in Missouri, presumably for burial, but no other information is available regarding this incident. Almost as soon as the Hxnsons settled in the Eastern part of the country they began a fan migration to the West. Some went North, others, South, and others even more West. Other early records show that in 1849 in El Morro, New Mexico an "A Henson", an "A W Hanson", and a "W Hanson" carved their names in Inscription Rock which is located in what is now Inscription Rock National Park. We know nothing else about them but it seems logical that they may have been headed for the gold fields of California. Yes, Hxnsons were pervasive throughout the history of this country and with these Volumes we hope to catalogue their existence.

*Although this research document is devoted to Hansons, Hensons, Hinsons, and Hynsons, it should not be considered to apply to only those spellings of the name. Other spellings may exist and may apply to the information contained here. We all know that early in the history of this country that misspellings and mispronunciations occurred, and quite often changes in spelling were made simply on a whim. Last name spelling, then, should not be a reason to discard the information. From now on in this Preface unless a specific spelling is definitely known, I'll simply refer to the name as Hxnson and imply it to mean any spelling of the name

TABLE OF CONTENTS

ALABAMA

LN	FIRSTNAME	IO	FATHER	MOM_SPOUSE	EVENT	EVENTDATE	CITY	COUNTY_PAR	ST	SOURCE
Hi				_Nancy	Wid bres of Streater	1775			NC	AL Barb 1860C #971
He					Indian Commissioner	1827	Ind Ter	Jackson	AL	Spies of Blue & Gray
He					Indian Commission d	1839		Jackson	AL	Spies of Blue & Gray
He				_Elizabeth	C wid	1840		Walker	AL	12000 21001 p284
Hi				_Gathings Lucy	w of Sampson Gathing	1845		Monroe	MS	AL Bald Lucy of
Hi			William	Cole	b male	1849				AL Walk 1850C
He				_Ann	C wid	1850				AL Mobi p435
He				_Louisa	C wid	1850				AL Jeff p163
He				_Margarett	C wid	1850				AL Walk p300
He				_Mary	C wid	1850				AL Rand p291
He				_Nancy	C wid	1850				AL Shel p251
Hi				_Sarah A	C wid	1850		Choc	AL	p171
He				_Emaline	C wid	1850		Jefferson	AL	p160
Hi				_Mary	C wid	1850	Mobile	Mobile	AL	p435
He				_Ann	C wid	1850		Mobile	AL	p435
Hi				_Jane E	C wid	1850	Marion	Perry	AL	p378
He	A				War Cvl Conf CoD	1863			AL	11thCav NARS
Hi	A	C			C Artless?	1840		Wilcox	AL	p312
He	Aaron			_Thompson Mary	m				AL	
Hi	Aaron			_Watkins Mary Ann wid	m	16 Aug 1827		Bibb	AL	BkA p178
Hi	Aaron				w	03 Jul 1830		Bibb	AL	Deed BkA p127
Hi	Aaron				C	1830		Bibb	AL	p158
Hi	Aaron			_ Sumberlin M J	b	1833			NC	AL Mare 1860C
He	Aaron				b War Cvl 43ALInf	1841			GA	AL Wash res
Hi	Aaron			_Sumberlin Mourning J	m	07 Apr 1857		Wilcox	AL	
He	Aaron				War Cvl Conf CoB enl	15 May 1862		Marengo	AL	43rdInf NARS
He	Aaron				res War Cvl Conf Pvt	15 May 1862		Washington	AL	43Inf CoB
Hi	Aaron	M	Needham	_Price Nancy	m	27 Feb 1853	Clayton	Barbour	AL	
Hi	Aaron	M	Needham	Lanney_Price Nancy	LG 79 Acr	01 Nov 1858		Barbour	AL	#21574
Hi	Aaron	M	Needham	Lanney_Price Nancy	War Cvl CoB 57th Rgt	1863	Clayton	Barbour	AL	AL Lown Pen Appl
He	Aaron	M	Needham	Lanney_Price Nancy	War Cvl Conf POW d	13 Dec 1863	Greenville	Butler	AL	CoB 57thRgt
He	Aaron	M	Needham	Lanney_Price Nancy	Wid War Cvl Pen App	1900			AL	COD War Cvl
He	Abner	H	John C Sr	Murray_Elvira	b	1805			SC	AL Mari 1830C p176
He	Abner	H	John C Sr	_Elvira	C 20-30	1830		Marion	AL	00001 1001 p176
He	Abraham				C	1830	Southern D	Dale	AL	p218
Hi	Abraham	C	William	Johnson	Wagoner b A C	1840	Clayton	Barbour	AL	1860C #69
He	Abraham	C	William	Johnson	b	1840		Barbour	AL	COD War Cvl

LN	FIRSTNAME	IO	FATHER	MOM_SPOUSE	EVENT	EVENTDATE	CITY	COUNTY_PAR	ST	SOURCE
Hi	Abraham	C	William	Johnson	War Cvl d CoI enl	10 Mar 1862	Opelika		AL	39th Inf
He	Adaline		Lazarus	Ceny/Carry_Lawler Riley	b C under Lawler	1820		Tuscaloosa	AL	MS Choc 1860C #1478
Hi	Adella		James	_Middlebrook John Edwar	b mom Warren	1860			AL	AL Wilc #195
He	Adolphus				C Adopas	1840		Sumpter	AL	p86
Hi	Albenia		William	Johnson	b f	1848	Clayton	Barbour	AL	1860C #69
Hi	Alexander		Asa Ed	Sartor	b	1849		Butler	AL	1850C
He	Alfred				res				AL	MO Hist of
He	Alice	Ad	Abner H	Elvira_Milton Davis	b Adaline	1830		Marion	AL	AR HotS 1860C p58
He	Alice	Ad	Abner H	_Davis Milton	b d1894	30 Jan 1830		Marion	AL	
Hi	Alice	J	M W	Margaret	b in res Whitten	1847			GA	AL Barb 1860C #68
Hi	Amanda		John W		b	1843				AL Maco 1850C IGI
He	Ambrose	P	Armstead	_Mary L	b in res Jn Cats	1837			GA	AL Cleb 1870C
Hi	Amos	Bu	Asa Miles	_Bowman Fannie Mae	b d17May1963	01 Sep 1889		Greenville	AL	AL Mont d
He	Ancil				C	1850	Dist 1	Lauderdale	AL	p248
Hi	Anderson				L 80 Acr			Marengo	AL	p340
Hi	Andrew		Samuel Sr		b Andy	1833				AL Morg 1850C IGI
Hi	Andrew	Jr	Andrew Sr	Elizabeth	b	1847				AL Cone 1850C IGI
He	Andrew	Sr		_ Elizabeth	War Creek vol	02 Jun 1836	Pine Orcha		AL	
He	Andrew	Sr		_ Elizabeth	War Creek disch	25 Jul 1836	Irwington	Mobile	AL	
Hi	Andrew	Sr		_ Elizabeth	C	1840		Conecuh	AL	p280
He	Andrew	Sr		_Elizabeth	C	1850			GA	AL Cone p372
He	Angeline		Wright	Elizabeth	b	1838		Bibb	AL	MS Leak 1850C p26
Hi	Ann		William	Martha	b	1843			AL	AL Coff 1870C #521
He	Ansel		William Jr	_Shackley Elizabeth	b Ancil	1839			TN	AL Laud 1850C p248
He	Ansel				C	1840		Walker	AL	110000 121001 p293
He	Aquilla		William	Lamberth_Hopkins Lucind	b	1825		Randolph	AL	1860C
He	Archibald		Lazarus	Narvel_Mary J	Wid res	1880		Marshall	AL	1880C
Ha	Armerintha		Sanford	White	b	1868		Cleburne	AL	
He	Armstead			_ Jane Petty	Wid res	1860		Randolph	AL	
Ha	Artelia		Sanford	_Whitley Good	b Teelie	1866		Randolph	AL	
Hi	Asa		Caleb Sr	Margaret_Moore Jane	b	1796		Wilkes	GA	AL Butl 1850C p193
Hi	Asa			_Holmes?	L t Abner Proctor	Dec 1831	Goulds For	Anson	NC	AL Perr Asa of BkY
He	Asa		Caleb Sr	Margaret_Moore Jane	C	1840		Butler	AL	p148
Hi	Asa				C	1840		Perry	AL	p264
Hi	Asa				C	1850	Gaston	Sumter	AL	p316
Hi	Asa	B			C	1850		Butler	AL	p234
Hi	Asa	Ed	Asa	Moore_Sartor Sarah H	b	1824		Twiggs	GA	AL Butl 1850C p193

2

LN	FIRSTNAME	IO	FATHER	MOM_SPOUSE	EVENT	EVENTDATE	CITY	COUNTY_PAR	ST	SOURCE
Hi	Asa	Ed	Asa	_Sartor Sarah H	m	15 Nov 1843		Butler	AL	IGI
Hi	Asa	Mi	Asa Edward	Sartor_Bush Nancy Ann	b Asa Miles d1943	01 Sep 1858		Greenville	AL	
Hi	Asa	Mi	Asa Edward	_Bush Nancy Ann	m Asa Miles	09 Nov 1882		Greenville	AL	FL Pensacola t
Hi	Asa	T	Isaac		b	1837			AL	Mari 1850C IGI
Hi	Asbury		William F	Pugh_Rushing Lucinda	b see Mastin	1844		Pike	AL	1850C
He	Asbury	Wh	Reuben Sr?	_ Hudson Mary	b	1827		Franklin	TN	AL Mars 1850C p190
He	Asbury	Wh		_Hudson Mary	m Ashbury	12 Feb 1843		Marshall	AL	
He	Asbury	Wh		_ Hudson Mary	Wid C	1870	Falkville	Morgan	AL	
Hi	Atlas	C		_Blakney Mary	m Artless?	29 Oct 1836		Wilcox	AL	
He	Attless				C Artless?	1850				AL Wilc p355
Ha	Azzie	Op	Augustus E	Hutchinson_Preskitt Dav	b d14Dec1956	06 Nov 1876		Floyd	GA	AL Birm d
He	Barbara		J D	Clarisa	b	1843			AL	MS Tish 1850C p838
He	Bartlett	A	Hadley	Avery	b	1833			AL	?
Hi	Bartley	M		_Boykins Mary J Leanna?	b Jms? d1920	02 Jun 1846			AL	MS d
Ha	Benjamin				C	1830	Southern D	Shelby	AL	p257
Hi	Benjamin		Thomas Sr		b	1831			AL	Laud 1850C p275
Ha	Berdie		Sanford	White	Twin b d at birth	15 May 1862		Randolph	AL	
Hi	Britta		William	Pugh	b	1842			AL	Pike 1850C
He	Burrell		John		b Burwell?	1848			AL	Mare 1850C IGI
Hi	Caleb				C	1850			GA	AL Butl p193
Hi	Caleb	Sr		_ Margaret	b of son Asa	1796		Wilkes	GA	AL Butl 1850C p193
He	Caroline			_Pollard Edward	m	11 Feb 1839		Marshall	AL	
Ha	Caroline		Andrew Sr	Elizabeth	b	1843			AL	Cone 1850C
Hi	Caroline		William	Pugh	b	1846			AL	Pike 1850C
He	Caroline		Andrew Sr	_Parker Miles S	m Nancy Caroline	07 Oct 1859	Greenville	Butler	AL	TX t
Hi	Catherine		Jesse	Catherine_Price	b	1830			GA	AL Barb 1860C p177
He	Catherine		Abner H	Elvira_Easley Wm	b Pauline Catherine	1833		Marion	AL	AR HotS 1850C p284
Hi	Catherine		Jesse	_Price	b	1833			GA	AL Barb 1870C #1792
Hi	Celia			_Thrailkill Anderson	m	06 Apr 1853		Bibb	AL	IGI
He	Cennie			_ Sexton Christopher C	b Sena d1896	1870	Huntsville	Madison	AL	TN Maur d
He	Charity	Ad	Lazarus	_Lollar William R	m Adeline	18 Apr 1841		Madison	AL	Lawler Riley no iss
Hi	Charles				C State	1820		Conecuh	AL	02 00 02 00 04 AHQ
He	Charles				C State	1820		Limestone	AL	01 06 01 01 09 AHQ
Hi	Charles				C State	1823		Conecuh	AL	AIS#2
He	Charles		James		b	1847			AL	Rand 1850C AL
Hi	Charles	H	William	Johnson	b C H	1850	Clayton	Barbour	AL	1860C #69
Hi	Charles	H	William	Johnson	b	1850	Clayton	Barbour	AL	GA Fult Atlanta t

LN	FIRSTNAME	IO	FATHER	MOM_SPOUSE	EVENT	EVENTDATE	CITY	COUNTY_PAR	ST	SOURCE
He	Charlotte		Martin		b	1795			AL	Pike 1850C IGI
He	Christophe		John		b	1843			AL	Cher 1850C
He	Clarissa		John		b	1847			AL	Cher 1850C
Hi	Clement				C	1840		Marengo	AL	p41
He	Curt		Eli Sr	Eady	b bro of Eliz Lenior				AL	Walk Lenior Cem
He	Cynthia		Lazarus	Ceny/Carry_Taylor Jacob	b	1818			TN	AL Tusca m
He	Cynthia		Lazarus	_Taylor Jacob	m	04 Apr 1832		Tuscaloosa	AL	
He	Cynthia		Ancil	_Perdue T W	b Synthia	1836			AL	Laud 1850C IGI
He	Cynthia	An	Abner H	Elvira_Waldrum Littleto	b	1840			AL	AR HotS 1850Cp284
Hi	David				C	1840	Reg 6	Morgan	AL	p6
He	Delina				C	1850			AL	Tall p404
He	Desina	C	William	Mary_Lindsey John G	b	1836			AL	KY Mars 1850C p477
He	Devinport		John		b	1848			AL	Laud 1850C
He	Dora	B			Ward of J M Henson	07 Jan 1870		Tuscaloosa	AL	MS Monr res
Ha	E	A			b	1822			AL	CA Cala 1850C p246
Hi	Edith	An	Needham	Lanney_Ward John	b Eady Ann	1823		Lenoir	NC	AL Mare 1860C #296
He	Edmond			_Rachael	b	1840			AL	AL Walk 1870C #80
He	Edmond			_Carolina	b	1842			AL	AL Walk 1870C #78
He	Eli		John		b	1843			AL	Walk 1850C
He	Eli	Jr	Eli Sr	Eady_James Elizabeth	b Ely	1828		Giles	TN	AL Walk 1850C p314
He	Eli	Jr	Eli Sr	Eady_James Elizabeth 1	b Ely	1838		Giles	TN	AL Walk 1880C ED281
He	Eli	Jr	Eli Sr	_James Elizabeth 1	War Cvl Conf enl	Nov 1862	Jasper	Walker	AL	CoF 56th AL
He	Eli	Jr	Eli Sr	_Childress Lucy 2	Wid War Cvl Pen Appl	1899		Walker	AL	#6329·
He	Eli	Sr	John Sr	Elizabeth_Eady Edith	b Wm Eli	1802			TN	AL Walk 1850C p314
He	Eli	Sr	John Sr	_Eady Edith	b d1883	1806			TN	AL Walk Lenior Cem
He	Eli	Sr	John Sr	Elizabeth_Eady Edith	b of dau Elizb	1838		Jefferson	IL	AL Walk 1850C p314
He	Elial				Tax 1824-	1823		Calloway	KY	AL Jack t?
He	Elias				C	1830		Jackson	AL	Ind Commiss?
He	Elias			_ Letticia Findley	Res	1842		Marshall	AL	Gandrud Records V96
He	Elijah			_ Daniel Nancy Ann	b	1831			NC	AL Mare MR
Hi	Elijah				b	1832			AL	AL Barb 1860C #997
He	Elijah				C	1840		Butler	AL	p148
Hi	Elijah				C	1850		Marengo	AL	p31
Hi	Elijah			_Daniel Nancy Ann	m	30 Jun 1854		Marengo	AL	
He	Elijah			_Sealy Mary Ann	m	19 Sep 1869		Marengo	AL	IGI
He	Elisha		James B		b	1849			AL	Cham 1850C
He	Elisha	B			War Cvl CoC Sgt1865-	1861			AL	6thInf NARS

4

LN	FIRSTNAME	IO	FATHER	MOM_SPOUSE	EVENT	EVENTDATE	CITY	COUNTY_PAR	ST	SOURCE
He	Eliza		Thomas Sr		b	1836				AL Laud 1850C
He	Eliza		Mathew		b	1836				AL Maco 1850C
He	Elizabeth		John Sr	Elizabeth	b res of bro Wm Sr	1795			NC	AL Walk 1850C p300
Hi	Elizabeth		Needham	Lanney_Hayes Charles	b	1818	Lenoir		NC	AL Wash 1860C
He	Elizabeth		Lazarus	Narvel	b res of Mary J	1830	Cass		GA	AL Mars 1880C
He	Elizabeth		Ancil	Shackley	b	1831				AL Laud 1850C
He	Elizabeth		Eli Sr	Eady_Lenior John	b sis of Curt	09 Sep 1833				AL Walk Lenior Cem
He	Elizabeth		William	Gilmore	b	1834		Marengo	AL	1850C IGI
He	Elizabeth		John	Elizabeth	b	1835			AL	AL Walk 1850C #11
He	Elizabeth		John		b	1836				AL Mare 1850C
He	Elizabeth		Hadley	_Strains	b	1836			AL	Avery mom
He	Elizabeth		Eli Sr	_Lenoir John	b	1838	Jefferson		IL	AL Walk 1850C p314
He	Elizabeth		James		b	1841				AL Rand 1850C IGI
He	Elizabeth		John W	_Foster Hiram	w of Jn W	1844		Marengo	AL	
He	Elizabeth		John		b	1849				AL Cher 1850C
He	Elizabeth		Asbury Wh	_Prichard John 2	b Joanah d1912	1855		Marshall	AL	AL Morgan 1870C
He	Elizabeth		Asbury Wh	Hudson_Sullivan Wm	b Annie	1856		Marshall	AL	AL Morgan 1870C
Ha	Ella	Ad	Sanford	White_Cavender Lemuel	b	Aug 1876		Cleburne	AL	
Ha	Ella	Ad	Sanford	_Cavender Lemuel	m	23 Apr 1896		Cleburne	AL	
He	Ellen		William	Gilmore	b	1837				AL Mare 1850C
He	Ellender		Mathew	McFarland	b	1845		Marengo	AL	1850C IGI
Ha	Emma	E	Sanford	_Wade Joseph H	b	Jun 1868		Cleburne	AL	White mom
He	Etta		Hadly	Avery_Hutchinson Allen	b d bf1889?	1838			AL	MS t
He	Eudora		Samuel	Sarah E	b	1852			AL	AL Barb 1870C p192
He	Evans		Joseph Lem	Daniel	b	1876		Lowdnes	AL	
Hi	Everett	E	William	_Amanda	Farmer b	1848			AL	AL Coff 1870C #566
He	Everett	E	William	Pugh_Amanda	b	1849			AL	AL Pike 1850C
Ha	Felan		Sanford	_Armstrong Margaret I	Twin b	15 May 1862		Randolph	AL	White mom
He	Felix		Robert L	Clayton	b	1836		DeKalb?	AL	TX Titu 1850C p97
He	Felix	C			War Cvl CoK Pvt	1863			AL	42ndInf NARS
Hi	Ferbe	F	James	Warren	b Phoebe?	1849			AL	AL Wilc #195
He	Fielding		John		b	1849				AL Rand 1850C
He	Frances		Andrew Sr	Elizabeth	b	1844				AL Cone 1850C IGI
Ha	Francis				C State	1820		Wilcox	AL	01 02 00 01 04 AHQ
He	Francis		Wright	Elizabeth	b	1834		Bibb	AL	MS Leak 1850C p26
He	Frank	P	William	_ Ellen Jones	Farmer b	04 Jun 1858			AL	TN Fran d
He	Frank	W			War Cvl CoI Pvt	1863			AL	Rosebells Cav NARS

LN	FIRSTNAME	IO	FATHER	MOM_SPOUSE	EVENT	EVENTDATE	CITY	COUNTY_PAR	ST	SOURCE
Hi	George				C	1830		Pike	AL	p66
He	George		Thomas Sr		b	1843				AL Laud 1850C IGI
Hi	George		William J	Elender	b	1847			GA	AL Covi 1850C p163
Hi	George				C	1850		Mare	AL	p65
Hi	George		James	Warren	b	1854			AL	AL Wilc #195
He	George	H			C Geo	1830		Perry	AL	
He	George	H			b of son Jms M	1844		Perry	AL	1850C
He	George	Ru		_Cathy Nancy	m	02 Dec 1840		Marshall	AL	
He	George	S	Samuel	Sarah E	b	1862			AL	AL Barb 1870C p192
He	George	Th	Alfred		res				AL	MO Hist of
He	George	W	George H		b	1834				AL Perr 1850C
Ha	George	Wa	George Was		b Jr	1836				AL Cham 1850C
Ha	George	Wa			C Sr	1840		Chambers	AL	p227
He	Gilbert			_Morgan Permelia	m	01 Mar 1857		Talapoosa	AL	IGI
Hi	Green			_Lucinda	b	1843			NC	AL Coff 1870C #81
He	Green	A	Hadley	Avery	b	1835			AL	FL t?
Hy	Grover	Cl	Louis Hutc	Corley_Brown Maude R	b	04 Mar 1885	Montgomery	Montgomery	AL	OK t
Hi	Gurinda				C	1850	Mobile	Mobile	AL	p394
He	Gus		Robert L S	Smith	b	1897		Jackson	AL	TN Monr t
He	Hadly		Bartlett S	_ Avery Elizabeth	b of son Jms	1834		Marengo?	AL	?
He	Hannah		William		b	1848				AL Blou 1850C
He	Hannah	E	Samuel Sr		b	1844				AL Morg 1850C
Ha	Hans	Pe		_Nelson Sarah Francis	b of son Henry Hall	1865				AL Bald IGI
Hi	Hardy				L 40 Acr	16 Sep 1835		Marengo	AL	Twp15N R56 Sec8 p1
Hi	Hardy				C	1840		Mobile	AL	p137
He	Harriet		Ancil	Shackley	b	1842				AL Laud 1850C
Ha	Harriet		Joseph	Susan	b	1850			AL	AL Covi 1860C #974
He	Harrison				C	1830	Southern D	Dale	AL	p218
Hi	Harrison				C	1840		Dale	AL	p12
He	Harry	R			War Cvl Union NG	1863			AL	Battery A NARS
Hi	Henderson				C	1830		Bibb	AL	p154
Hi	Henrietta		Thomas		b	1832				AL Monr 1850C
Hi	Henry			_Kensaw Martha					AL	?
Ha	Henry				C	1840		Dallas	AL	p72
Hi	Henry				C	1850	Mobile	Mobile	AL	p435
Hi	Henry		James	Warren	b	1856			AL	AL Wilc #195
He	Henry	C	George Was		b	1846				AL Cham 1850C

LN	FIRSTNAME	IO	FATHER	MOM_SPOUSE	EVENT	EVENTDATE	CITY	COUNTY_PAR	ST	SOURCE
He	Henry	Cl	Henry W	Pinelope	b C res of H Boston	1842			AL	AL Walk 1850C p326
He	Henry	Ha	Hans Pe	Nelson	b Henry Hall	1865		Baldwin	AL	IGI
He	Henry	K	Isaac		b	1845				AL Mari 1850C
Hi	Henry	L	John	Mary	b	1821			NC	AL Lown 1850C
He	Hester	An			b C res of H Boston	1838		Walker	AL	1850C p326
Ha	Ida		Sanford	_Harper Martin Ashley	b m 5 times	1879		Cleburne	AL	White mom
He	Isaac				b	1785				AL Mari 1830C p180
He	Isaac				C 30-40	1830		Marion	AL	100001 21001 p180
He	Isaac				C	1850		Lauderdale	AL	p275
He	Isaac				C	1850		Marion	AL	p132
He	Isaac				L 80 Acr Sec35	27 Oct 1858		Winston	AL	Cert#29299
He	Isaac			_King Sarah	m	09 Aug 1868		Calhoun	AL	IGI
He	Isaac	Jr	Isaac Sr	Sarah	b	1847			AL	AL Walk 1850C p325
He	Isaac	N	Isaac		b	1842				AL Mari 1850C
He	Isaac	Sr		_Sarah	b C inres A Griffon	1802			SC	AL Walk 1850C p325
Ha	J	C		_Rebecca	Carpenter b	1812			GA	AL Covi 1860C p444
He	J	D		_ Clarisa	b of son Joshua	1838			AL	MS Tish 1850C p838
He	J	M			gaurd of Dora B	07 Jan 1870		Tuscaloosa	AL	MS Monr ward res
He	J	M		_King E S	m	03 Jan 1878		Marengo	AL	
Hi	J	S			C	1840		Cherokee	AL	p145
Hi	J	T		_Burson Phoebe J	m	17 Sep 1857		Wilcox	AL	
Hi	J	W			C	1840		Macon	AL	p5
He	Jackson		John		b	1849				AL Rand 1850C
Ha	Jacob				C	1840		Autauga	AL	p38
He	Jacob		James	Martha	b	1862			AL	AL Barb 1870C p185
Ha	Jacob	Ge	James	Wiley_Jones Eloia	b C res of A Wiley	1850		Talladega	AL	1860C
He	Jacob	Ge	James	Wiley_Jones Eloia	b Jacob Genkins	31 Oct 1850		Talladega	AL	
He	Jacob	Ge	James	_Jones Eloia	m d25Sep1932	29 Jan 1869		Monroe	AL	TX Bast d
He	James			_Martha	b	1814			GA	AL Barb 1870C p185
Hi	James			_Warren Martha Ellen	b	1825			AL	AL Wilc 1860C #195
He	James		John W	Moore_Wiley Rebecca Ell	b d1864	1828			GA	AL Tall 1850C p405
Ha	James		John		b	1829				AL Madi 1850C
He	James		John		b	1832				AL Cher 1850C
He	James		Armstead	Petty_Curry Harriet E	b d1911	1832			GA	AL Cleb 1870C
He	James		Hadley	Avery	b	1834			AL	?
He	James		Samuel Sr		b	1835				AL Morg 1850C
Hi	James		William	_M D	Shoemaker b	1835	Clayton	Barbour	AL	1860C #56

ALABAMA

LN	FIRSTNAME	IO	FATHER	MOM_SPOUSE	EVENT	EVENTDATE	CITY	COUNTY_PAR	ST	SOURCE
He	James		William	Johnson_M D	b	1835	Clayton	Barbour	AL	IL wid t
He	James		William		b	1838				AL Blou 1850C
He	James				C	1840		Butler	AL	p137
He	James				C	1840		Randolph	AL	p211
He	James				C	1840		Tallapoosa	AL	p183
He	James		John		b	1842				AL Mare 1850C
He	James		Rutherford		b	1843				AL Rand 1850C IGI
He	James		John W	Moore_Wiley Rebecca Ell	w of Jn W	1844		Marengo	AL	
Ha	James		Andrew Sr	Elizabeth	b	1845				AL Cone 1850C IGI
He	James		John W	_Wiley Rebecca Ellen	m	1848		Talladega	AL	?
Hi	James				C	1850		Coff	AL	p295
He	James		James	Warren	b	1852			AL	AL Barb 1870C p185
Hi	James		James	Warren	b	1852			AL	AL Wilc #195
Hi	James				Pwr Atty t Richard	05 Feb 1863		Wayne	NC	AL Barb James in
He	James	A	William	Cole	b	1849			AL	AL Walk 1850C
Hi	James	A	Noah	McDaniel	b	1856			AL	AL Wash #278
Hi	James	A			War Cvl CoC Pvt enl	26 Apr 1862	Camden	Wilcox	AL	42nd Inf
Hi	James	A			War Cvl CoC muster	16 May 1862	Columbus	Lowndes	MS	AL Wilc f 42nd Inf
He	James	A			War Cvl Union CoE	1863			AL	1stCal NARS
Hi	James	B		_Robertson Elenor	m	1845		Washington	AL	
He	James	B			b of son Elisha	1849				AL Cham 1850C
Hi	James	Ba		_ Boykins Mary J	b Bartley M?	02 Jun 1846		Choctaw	AL	
He	James	D	John	Elizabeth	b	1847				AL Walk 1850C
Hi	James	J		_Rivere Mary E	m	12 Sep 1861		Wilcox	AL	
He	James	Jr	James Sr		b	1843				AL Rand 1850C
He	James	M	George H		b	1844				AL Perr 1850C
He	James	M	Archibald	Mary J	b	1860		Hamilton	TN	AL Mars 1880C
He	James	Sr			C Jms	1850		Randolph	AL	p294
Hi	Jane		William	Pugh	b	1847				AL Pike 1850C
He	Jane	G	William	Gilmore	b	1844		Marengo	AL	1850C
He	Jennette		Asberry	Hudson	b	1848			TN	AL Mars 1850C p190
He	Jeremiah				L 80 Acr Sec26	27 Jun 1855		Winston	AL	Cert#24386
He	Jeremiah				L 40 Acr Sec27	27 Jun 1855		Winston	AL	Cert#24386
He	Jeremiah				L 120 Acr Sec26	05 Nov 1857		Winston	AL	Cert#28137
He	Jeremiah				L 80 Acr Sec27	05 Nov 1857		Winston	AL	Cert#28137
He	Jeremiah				L 40 Acr Sec35	05 Nov 1857		Winston	AL	Cert#28137
He	Jeremiah	Sr		_ Lyles Fannie	C as J	1840		DeKalb	AL	p181

LN	FIRSTNAME	IO	FATHER	MOM_SPOUSE	EVENT	EVENTDATE	CITY	COUNTY_PAR	ST	SOURCE
Hi	Jeremiah	Sr		_ Liles Fannie	Tax	1844		Harrison	TX	AL DeKa f?
He	Jerry			_Cummins Ellen/Eleanor	b	1850		Franklin	AL	
He	Jesse				b	1785				AL Walk 1840C p293
He	Jesse				C	1830		Lauderdale	AL	p216
Hi	Jesse			_ Catherine	b of dau	1830			GA	AL Barb 1860C p177
Hi	Jesse		William	Johnson_Hinson Lucy	Shoemaker b	1835	Clayton	Barbour	AL	1860C #69
Hi	Jesse		William	Martha	b	1839			AL	AL Coff 1870C #521
Ha	Jesse				C	1840		Sumpter	AL	p134
He	Jesse				C 50-60	1840		Walker	AL	1f 50-60 p293
He	Jesse		Rutherford		b	1844				AL Rand 1850C
He	Jesse		John		b	1848				AL Cher 1850C
He	Jesse				C	1850				AL Tall p404
Hi	Jesse		William Sr	Johnson_Hinson Lucy Mal	War Cvl CoI 39Vol	15 May 1862		Barbour	AL	Wid Pen Jul 1900
Hi	Jesse		William Sr	Johnson_Hinson Lucy Mal	War Cvl disc	1863		Montgomery	AL	
Hi	Jesse		William Sr	Johnson_Hinson Lucy Mal	Pwr Atty t Richard	05 Feb 1863		Wayne	NC	AL Barb Jesse in
Hi	Jesse		William Sr	_Hinson Lucy Malinda	m dau of Needham	28 Feb 1866	Troy	Pike	AL	FL t
He	Jesse		William Sr	Johnson_Hinson Lucy	Wid War Cvl Pen App	Jul 1900			AL	FL?
He	Jesse	Jr	Jesse Sr	_Irvin Sally	b	14 Aug 1847	Wedowee	Randolph	AL	Walls mom
He	Jesse	Sr		_ Elizabeth Crawford	b	1767			VA	AL Rand 1850C
Hi	Jesse	Sr		_Catherine	b	1785			NC	AL Barb 1860C p177
Hi	Jesse	Sr		_ Catherine	b C res of Buston	1785			NC	AL Barb 1870C #1791
He	Jesse	Sr		_ Elizabeth Crawford	C Jesse	1840		Randolph	AL	p209
He	Jesse	Sr	William	_Walls Elizabeth	m dau of Jerry	1846	Wedowee	Randolph	AL	
Hi	Jesse	Sr		_ Mary Murphy 2	LW War 1812?	1850		Randolph	AL	
He	Jesse	Sr		_ Murphy Mary 2	d	07 Mar 1852		Randolph	AL	
He	Jim		Robert L S	Smith	Ind Cher? b	1901		Jackson	AL	TN Monr t
He	Jincy		Ancil	Shackley	b	1828				AL Laud 1850C
He	Joanah		Asbury W	_Sullivan Wm Henry 1	b Elizabeth	11 Apr 1856		Marshall	AL	AR t
He	Joanah		Asbury Wh	Hudson_Prichard John 2	b Elizb d01Dec1912	11 Apr 1856		Marshall	AL	AR t
He	Joe	R	Robert L S	Smith	Ind Cher? b	1895		Jackson	AL	TN Monr t
He	John				b	1765				AL Walk 1840C p293
He	John				b John C?	1775				AL Mari 1830C p176
Hi	John			_Mary	b	1787			NC	AL Lowd 1850C
Hi	John				L	1804		Washington	AL	
He	John			_Elizabeth	b	1806			KY	AL Walk 1850C p327
Hi	John				Tax	1816	AL Terr	Baldwin	AL	AIS#1
He	John				Tax	1816	AL Terr	Monroe	AL	AIS#1

LN	FIRSTNAME	IO	FATHER	MOM_SPOUSE	EVENT	EVENTDATE	CITY	COUNTY_PAR	ST	SOURCE
Hi	John				C State	1820		Baldwin	AL	01 02 01 01 05
Hi	John				Tax	1821		Baldwin	AL	AIS#2
Hi	John				Tax	1823		Baldwin	AL	AIS#2
He	John			_S A	b	1827			AL	AR Pike 1860C p443
Hi	John				b res of Jn Roberts	1828			AL	AL Choc 1850C p157
He	John				C	1830		Lauderdale	AL	p210
He	John				C	1830		Walker	AL	p268
Hi	John		Mathew		b	1832				AL Maco 1850C
He	John				L	22 Jul 1836		Walker	AL	Sec25 Twp15 Rnge5
He	John		Eli Sr	_Emily	b in res H Thomas	1836		Jefferson	IL	AL Walk 1880C ED281
He	John		P A	_Price Annette	b d1906	1837			AL	TX Cass 1860C p375B
He	John		P A	Elizabeth_Annete Price	b	02 Feb 1838			AL	
He	John		P A	Elizabeth_Annete Price	b C res of Eliz Bas	1838			AL	TX Cass 1850C p765
He	John		P A	Elizabeth_Annete Price	b	1838			AL	TX Madi 1900C ED28
He	John		Eli Sr	Eady_Emily	b	1838		Jefferson	IL	AL Walk 1850C p314
He	John				C	1840		Randolph	AL	p215
He	John				C 70-80	1840		Walker	AL	1f 70-80 p293
Hi	John				C	1840		Wilcox	AL	p337
Ha	John		Asa Edward	Sartor	b	1843				AL Butl 1850C
He	John		William		b	1844				AL Blou 1850C IGI
Hi	John		Asa	Moore	b	1844				AL Butl 1850C IGI
He	John		Mathew	McFarland	b	1847				AL Mare 1850C
He	John		Thomas		b	1848				AL Laud 1850C IGI
He	John		John	_Malinda	b	1849			AL	AL Walk 1870C
He	John		John	Elizabeth_Malinda	b	1850			AL	AL Walk 1850C
Hi	John				C	1850		Cher	AL	p116
Hi	John				C	1850		Cone	AL	p354
He	John				C	1850		Lauderdale	AL	p249
He	John				C	1850		Randolph	AL	p291
He	John		Eli Sr	Eady_Emily	War Cvl Conf enl	15 Feb 1862	Jasper	Walker	AL	CoF 28th AL Inf
He	John	A	Asbury Wh	Hudson	b	1848				AL Mars 1850C
He	John	C	John W	Moore_Wilkinson Malinda	b	1815				AL Mare MR
He	John	C			C 50-60 Sr p176 (2)	1830		Marion	AL	01121001 00110001
He	John	C	Abner H Sr	Elvira_Compton Margaret	b	1832		Marion	AL	AR HotS 1860C p57
He	John	C	Abner H Sr	Elvira_Compton Margaret	b	1832		Marion	AL	AR HotS 1850Cp284
He	John	C	John W	_Wilkinson Malinda	m	13 Aug 1834		Marengo	AL	
Ha	John	C			C	1840		Randolph	AL	p193

LN	FIRSTNAME	IO	FATHER	MOM_SPOUSE	EVENT	EVENTDATE	CITY	COUNTY_PAR	ST	SOURCE
He	John	C	John W	Moore_Wilkinson Malinda	w of John W	1844		Marengo	AL	
He	John	C	John W	Moore_Wilkinson Malinda	C	1850		Marengo	AL	p48
He	John	F			C 20-30	1840		Walker	AL	00001 10010 p293
Hi	John	F	Green	Lucinda	b	1855			GA	AL Coff 1870C #81
He	John	G	William	Gilmore_Lester Pocohaon	b	1832		Marengo	AL	1850C & MR
He	John	G	William	_Lester Pocohantas	m	12 Jul 1858		Marengo	AL	
He	John	Ja	Eli Jr	James_Cross Sarah Jane	b Jn Jms	05 Sep 1855		Walker	AL	AR Hatt t
He	John	Jr	John Sr		b	1834				AL Cher 1850C
Ha	John	Jr	John Sr		b	1834				AL Madi 1850C
He	John	Jr			C	1840		Marengo	AL	p67
He	John	Jr	John Sr		b	1845				AL Maco 1850C
He	John	Jr	John Sr		b	1849				AL Mare 1850C
He	John	Jr	John Sr		b	1849				AL Walk 1850C
He	John	Jr	John Sr	Slaughter	b	17 Apr 1850		Walker	AL	IGI
He	John	R	Robert L S	_Davis Alice	Ind Cher b mom Smith	1890		Jackson	AL	TN Monr t
He	John	Sr		_Elizabeth	b	1767			NC	AL Walk 1850C p314
He	John	Sr			C	1840		Marengo	AL	p67
He	John	Sr		_Slaughter Malinda	C	1850		Walker	AL	IGI
He	John	T	Lazarus	_Harriet E	b mom Ceny/Carry	1828			AL	MS Choc 1850C# 148
He	John	W		_ Moore Nelly	b of son Jms	1828			GA	AL Tall 1850C p405
Hi	John	W		_ Moore Nelly	C Jn	1830	Southern D	Marengo	AL	p359
Hi	John	W			C	1830	Mobile	Mobile	AL	p378
Hi	John	W	Thomas		b	1836				AL Monr 1850C
Hi	John	W			Indian Depredations	1836		Macon	AL	US Court of Claims
He	John	W	George H		b	1838				AL Perr 1850C
Ha	John	W	James		b	1844				AL Coff 1850C
He	John	W		_ Merritt Opelia Angeln	b d1884	1844			AL	MS Monr t
He	John	W		_Moore Nelly	w	07 Aug 1844		Marengo	AL	BkA p450
He	John	W			C	1850				AL Shel p235
Hi	John	W			C	1850		Mobile	AL	p452
Ha	John	W	John W	_King Alice	b Jr	1856		Pickens	AL	West mom
He	John	W		_ West	b of son Jn W Jr	1856		Pickens	AL	
Hi	Johnathan		William J	Elender	b	1849			FL	AL Covi p163
Ha	Joseph			_Susan	b	1827			GA	AL Covi 1860C #974
He	Joseph			_Thomas Mary	m	20 Jan 1829		Marengo	AL	
Hi	Joseph				C	1830	Southern D	Marengo	AL	p359
He	Joseph		Hadley	Avery_Cross Elena	b	1833			AL	

LN	FIRSTNAME	IO	FATHER	MOM_SPOUSE	EVENT	EVENTDATE	CITY	COUNTY_PAR	ST	SOURCE
He	Joseph				C	1840		Jackson	AL	p8
Hi	Joseph		William J	Elender	b	1845			GA	AL Covi p163
He	Joseph		Rutherford		b	1848			AL	Rand 1850C
He	Joseph				C	1850		Tall	AL	p401
He	Joseph		William	Lambert_Nolan Susan	L	1859		Talladega	AL	GS NC Meck
Hi	Joseph	Le	John	_Martin Mary	b Joseph Lemuel	11 Oct 1833			SC	ALSLA HHHH File
Hi	Joseph	Le	John	Mary_Martin Mary	b	1833			SC	AL Lown 1850C
He	Joseph	Le		_Daniel Martha Ella	son Evans b	1876		Lowndes	AL	NC Anso f
Hi	Joshua				C	1830		Walker	AL	p260
He	Joshua		John Sr	Elizabeth	b	1830			Al	AL Walk 1850C #11
He	Joshua				L	06 Oct 1833		Walker	AL	Sec19 Twp14 Rnge5
He	Joshua		J D	Clarisa	b	1838			AL	MS Tish 1850C p838
He	Joshua				d	1839		Walker	AL	Barton Absolom Admin
Hi	Joshua	J	Thomas		b	1834			AL	Monr 1850C
He	Jsem		Ancil	Shackley	b	1837			AL	Laud 1850C
He	Judy		William Ri	_Peak James	Ind Cher son Richd b	1830		Habersham	GA	AL Jack Pendergrass
Ha	Julia		Sanford Ha	White_Cavender Wm Jacks	b d22Dec1943	07 Mar 1874		Cleburne	AL	
Ha	Julia		Sanford Ha	_Cavender Wm Jackson	m	13 Dec 1888		Cleburne	AL	
He	L	M			C	1850			AL	Lawr p400
He	Larkin				Res				AL	LDS film #15144
Ha	Lazarus			_ Ceny/Carrie	b of dau Cynthia	1818			TN	AL Tusc t
He	Lazarus			_ Ceny/Carrie	C 40-50 as L	1830		Tuscaloosa	AL	1000101 112101
He	Lazarus			_ Ceny/Carry	C 50-60	1840		Tuscaloosa	AL	02000001 0121001p210
Hi	Lemuel	C		_Gibson? Elizabeth	b L C in res Gibson	1826			NC	AL Barb 1860C #55
He	Lena		James	Martha	b	1865			AL	AL Barb 1870C p185
Hi	Leona		Asa	Moore	b				GA	AL Butl 1850C p193
He	Lett	T	John		b	1844			AL	Rand 1850C
He	Letta				b				AL	Blou 1850C p108
Hi	Levi			_ McDowell Rebecca	b	1812			NC	AL Mare 1850C p89
He	Levi			_Korntz Martha	b d26Aug1915	27 Jul 1834			AL	Hawthorn res
He	Levi		Eli Sr	Eady	b	1843		Jefferson	IL	AL Walk 1850C p314
He	Levi			_McDowell Rebecca	m	06 Oct 1846		Marengo	AL	
Hi	Levi	H	Needham	Lanney_urm	b	1840		Wayne	NC	AL Barb 1860C #71
Ha	Levi	H	Needham	Lanney_urm	War Cvl Pvt CoF d	04 Jul 1864	Rock Islan	Rock Islan	IL	AL 28th POW bur N
He	Lizzie	Le			Ward of J M Henson	07 Jan 1870		Tuscaloosa	AL	MS Monr res
Hy	Louis	Hu	Aaron	_Corley Louisa B	b	17 Sep 1855	Clayton	Barbour	AL	Price mom
Hi	Louisa		Asa	Moore	b			Twiggs	GA	AL Butl 1850C p193

LN	FIRSTNAME	IO	FATHER	MOM_SPOUSE	EVENT	EVENTDATE	CITY	COUNTY_PAR	ST	SOURCE
He	Lovely	M	James	Martha	b	1854			AL	AL Barb 1870C p185
Hi	Lucretia		Asa	Moore	b					AL Butl 1850C p193
Hi	Lucy	J	Martin M	Albritton	b	1857			GA	AL Barb 1860C
Hi	Lucy	Ma	Needham	Lanney_Jesse Hinson	b	1838		Wayne	NC	AL Barb 1860C #71
Hi	Lucy	Ma	Needham	Lanney_Hinson Jesse	b Lucy Malinda Winni	1839		Wayne	NC	AL Pike 1850C
Hi	Lucy	Ma	Needham	_Hinson Jesse	m son of Wm	28 Feb 1866	Troy	Pike	AL	Fl t
Hi	M	C	Jesse	Hinson	b	1855			AL	AL Barb 1860C p177
He	M	S	P A	Elizabeth	b C res of Eliz Bas	1841			AL	TX Cass 1850C p765
Hi	M	W		_Margaret	b Sr in res Whitten	1840			NC	AL Barb 1860C #68
He	M	W		_ Margaret	b of dau Alice J	1847			GA	AL Barb 1860C #68
Hi	M	W	M W	Margaret	b Jr	1860		Barbour	AL	1860C #68
He	Mahala		P A	Elizabeth	b C res of Eliz Bas	1838			AL	TX Cass 1850C p765
He	Malissa	C	Asbury	Mary	b	1845			TN	AL Mars 1850C p190
He	Marcus	H	Isaac		b	1832				AL Mari 1850C
Hi	Margaret		Asa	Moore	b			Twiggs	GA	AL Butl 1850C p193
He	Margaret		John Sr	Elizabeth	b res of bro Wm Sr	1790			NC	AL Walk 1850C
He	Margaret				b C res of J Daniel	1837			AL	AL Walk 1850C #9
He	Margaret		Ancil	Shackley	b	1840				AL Laud 1850C IGI
He	Margaret		James	Warren	b	1843			AL	AL Barb 1870C p185
Hi	Margaret		Noah	McDaniel	b	1853			AL	AL Wash #278
Ha	Margaret	I	James		b	1849				AL Coff 1850C
He	Margaret	J	Samuel Sr		b	1843				AL Morg 1850C IGI
Ha	Margaret	J	Sanford	_Harper David	m	13 Aug 1874		Randolph	AL	
Hi	Margaret	Ja		_Sartor William C	m	22 Jun 1844		Butler	AL	IGI
He	Margaret	M	Asberry	Hudson	b	1849			TN	AL Mars 1850C p190
He	Mariah		William	Cole	b Marian	1825			AL	AL Walk 1850C p314
Hi	Mariah			_Lang John M	m	10 Jun 1851	Bay Minett	Baldwin	AL	IGI
He	Marion				L 80 Acr Sec36	20 Jan 1859		Winston	AL	Cert#29765
He	Marion				L 120 Acr Sec36	11 Dec 1860		Winston	AL	Cert#32619
He	Martha		Nicholas	Sarah	b	1832			AL	KY Mars 1850C p469
He	Martha		Thomas Sr		b	1834				AL Laud 1850C
Hi	Martha		William J	Elender	b	1836			SC	AL Covi 1850C p163
He	Martha		John		b	1837				AL Mare 1850C
He	Martha		John		b	1838				AL Cher 1850C
He	Martha		James	Warren	b	1846			AL	AL Barb 1870C p185
He	Martha		William		b	1849				AL Blou 1850C
Hi	Martha	An	Asa	_Liddle John	b mom Moore	1838		Twiggs	GA	AL Butl 1850C p193

LN	FIRSTNAME	IO	FATHER	MOM_SPOUSE	EVENT	EVENTDATE	CITY	COUNTY_PAR	ST	SOURCE
Hi	Martha	An	Elijah	Daniel	b	01 Jul 1861		Marango	AL	IGI
Hi	Martha	J	Thomas		b	1838				AL Monr 1850C
Ha	Martha	M	John		b	1841				AL Madi 1850C
He	Martha	Ma		Dilday_Daly	Ind Cher? b of dau	1842	Jasper	Marion	TN	AL Jack 1870C
He	Martha	Ma		Dilday_Patrick Daly	Ind Cher Confirmed	05 Oct 1869	Bridgeport	Jackson	AL	Sacred Heart Church
He	Martha	Ma	Charles?	Dilday_Patrick Daly	Ind Cher d	16 Mar 1899		Jackson	AL	Hubbs Frost TNSLA
Hi	Martin		William J	Elender	b	1843			FL	AL Covi 1850C p163
Hi	Martin	F			b	1757		Dobbs	NC	AL Pike 1850C p229
Hi	Martin	F			C	1840		Russell	AL	p28
He	Martin	F			War Rev Pen Appl	31 Jan 1850		Pike	AL	#5040 rej
Hi	Martin	L		_Lucinda	b	1843			AL	AL Coff 1870C #524
Hi	Martin	M	Needham	Lanney_Albritton Mary	b C inres Albritton	1830		Lenoir	NC	AL Barb 1860C #55
Hi	Martin	M	Needham	_Albritton Mary	m	02 Oct 1856		Barbour	AL	
Hi	Martin	M	Needham	Lanney_Albritton Mary	b of dau Lucy	1857			GA	AL Barb 1860C #55
Hi	Martin	M	Needham	Lanny_Albritton	LG 79 Acr	01 Nov 1858		Barbour	AL	#22476
He	Mary		John		b	1838				AL Cher 1850C
Hi	Mary		Mathew		b	1838				AL Maco 1850C
He	Mary		James		b	1838				AL Rand 1850C
He	Mary		John		b	1843				AL Mare 1850C
He	Mary		John W	_Hammond Sherrod	w of Jn W	1844		Marengo	AL	Moore mom
He	Mary		William		b	1846				AL Blou 1850C
He	Mary	A	Samuel		b	1839				AL Morg 1850C
Hi	Mary	A	Thomas		b	1840				AL Monr 1850C
Hi	Mary	A	Levi	Rebecca	b	1847				AL Mare 1850C p89
Hi	Mary	Al	Needham	_Jackson Warren D	m	02 Nov 1856	Clayton	Barbour	AL	
He	Mary	Do			b res of Jn	1824			TN	AL Walk 1850C #203
He	Mary	E	Abner H	Elvira_Holliman James W	b	1842			AL	AR HotS 1850Cp284
Ha	Mary	E	John		b	1848				AL Mobi 1850C
Ha	Mary	E	Sanford	White_Beam Jms B	b	1859		Randolph	AL	
Ha	Mary	E	Sanford	_Beam Jms B	m	13 Aug 1874		Randolph	AL	
Ha	Mary	M	John		b	1838				AL Madi 1850C
He	Mary	Re	Richard	Francis_Mardis John	b	1835			AL	MS Kemp 1870C
He	Mary	Re	Richard	Francis_Mardis John	b	1835		Bibb?	AL	MS Kemp 1850C #486
He	Mary	Re	Richard	_Mardis John W	b in res J Perkins	1836			AL	MS Kemp 1860C #402
He	Mary	W	Samuel	Sarah E	b	1859			AL	AL Barb 1870C p192
Hi	Mastin	As	William F	Pugh_Rushing Lucinda	b Asbury	18 Mar 1843		Pike	AL	
Hi	Mastin	As	William F	_Rushing Lucinda	m	05 Oct 1865		Pike	AL	

LN	FIRSTNAME	IO	FATHER	MOM_SPOUSE	EVENT	EVENTDATE	CITY	COUNTY_PAR	ST	SOURCE
He	Mathew				C State	1820		Shelby	AL	01 00 01 01 03 AIS
Hi	Mathew				C	1830		Bibb	AL	p155
Hi	Mathew				C	1840		Macon	AL	p9
He	Mathew		John W	_McFarland Mary	m	21 Mar 1842		Marengo	AL	
Hi	Mathew		Simeon		b	1849				AL Maco 1850C
He	Mathew		John W	Moore_McFarland Mary	C	1850				AL Mare p48
He	Mathew				C	1850				AL Maco IGI
He	Mathew	Wi			b C res of H Boston	1772			SC	AL Walk 1850C p326
He	Matilda		Lazarus	Ceny/Carry_Lollar Redde	b	1834		Tuscaloosa	AL	MS Choc 1850C #148
Ha	Milly	P	Sanford	_Green John W	b	Feb 1872		Cleburne	AL	White mom
He	Minerva		Wright	Elizabeth	b	1841		Bibb?	AL	MS Leak 1850C p26
Hi	Moses	Ol			Tax	1769		Dobbs	NC	AL Russ t
Hi	Moses	Ol			Tax	1793		Glasgow	NC	AL Russ t
Hi	Moses	Ol	Jesse?		War Rev Pen	07 Aug 1838	Girard	Russell	AL	NC Dobbs f #5041
Hi	N	H	Martin M	Albritton	b	1859			AL	AL Barb 1860C #55
He	Nancy			_Williams Henry	m son of RS David	1825		Greene	AL	NC White?
He	Nancy		John		b	1833				AL Cher 1850C
He	Nancy		Wright	Elizabeth	b	1836			AL	MS Leak 1850C p26
He	Nancy		William		b	1843				AL Blou 1850C
He	Nancy		Rutherford		b	1846				AL Rand 1850C
Ha	Nancy	C	Sanford	White_Ballenger Jn D	b	1860		Randolph	AL	
Ha	Nancy	C	Sanford	_Ballenger John D	m	26 Feb 1878		Randolph	AL	
He	Nancy	J	Samuel Sr		b	1841				AL Morg 1850C IGI
Hi	Nancy	J	Thomas		b	1842				AL Monr 1850C
He	Nathan		James	Warren	b	1856			AL	AL Barb 1870C p185
He	Nathan	G	William	Gilmore	b	1846				AL Mare 1850C
Hi	Needham		Martin Ol?	_ Lanney	b	1787		Dobbs	NC	AL Pike 1850C
Hi	Needham			_ Lanney/Lena	Wid C	1860		Barbour	AL	#71
He	Nicholas			_ Sarah	b of dau Martha	1832			AL	KY Mars 1850C
Hi	Noah			_ McDaniel Frances Emel	b	1810			NC	AL Mare 1850C p89
Hi	Noah			_ McDaniel Emeline Fran	b	1810			NC	AL Wash #278
He	Noah		John		b	1845				AL Cher 1850C
Hi	Noah			_McDaniel Emeline Franc	m	27 Jan 1848		Marengo	AL	
Hi	Nora			_Elmore John 1	b Heddie/Hardy?	1826		Lenoir	NC	AL Mare 1860C #73
Ha	Obel				C Able?	1830		Conecuh	AL	p101
He	P	A		_ Elizabeth	b of son Jn	02 Feb 1838			AL	
He	Pauline	Ca	Abner H	_Easley William	b Catherine	1833		Marion	AL	AR HotS 1880C

LN	FIRSTNAME	IO	FATHER	MOM_SPOUSE	EVENT	EVENTDATE	CITY	COUNTY_PAR	ST	SOURCE
Ha	Perthery			_Chandler Thomas	Ind Cher m	07 Jul 1812		Madison	AL	IGI
He	Phillip		Elias?	_Hutchinson Celestine	b dad Ind Commiss	12 Dec 1827	Ind Ter	Jackson	AL	Spies of Blue & Grey
He	Phillip				C	1850				AL Perr p308
He	Phillip			_ Hutchinson Celestine	War Cvl Spy Arrested	20 May 1864	Ind Ter	Jackson	AL	Spies of Blue & Gray
He	Polly			_Goodbread Phillip R 2?	m	04 Jul 1830		Marengo	AL	TX Wils d
He	Polly		Thomas Sr		b	1832				AL Laud 1850C
He	Polly		Rutherford		b	1847				AL Rand 1850C
He	Polly	An	Ancil	Shackley	b	1833				AL Laud 1850C
He	R	A		_Dearing Mary R	m	25 Sep 1849		Tuscaloosa	AL	SC Mag of Ances Rch
He	R	A		_Cobb Thomas	m	09 Jul 1856		Madison	AL	IGI
He .	R	S			C Robert L?	1840		DeKalb	AL	p178
Ha	Rachael		James	Wiley?	b	1849			AL	AL Tall 1850C p405
Ha	Rachael		James	Wiley?	b C res of A Wiley	1849			AL	AL Tall 1860C
He	Rebecca		Solomon	_Buleson Michael	w of Solomon	10 Dec 1822		Jefferson	AL	
Hi	Rebecca		Thomas		b	1830				AL Monr 1850C
He	Rebecca			Mary_Satefield	b	1837			AL	MS Kemp 1850C #496
He	Reed		Robert L S	Smith	Ind Cher? b	1899		Jackson	AL	TN Monr t
He	Reuben	Sr			C State	1832		Franklin	TN	AL Mars t?
He	Reuben	Sr			C 50-60	1840		Marshall	AL	02111001 0010001 p72
He	Reuben	Sr			Democratic Meeting	25 Jul 1840		Marshall	AL	Gandrud V12 p74
He	Reuben	Sr			L Claims intrest in	08 Feb 1844		Marshall	AL	Gandrud V15 p79
He	Reuben	Sr		_ Joannah?	C Wid	1850		Marshall	AL	
He	Richard			_ Frances	b of son Wm M	1834			AL	MS Kemp 1860C #396
He	Richard			_ Frances	b of dau Mary R	1836			AL	MS Kemp #402
Hi	Richard	A	Aaron	Mary Ann_Mary Ann	w of Aron	03 Jul 1830		Bibb	AL	Deed BkA p127
He	Richard	C	Abner H	Elvira_Penderslice Mary	b	1836		Marion	AL	AR HotS 1850C p284
He	Richard	C	Abner H	Elvira_Penderslice Mary	b	1837		Marion	AL	AR HotS 1860C p57
Hi	Right				C Wright?	1840		Bibb	AL	MS t? p128
He	Robert		Thomas Sr		b	1833				AL Laud 1850C
He	Robert				C	1840		Randolph	AL	p194
He	Robert		John		b	1842				AL Cher 1850C
He	Robert			_ Mary	b	1847			SC	AL Walk 1870C #75
He	Robert		John		b	1849				AL Laud 1850C
He	Robert				C	1850				AL Blou p108
He	Robert				C	1850				AL Faye p93
He	Robert	L	John R	_Smith	Ind Cher? Sr res		Tellico Pl	Monroe	TN	AL Jack f
He	Robert	L		_Clayton Harriet 1	b of son Felix	1836		DeKalb	AL	TX Titu 1850C

LN	FIRSTNAME	IO	FATHER	MOM_SPOUSE	EVENT	EVENTDATE	CITY	COUNTY_PAR	ST	SOURCE
He	Robert	L		_ Clayton Harriet 1	C as R S?	1840		DeKalb	AL	
He	Robert	L	Robert L S	Smith_Zona	Ind Cher? b Jr	1903		Jackson	AL	TN Monr t
Hi	Robert	W			b C res of Green	1850			GA	AL Coff 1870C #81
Hi	Rufus	Ro	Thomas Mar		b Rufus Roy d1976	1898		Pike	AL	
He	Rutherford				b of son Jms	1843				AL Rand 1850C
He	Rutherford				C	1850				AL Rand p294
He	Samuel			_Sarah E	b in res Poll Gibson	1825			NC	AL Barb 1870C p192
He	Samuel		Lazarus	_Elondar	b	1833		Tuscaloosa	AL	MS m
He	Samuel		William		b	1837				AL Blou 1850C
Hi	Samuel				C	1840		Franklin	AL	p227
He	Samuel		Thomas		b	1847				AL Laud 1850C
He	Samuel				C	1850				AL Laud p248
Hi	Samuel		Green	Lucinda	b	1853			GA	AL Coff 1870C #81
Ha	Samuel	A	George W		b	1828				AL Cham 1850C
He	Samuel	Al	Asbury	Hudson	b Sml Alfred	1861		Marshall	AL	AR t AL Morg 1870C
He	Samuel	Jr	Samuel Sr		b	1837				AL Morg 1850C
He	Samuel	Sr			C	1850				AL Morg p272
He	Sanford	Ha	Armstead	Petty_White Nancy	b d15May1892	1823		Morgan	GA	AL Cleb 1870C
He	Sanford	Ha	Armstead	_White Nancy C	b Sr	1823		Morgan	GA	AL Rand 1860C
He	Sarah		John		b	1815				AL Lown 1850C
Hi	Sarah		Mathew		b	1834				AL Maco 1850C
He	Sarah		Ancil	Shackley	b	1839				AL Laud 1850C
Ha	Sarah		William		b	1840				AL Blou 1850C
He	Sarah		John		b	1841				AL Cher 1850C
He	Sarah		John	Elizabeth	b	1844			AL	AL Walk 1850C p327
He	Sarah	A	William	Gilmore	b	1840				AL Mare 1850C
He	Sarah	A	John		b	1845				AL Mare 1850C IGI
Hi	Sarah	E	Thomas		b	1844				AL Monr 1850C
He	Sarah	E	Abner H	Elvira	b	1844			AL	AR HotS 1850Cp284
He	Sarah	E	John		b	1846				AL Rand 1850C
Hi	Sarah	J	Levi	Rebecca	b	1849				AL Mare 1850C p89
Hi	Sarah	J	Noah	McDaniel	b	1858			AL	AL Wash #278
He	Scott		Thomas	Hulsey_Denton Susann	b Sawmill d13Mar1946	13 Jan 1861			AL	TN Lewi d
He	Sena	S	James	Warren	b	1850			AL	AL Barb 1870C p185
He	Silas		John		b	1835				AL Cher 1850C
Hi	Simeon				C	1850				AL Maco IGI
Hi	Solomon				Tax	1816	AL Ter	Monroe	AL	AIS#1

LN	FIRSTNAME	IO	FATHER	MOM_SPOUSE	EVENT	EVENTDATE	CITY	COUNTY_PAR	ST	SOURCE
He	Solomon				w	10 Dec 1822		Jefferson	AL	p19
He	Solomon			Elizabeth	b	1832			AL	AL Walk 1850C #11
He	Solomon		Isaac Sr	Sarah	b C inres P McElroy	1843			AL	AL Walk 1850C #365
He	Susan			_Noble Yancy	m	22 Nov 1837		Marshall	AL	NC b
He	Susanna		Jesse Sr	_Driver W M	b d22Apr1932	21 Sep 1849	Wedowee	Randolph	AL	
Ha	T	J			C	1840		Barbour	AL	p47
He	Tapley	Sr	Tapley Old	Holder_Kilgare Mariah	C	1860	Center	Cherokee	AL	GA Morg Mariah res
Ha	Thaddeus		George W		b	1843			AL	Cham 1850C
Hi	Thomas				C State	1820		Conecuh	AL	01 06 01 04 12 AHQ
Hi	Thomas				Tax	1821		Conecuh	AL	AIS#2
Hi	Thomas				Tax	1823		Conecuh	AL	AIS#2
Hy	Thomas				C	1830		Conecuh	AL	p110
He	Thomas		William Jr	Millie_Hulsey Terri Jan	b d1908	Oct 1833		Walker	AL	TN Lawr d
He	Thomas		John		b	1836			AL	Cher 1850C
Hi	Thomas				C	1840		Franklin	AL	p227
Hi	Thomas				C	1840		Monroe	AL	p242
He	Thomas		William		b	1841			AL	Blou 1850C
Hi	Thomas			_Sanders Areaney	m	15 Jan 1843		Tallapoosa	AL	IGI
Ha	Thomas		Andrew	Elizabeth	b	1849			AL	Cone 1850C
He	Thomas				C (2)	1850			AL	Laud p24
He	Thomas				C	1850			AL	Auta p68
Hi	Thomas				C	1850		Monroe	AL	p9
He	Thomas		William Jr	_Hulsey Terri Jane	m	1858		Winston	AL	
He	Thomas		William Jr	Milly_Hyulsey Teri	War Cvl avoided	1863		Winston	AL	Hid in caves
He	Thomas	G	William	Gilmore	b	1848			AL	Mare 1850C
He	Thomas	J	George H		b	1849			AL	Perr 1850C
He	Thomas	Jr	Thomas Sr		b	1847			AL	Laud 1850C
Hi	Thomas	Ma	Mastin Asb	Rushing	b Tms Martin d1954	1868		Pike	AL	
He	Thomas	P			C	1850			AL	Walk p305
He	Thomas	Sr			C	1830		Lauderdale	AL	p240
Hi	Tilmon	G	Asa	Moore	b	1841			GA	AL Butl 1850C p193
He	Timothy		William		b	1836			AL	Blou 1850C
He	Virginia		Tapley Sr	Kilgare	b	1842			GA	AL Cher 1860C
He	W				C	1840		Blount	AL	p85
He	W	C			War Cvl CoI Pvt1865-	1861			AL	53rd Rangers NARS
Hi	W	E			C	1830		Montgomery	AL	p177
Hi	W	J			C	1840		Russell	AL	p3

LN	FIRSTNAME	IO	FATHER	MOM_SPOUSE	EVENT	EVENTDATE	CITY	COUNTY_PAR	ST	SOURCE
Hi	W	W			C	1850		Choctaw	AL	p161
Hi	William			_ Martha	Farmer b	1811			NC	AL Coff 1870C #521
He	William			_Millie	b	1812			GA	AL Lawr 1860C #274
He	William		John W	_Gilmore Ann	m	21 Dec 1829		Marengo	AL	
He	William				C	1830		Blount	AL	p23
He	William				C	1830		Dallas	AL	p69
He	William				C	1830		Marion	AL	p181
Hi	William		John W	Moore_Gilmore Anna	C	1830		Merengo	AL	p359
He	William		Ancil	Shackley	b	1834				AL Laud 1850C IGI
He	William		James		b	1834				AL Rand 1850C
He	William			_ Mary	b of dau Desina	1836				AL KY Mars 1850C
Hi	William			_Thompson Elizabeth M	m	31 May 1836		Wilcox	AL	
Hi	William		Asa	Moore	b	1838				AL Butl 1850C IGI
Ha	William		Andrew Sr	Elizabeth	b	1839		Conecuh	AL	1850C IGI
He	William		Robert L	Clayton	b	1839		DeKalb	AL	TX Titu 1850C p97
He	William				C	1840		Benton	AL	p14
He	William		Andrew Sr	Elizabeth	b	15 Oct 1840		Conecuh	AL	
He	William		John W	Moore_Gilmore Anna	C	1840		Marengo	AL	p67
He	William				C	1840		Randolph	AL	p209
He	William			Elizabeth	b	1842			AL	AL Walk 1850C #11
He	William		John W	Moore_Gilmore Anna	Exec w of John W	07 Aug 1844		Marengo	AL	
Hi	William		Asa		b	1846				AL Butl 1850C
Hi	William		John		b	1847				AL Maco 1850C
Ha	William		John W		b	1849				AL Russ 1850C
He	William				C	1850		Blount	AL	p124
He	William		John W	Moore_Gilmore Ann	C	1850		Marengo	AL	p48
He	William				C	1850		Randolph	AL	p289
He	William				L 80 Acr Sec35	23 Jun 1855		Winston	AL	Cert#24367
He	William				L 80 Acr Sec36	21 Aug 1855		Winston	AL	Cert#24807
He	William				L 40 Acr Sec36	21 Sep 1855		Winston	AL	Cert#25123
He	William				L 40 Acr Sec3 SWofNW	23 Feb 1859		Winston	AL	Cert#30020
He	William				L 80 Acr Sec35	20 Jan 1859		Winston	AL	Cert#29764
He	William				War Cvl CoC Pvt1865-	1861			AL	21stInf NARS
He	William				War Cvl CoE 28AL Inf	1863		Winston	AL	SLA
Hi	William				Ind Cher rej	1909	Local		AL	#6366 Creek Case
He	William	A	Armstead	Petty	b				GA	AL Rand 1860C
He	William	Ab	Abner H	Elvira	b	1847			AL	AR HotS 1850C p284

19

LN	FIRSTNAME	IO	FATHER	MOM_SPOUSE	EVENT	EVENTDATE	CITY	COUNTY_PAR	ST	SOURCE
He	William	C			C	1850		Marion	AL	p132
Hi	William	Ca	Asa	_Wallace Barbara E	Police Dept				AL	
Hi	William	El	Bartley M	_Roberson Martha Eliza	b d1938 mom Boykins	26 Nov 1877			AL	TX Lubbock d
Hi	William	F	Joshua	_ Martha Ann Pugh	b	1810		Robeson	NC	AL Pike 1850C p138
Hi	William	F	Joshua	_Pugh Martha Ann	m d30Dec1893	14 Dec 1839		Pike	AL	
Hi	William	F	Joshua	_ Pugh Martha?	C Wm	1840		Pike	AL	p390
Hi	William	Fe	William Sr	Johnson_Nunes Euphemia	Shoemaker b Wm Felix	1845	Clayton	Barbour	AL	1860C #69
Hi	William	Fe	William Sr	Johnson_Nunes Euphemia	War Cvl CoB enl	01 Mar 1862	Clayton	Barbour	AL	57Rgt Inf
Hi	William	Fe	William Sr	_Nunes Euphemia O	m dau of Hnry A	01 Mar 1867		Barbour	AL	AL Mare t
He	William	G	William	Gilmore	b	1838				AL Mare 1850C
He	William	H	John Sr	Elizabeth	b	1840		Walker	AL	1850C p327
Hi	William	J		_Elender	b	1801			NC	AL Covi 1850C p163
Hi	William	J		_ Elender	b of dau Martha	1836			SC	AL Covi 1850C p163
Hi	William	J		_ Elender	b of son Martin	1843			FL	AL Covi 1850C p163
Ha	William	J	James		b	1845				AL Coff 1850C
Hi	William	J		_ Elender	b of son Joseph	1845			GA	AL Covi 1850C p163
He	William	Jr		_ Millie	C 30-40	1840		Walker	AL	221001 000001 p293
He	William	M	Richard	Frances_Margaret	b	1834			AL	MS Kemp 1860C #396
He	William	M	Tapley Jr	Kilgare	b	1844			GA	AL Cher 1860C
He	William	R	George W		b	1846				AL Perr 1850C
He	William	R			War Cvl CoC Pvt1865-	1861			AL	21stInf NARS
He	William	Sr	John Sr	Elizabeth_Cole Isabella	b Wm D?	1798		Rutherford	NC	AL Walk 1850C p300
Hi	William	Sr	Jesse Sr	Catherine_Johnson Maria	Shoemaker b	1809			NC	AL Barb 1860C #69
Hi	William	Sr	Jesse Sr	_Johnson Maria	m dau of Jim	1835	Clayton	Barbour	AL	
Hi	William	Sr	Jesse Sr	Catherine_Johnson Marie	LG ent	1836		Barbour	AL	Twp10 R26 Sec22
Hi	William	Sr	Jesse Sr	Catherine_Johnson Marie	LG	20 Sep 1839	Sparta	Sparta	AL	#5146 bro Jesse?
He	William	Sr	John Sr	Elizabeth_Cole Isabelle	C 40-50	1840		Walker	AL	0110001 101001 p293
He	Winifred		William		b Winnafer	1845				AL Blou 1850C

FLORIDA

LN	FIRSTNAME	IO	FATHER	MOM_SPOUSE	EVENT	EVENTDATE	CITY	COUNTY_PAR	ST	SOURCE
Hi	A	W		_Bishop Sarah Nancy	m	19 Mar 1857		Putnam	FL	IGI
Hi	Albert			_Sterling Mary Ann	m	01 Jan 1857		Hillsborou	FL	IGI
Hi	Albert	G	Henry Brig	_Dolan Mary	b	09 Oct 1881		Clay	FL	Moore mom
Hi	Albert	P	Joseph E H	Jane L	b?	1879			FL	
Hi	Alcy			_Miller Arthur	m	09 Oct 1866		Jackson	FL	IGI
Hi	Alma		Thomas Jef	_Asson Thomas	b	1883		Lake	FL	Bundy mom
Hi	Almira		Thomas Jef	Cannady_Kinsey L	Husb wit Wid Pen App	20 Mar 1893		Lake	FL	of mom Eliza Cannady
Hi	Andrew	Ja	Thomas Jef	Cannady_Sullivan Sarah	b d12Feb1924	10 Jan 1846	Lake Park	Lowndes	GA	FL Lake Altoona Cem
Hi	Andrew	Ja	Thomas Jef	_Sullivan Sarah	m	24 Dec 1868	Waldo	Alachua	FL	
Hi	Anna	Lo	Thomas Jef	_Bevil L	b Anna Louise	29 Mar 1877		Lake	FL	Bundy mom
Hi	Asa	Mi	Asa Edward	_Bush Nancy Ann	m Asa Miles	09 Nov 1882	Greenville	AL		FL Pensacola t
Hi	Augustine	W		_Matthison Ruth	m	07 Dec 1849		Gadsden	FL	IGI
Hi	Bartlett			_Alderman Margaret Ann	m	1847			FL	GA Pio of Wiregrass
Hi	Bartlett	F		_Laing Margaretta M	m	20 Dec 1865	Quincy	Gadsden	FL	IGI
Hi	Benjamin	A		_Alderman Sarah J	m	26 Dec 1855		Gadsden	FL	IGI
He	Burr				C	1840		Gadsden	FL	p97
He	Burr				Tax	1845		Gadsden	FL	AIS#4
Hi	Caswell		Andrew Jac	Sullivan	b	27 Jan 1875		Lake	FL	
Hi	Charity			_Faircloth Alexander	m	05 Oct 1866		Jackson	FL	IGI
Hi	Charles			_Hinson Mary	m	09 Oct 1866		Jackson	FL	IGI
Hi	Charles	E	Andrew Jac	_Earhart Mary	b	10 Mar 1870		Lake	FL	Sullivan mom
Hi	Charles	L	Henry Brig	_Mattie L	b	17 Jan 1886		Clay	FL	Moore mom
Hi	Charlotte			_Chapple George	m	07 Oct 1866		Gadsden	FL	IGI
Hi	Colonel	De	Thomas Jef	Bundy	b Colonel Desoto	Apr 1878		Lake	FL	
Hi	Cornelius			_Hinson Gracy	m	14 Oct 1866		Gadsden	FL	IGI
Hi	Daniel	M			C as D M	1830		Gadsden	FL	p156
Hi	Daniel	M			C	1840		Gadsden	FL	p97
Hi	Daniel	M			C State	1845		Gadsden	FL	AIS#4
Hi	Dolly	Lo		_Lyman Hall Jr	b Dolly Lovena	1874			FL	
Hi	Dora		Thomas Jef	Bundy	b	1879		Lake	FL	
Hi	Elijah			_Butler Ellen	m	22 Aug 1869		Gadsden	FL	IGI
Hi	Elizabeth		Thomas Jef		b	1868			FL	
Hi	Elizabeth		George Was	Elizabeth Lizzie	b?	1868			FL	
Hi	Elizabeth	C	Andrew Jac	_Pepper	b	29 Dec 1871		Lake	FL	Sullivan mom
Hi	Ellen			_Gain Henry	m	21 Jul 1869		Gadsden	FL	IGI
Hi	Fannie			_Wyatt George B	m	31 May 1867		Gadsden	FL	IGI
Hi	Francis	J	Thomas Jef	Cannady_Mary L	d post	20 Mar 1893	Altoona	Lake	FL	

LN	FIRSTNAME	IO	FATHER	MOM_SPOUSE	EVENT	EVENTDATE	CITY	COUNTY_PAR	ST	SOURCE
Hi	Frank	He	Henry Brig	Moore_Mattie L	b Frank Henry	Apr 1872			FL	see Henry Frank
Hi	Franklin		Andrew Jac	Sullivan	b	1879		Lake	FL	
Hi	Fred		Andrew Jac	Sullivan	b	16 Mar 1894		Lake	FL	
Hi	George	Wa	Thomas Jef	_Elizabeth Lizzie	m?	1864			FL	
Hi	George	Wa	Henry Brig	_Green Estella	b d07Sep1934	14 Jul 1874	Waldo	Alachua	FL	
Hi	Gracy			_Hinson Cornelius	m	14 Oct 1866		Gadsden	FL	IGI
He	Green	A	Hadley	Avery	b	1835			AL	FL t?
Hi	H	E		_Harrison Daniel	m	30 Feb 1866		Alachua	FL	IGI
Hi	Hadly		Bartlett S	_ Elizabeth Avery	b d1889	1808			NC	FL d
Hi	Hadly			_Horn Lizzie L	m	08 Dec 1868		Jackson	FL	IGI
Hi	Hager			_Mitchell Charles	m	30 Aug 1866		Marion	FL	IGI
Hi	Harriet			_Grissett A C W	m	19 Dec 1837		Leon	FL	IGI
Hi	Harriet			_Cox John	m	10 Jan 1846		Leon	FL	IGI
Hi	Harriet	P		_Green George Washingtn	m	25 Feb 1847	Tallahasse	Leon	FL	IGI
Hi	Harry			_Mills Julia	m	11 Mar 1869		Gadsen	FL	IGI
Hi	Hattie		Andrew Jac	_Fish	b	27 Mar 1894		Lake	FL	Sullivan mom
Hi	Henrietta			_Anderson Charles	m	07 Oct 1866		Gadsen	FL	IGI
Hi	Henry			_Nelson Amanda	m	04 Oct 1866		Gadsen	FL	IGI
Hi	Henry			_McElvy Clara	m	24 Dec 1867		Gadsen	FL	IGI
He	Henry	Br	Thomas Jef	_Moore Martha A	b Henry Briggs Sr	1842	Lake Park	Lowndes	GA	FL Clay 1850C #792
He	Henry	Br	Henry Brig	Moore_unm	b Jr dy	Apr 1872	Saluda	Alachua	FL	
Hi	Henry	Fr		_Mattie L	b of son Jesse J	Sep 1893			FL	see Frank Henry
Hi	Horace	G	Andrew Jac	_Aileen	b	17 Aug 1887	Altoona	Lake	FL	Sullivan mom
Ha	J	H			Petition	1827	St Augusti	St Johns	FL	
Ha	J	M			Tax 1829-	1822	St Augusti	St Johns	FL	
Hi	James	Al	James H	McCrary	b Jms Alphe	17 Dec 1867		Jackson	FL	IGI
Hi	James	Fu	James L	Obedience_Douglas Eliza	Wit Wid Pen of Tms J	21 Apr 1893		Coffee	GA	FL Lake Wid Pen#1110
Hi	James	H		_McCrary Mary J	b of son Jms Alphe	17 Dec 1867		Jackson	FL	IGI
Hi	Jennie			_Young Tony	m	22 Mar 1866		Jackson	FL	IGI
Hi	Jesse		William Sr	_Hinson Lucy Malinda	m dau of Needham	28 Feb 1866	Troy	Pike	AL	FL t
He	Jesse		William Sr	Johnson_Hinson Lucy	Wid War Cvl Pen App	Jul 1900			AL	FL?
Hi	Jesse	J	Frank H	Mattie	b	Sep 1893			FL	
He	Jesse	Sr		_ Catherine	b	1785			NC	FL d
Ha	John				Petitioner	1824		Jackson	FL	
Hi	John		Henry Brig	Moore	b	17 Mar 1865			FL	
Hi	John			_Andrews Rose	m	08 Sep 1869		Jackson	FL	IGI
Hi	John	H	Andrew Jac	_Butler Dora Ann	b d23Nov1945	20 Feb 1865		Lake	FL	Sullivan mom

LN	FIRSTNAME	IO	FATHER	MOM_SPOUSE	EVENT	EVENTDATE	CITY	COUNTY_PAR	ST	SOURCE
Ha	John	M		_ Brebner Elizabeth	Gaurd of wifes prop		St Augusti	St Johns	FL	SC prop in
Ha	John	M		_Brebner Elizabeth	m	14 Nov 1826	St Augusti	St Johns	FL	IGI
Hi	Johnathan		William J	Elender	b	1849			FL	AL Covi p163
Hi	Joseph			_Brown Althis Ann	m	11 Mar 1856		Jackson	FL	IGI
Hi	Joseph		Andrew Jac	_Lanier Rosa Lee	b	05 Mar 1877		Lake	FL	Sullivan mom
Hi	Joseph	EH	Thomas Jef	Cannady_Jane L	m?	1878			FL	
Hi	Joseph	Ro	Henry Brig	Moore	b? Joseph Rowan	1873		Alachua	FL	
Hi	Josephine			_Laing Waltham E	m	16 Mar 1865		Gadsden	FL	IGI
Hi	Kate		Albert G	Eliza Lizzie	b	1871		Clay	FL	
Hi	Leon		Andrew Jac	Sullivan	b	29 Jun 1889		Lake	FL	
Hi	Lillie		Andrew Jac	_Menard John	b	14 Apr 1880		Lake	FL	Sullivan mom
Hi	Linda			_Jones Abram	m	09 Sep 1866		Marion	FL	IGI
Hi	M	H		_Bowl Ommie M	m	16 May 1865		Jackson	FL	IGI
Hi	Martha			_Mitchell Nelson	m	07 Oct 1866		Gadsden	FL	IGI
Hi	Martha	Ca		_Woodberry John H	m	11 Nov 1869		Gadsden	FL	IGI
Hi	Martha	Ja	Henry Brig	_Gnann Ephraim	b	29 Feb 1880		Clay	FL	Moore mom
Hi	Martin		William J	Elender	b	1843			FL	AL Covi 1850C p163
Hi	Mary			_Hinson Charles	m	09 Oct 1866		Jackson	FL	IGI
Hi	Mary	A		_Goodwin Solomon	m	26 Apr 1866		Hillsborou	FL	IGI
Hi	Mary	An	Thomas Jef	_Dees Lenord Bryant	m	14 Jan 1866			FL	
Hi	Mary	J		_Alderman George F	m	08 May 1856		Gadsden	FL	IGI
Hi	Milliard		John H	_Perry Clara	b	Jul 1899			FL	Butler mom
Hi	Minnie	T	Thomas Jef	Bundy_Hull Samuel Mor	b	1871		Lake	FL	
Hi	Minnie	T	Thomas Jef	_Hull Samuel Morgan	m	16 Apr 1893	Altoona	Lake	FL	FL Gen V5:1 p17
Hi	Nancy			_Bailey Jack	m	23 Sep 1866		Alachua	FL	IGI
Hi	Nancy			_Tanner James	m	09 Oct 1866		Jackson	FL	IGI
Hi	Nancy			_Harris William	m	16 Apr 1868		Polk	FL	IGI
Hi	Phillip			_Alderman Margaret	m	03 Feb 1850		Gadsden	FL	IGI
Hi	Phoebe			_Goodwin Francis	m	06 Oct 1866		Gadsden	FL	IGI
Ha	Reason				War Rev Muster Sgt	15 Jun 1783	St Augusti	St Johns	FL	Loy Sou Camp
Hi	Rhoda			_Williamson Benjamin	m	05 Oct 1867		Leon	FL	IGI
Hi	Robert		George Was	Eliza Lizzie	b	1866		Clay	FL	
Hi	Ruth	M	Joseph E H	Jane L	b?	1881			FL	
Hi	Ruth	M	John H	Butler	b	Dec 1887			FL	
Hi	Samuel				c	1840		Columbia	FL	p150
Hi	Samuel				Tax	1845		Columbia	FL	AIS#4
Hi	Solomon			_Browning Esther	m	28 Aug 1868		Gadsden	FL	IGI

LN	FIRSTNAME	IO	FATHER	MOM_SPOUSE	EVENT	EVENTDATE	CITY	COUNTY_PAR	ST	SOURCE
Hi	Sophia			_Agnew Jerry	m	10 Sep 1866		Marion	FL	IGI
Hi	Stella		Andrew Jac	Sullivan_Matteson Clare	b	18 Dec 1891		Lake	FL	
Hi	Stella		Andrew Jac	_Matteson Clarence	Adopted Wilbur Lee	19		Lake	FL	
Hi	Susan	V	Henry Brig	Moore_Hall John P	b	12 Apr 1866		Clay	FL	
Hi	Susan	V	Henry Brig	_Hall John P 1	m	20 Sep 1884		Clay	FL	
Hi	Susan	V	Henry Brig	_Hall Geo Washington 2	m	04 Oct 1896		Clay	FL	
Hi	Thomas	Je	James L	Obedience_Cannady Elizb	b Sr	25 Feb 1803			SC	FL Lake Altoona Cem
Hi	Thomas	Je	James L	Obedience_Cannady Elizb	b Tms Jefferson Sr	1803			SC	FL Oran 1870C
Hi	Thomas	Je	James L	Obedience_Cannady Eliza	War Indian disc	18 Dec 1837	Ft Gilland		FL	Smith Geo W Capt
Hi	Thomas	Je	Thomas Jef	Cannaday_Bundy Louisa A	b Jr d15Apr1918	26 Aug 1851		Lowndes	GA	FL Lake Altoona Cem
Hi	Thomas	Je	James L	Obedience_Cannady Eliza	War Ind L 80 Acr	Oct 1855			FL	LW#13888 Pen#1110
Hi	Thomas	Je	James L	Obedience_Cannady Eliza	C Sr	1860		New River	FL	
Hi	Thomas	Je	Thomas Jef	_Bundy Louisa Ann	m Jr	10 Sep 1869		Putnam	FL	IGI
Hi	Thomas	Je	Andrew Jac	_Ahern Grace	b	18 Jun 1873		Lake	FL	Sullivan mom
Hi	Thomas	Je	James L	Obedience_Cannady Eliza	C	1880		Lake	FL	
Hi	Thomas	Je	James L	Obedience_Cannady Eliza	d	07 Feb 1882	Altoona	Lake	FL	Hinson Cem
He	Thomas	Je	James L	Obedience_Cannady Eliza	Wid War Ind Pen Appl	13 Sep 1892	Altoona	Lake	FL	Kinsey L wit #1110
Hi	Thomas	Je	Thomas Jef	Cannady_Bundy Louisa An	Wit Wid Pen Appl of	13 Sep 1892	Altoona	Lake	FL	Cannady Eliza mom
Hi	Thomas	W	John	Elizabeth	Res	1874	Ocala	Ocala	FL	Conf Mil Hist V8p540
Hi	Wilbur	Le	Wilbur		Adopted by Stella &			Lake	FL	Matteson Clarence
Hi	William		Andrew Jac	Sullivan	b	14 Dec 1882		Lake	FL	
Hi	William		James L	Obedience_Haddock Nancy	Wit Wid Pen of Tms J	21 Apr 1893		Coffee	GA	FL Lake Wid Pen#1110
Hi	William	J		_ Elender	b of son Martin	1843			FL	AL Covi 1850C p163
Hi	Wilson			_Johnson Flora	m	30 Sep 1866		Gadsden	FL	IGI
Hi	Windham			_McAfee Elizabeth	m	09 Apr 1834		Leon	FL	IGI
Hi	Witherow		George Was	Elizabeth Lizzie	b?	1873			FL	

Georgia

LN	FIRSTNAME	IO	FATHER	MOM_SPOUSE	EVENT	EVENTDATE	CITY	COUNTY_PAR	ST	SOURCE
He				_Davis	m			Franklin	GA	Hist of p550
Ha				_Nancy	Wid b	1770			VA	GA Morg 1850C
Ha				_Ann	Wid b	1772			VA	GA Monr 1850C
Hi				_Sarah Ann	Wid m Deed Bk18	15 Oct 1795		Liberty	GA	Austin Joseph
Ha				_Margaret	Wid b	1795			MD	GA Wilk 1850C
He					Tax	1807		Franklin	GA	Middleton & #15
Ha				_ Elizabeth	Wid LL	1807		Wilkes	GA	#146 16 W
He					Tax	1808		Franklin	GA	Hulford & #30
He					Tax	1808		Franklin	GA	Ker & #18
He					Tax	1819		Franklin	GA	Garrott & #67
He					C wid/Mrs	1820		Chatham	GA	
Hi				_Sarah	C wid RS Isaac?	1820	Winnes Dis	Jackson	GA	
Hi					C Ind Cher?	1820		Richmond	GA	
Ha				_Elizabeth	C wid	1820		Wilkes	GA	p170
Ha				_ Sarah	Wid L 450 acres	17 Feb 1821			GA	Gen Mag VA
Ha				_ Elizabeth	C wid State	1824		Wilkes	GA	
Hi				_ Sarah	Wid RS LL res	1827	Winnes Dis	Jackson	GA	
Hi				_ Sarah	Wid RS LL	1827		Troup	GA	166 9
Hi					Tax Capt no Roone?	1830		Roone	AR	GA Kith&Kin of
Ha				_Ruth	C wid	1830		Morgan	GA	p252
He				_Marann	C wid	1830		Walton	GA	p173
Ha				_ Elizabeth	C wid	1830		Wilkes	GA	p324
He				_ Dilday Mary	Ind Cher bofson Chas	1832	Tunnel Hil		GA	
Ha				_ Elizabeth	Wid LL Cher Res	1832		Wilkes	GA	Lot28 Dist4 Sec1
Ha				_Francis	d post	1835			GA	
He				_ Walkingstick Elizabet	Ind Cher of #940 res	1835	Ind Ter		GA	Tally Robert gs
Ha				_Elizabeth	Wid LL res	1838		Newton	GA	#319
Ha				_ Elizabeth	Wid of J M? w t	09 Nov 1838		Wilkes	GA	Knox Jane p46
Ha				_Margaret	Wid m	28 Mar 1839			GA	Slaughter Beverly
He				_Holder	War Rev 7 bro d	1839		Paulding	GA	1858 lttr
He				_Eliza S	C wid	1840		Oglethorpe	GA	p65
He				_ Margaret	C wid	1840	Dist 166	Wilkes	GA	p272
He				_Burney Etta	m	1841			GA	McCall Collec GASLA
Hi			Caleb?	_Golden Noah	w of Caleb	1845		Twiggs	GA	
He				_Margaret	C wid	1850	Div 11	Carroll	GA	p15
He				_Mary	C wid	1850	Div 11	Carroll	GA	p68
He				_Martha	C wid	1850	Div 12	Cass	GA	p196

LN	FIRSTNAME	IO	FATHER	MOM_SPOUSE	EVENT	EVENTDATE	CITY	COUNTY_PAR	ST	SOURCE
He				_Martha	C wid	1850	Div 12	Cass	GA	p127
He				_Wealthy	C wid of Jms?	1850	Scull Sh	Clarke	GA	p80
Hi				_Sarah	C wid	1850	Dist 19	Coweta	GA	p338
Hi				_Rachael C	C wid	1850	Dist 69	Pulaski	GA	p240
He				_Mary	C wid	1850	Mineral	Stewart	GA	p127
He				_Sarah	C wid	1850	Mineral	Stewart	GA	p127
He				_Mary	C wid	1850	Dist 23	Talbot	GA	p308
He				_Irla H	C wid	1850	Div 88	Walton	GA	p30
Hi				_Lamb Axie Elizabeth	b of son Jacob Bucha	27 May 1857	Cochran	Pulaski	GA	IGI
He				_Athan Fanny	b of son Nathaniel	12 Aug 1872		Stewart	GA	IGI
He			William C	_ Thompson	Ind Cher #17442	1908	Blue Ridge		GA	#117 dup rej
He				_ Walkingstick Elizabet	Ind Cher of #940	1909		Jasper	GA	Tally Robert gs
Hi	-----				Tax	1807		Franklin	GA	#31
He	-----				Tax	1807		Franklin	GA	#32
He	-----				Tax	1807		Franklin	GA	#118
He	-----				Tax	1807		Franklin	GA	#70
He	-----				Tax	1807		Franklin	GA	#71
He	-----				Tax	1808		Franklin	GA	#28
He	-----				Tax	1819		Franklin	GA	#49
He	-----				Tax	1819		Franklin	GA	#69
He	-----				Tax	1819		Franklin	GA	#89
He	------				Tax	1807		Franklin	GA	#78
Hi	------				Tax	1819		Franklin	GA	#140 ·
Hi	------				Tax	1819		Franklin	GA	#144
He	------				Tax	1819		Franklin	GA	#145
He	------				Tax	1819		Franklin	GA	#146
He	------				Tax	1819		Franklin	GA	#71
He	------				Tax	1819		Franklin	GA	#66
He	------				Tax	1819		Franklin	GA	#135
He	--------				Tax	1819		Franklin	GA	#143
He	A	A			War Cvl Conf Gamblin	1863			GA	Capt State Troop
He	A	J		_King Rebecca	m	04 Jan 1880		Fulton	GA	IGI
He	Aaron				b	1765				GA Fran 1830C p231
He	Aaron			_Mary	Tax 1831	1826	Dist 4	Appling	GA	
He	Aaron			_ Mary	Tax 3 lots won by	1826		Franklin	GA	Lazarus bro?
He	Aaron				C 60-70 p231	1830		Franklin	GA	000110011 01121001
He	Aaron				Appraiser f	06 Jul 1830		Franklin	GA	York Wm p19

LN	FIRSTNAME	IO	FATHER	MOM_SPOUSE	EVENT	EVENTDATE	CITY	COUNTY_PAR	ST	SOURCE
He	Aaron			_ Mary	Tax 1 poll	1832		Carroll	GA	
He	Aaron			_ Mary	LL Cher	1832		Walker	GA	#271 Dist26 sec3
He	Aaron				Juror	05 Jan 1833		Carroll	GA	Inf Crt Min1827-47
He	Aaron			_ Mary	d	1835		Carroll	GA	
He	Aaron				b War Cvl 43ALInf	1841			GA	AL Wash res
He	Aaron				L 202 Acr Tax 1 poll	1844		Carroll	GA	Orren A?
He	Aaron				L 40 Acr Tax 1 poll	1844		Paulding	GA	
He	Aaron				L 160 Acr Tax 1 poll	1844		Walker	GA	
He	Aaron	Wi	Orren A	_Brown Louisa	b d25Jan1933	24 Nov 1847		Carroll	GA	TX Wood d
Ha	Aaron	Wi	Orren A	Cartwright_Brown Louisa	War Cvl enl	1863		Carroll	GA	GSLA
Ha	Abner				b	1814			NC	GA Cass Mort Sched
Ha	Abner				LL Res	1838		Jefferson	GA	#193
Ha	Abner				d	Apr 1849		Cass	GA	1850 Mort Sched
He	Abraham				War Cvl Conf CoC	1863			GA	31stInf NARS
He	Ada			_Fleming Charles	m	1896		Gwinnett	GA	
He	Ada	A	Andrew Ber	Angelina	b	1843			GA	GA Cass 1850C #1373
Hi	Addison				C	1850	Dist 69	Pulaski	GA	p235
He	Aggie		William Ri	Blair_Rhodes Samuel	Ind Cher b as Margar	1836			GA	NC Cher 1850C #63
He	Agnes		Archibald		Ind Cher? b	1832		Buncombe	NC	GA Unio 1850C p235
He	Albert	G	Thomas Jef	Cannaday	b	1831		Telfair	GA	GA Lown 1850C #792
Hi	Albert	G	Thomas Jef	Cannady	Unc Jms appt Gaurd	05 Mar 1845		Telfair	GA	
Ha	Alexander	C		_Cleveland Ellen Hanson	m	06 Jun 1852			GA	GSLA DAR Bible R
Ha	Aley		Samuel	_Aldridge Nathan	m Alizannah	11 Aug 1810		Jackson	GA	37,000 MR
He	Alford				War Cvl Conf CoF	1863			GA	38thInf NARS
He	Alfred		James	Costen_Adams Elizabeth	Ind Cher? b d1932	17 Apr 1852		Forsyth	GA	MS d
He	Alfred	W		_Gliddings Letta	m	10 Nov 1868		Pulaski	GA	
Hi	Alice	F	William	_Gaskins Daniel	b mom McDuffie	28 Apr 1848		Telfair	GA	Pio of Wiregrass
Hi	Alice	J	M W	Margaret	b in res Whitten	1847			GA	AL Barb 1860C #68
Ha	Alizannah		Samuel	Simms_Aldridge Nathanie	m	11 Oct 1810		Jackson	GA	So Kith&Kin p109
He	Allen		Daniel Sr	Pool_Blaylock Elizabeth	b	1794		Anson	NC	GA Unio 1850C p206
He	Allen			_Maxwell Rhoda L	m	06 Feb 1853		Cass	GA	
He	Almira		Thomas Jef	Cannady_Kinsey L	b	1835		Lowndes	GA	1850C #792
Hi	Almira		Thomas Jef	_Kinsey L	m	1853			GA	
Hi	Almira		William	_Enzor William	b	28 Mar 1859		Coffee	GA	McDuffie mom
He	Alsey			_Johnson Jesse	m	01 Jan 1829		Franklin	GA	Hist Col DAR
He	Alsey		Joseph Jr	Clark	Ind Cher? b Elsey	1833		Union	GA	
He	Amanda		George W S	Lambert_	b	1834		Coweta	GA	GS NC Meck

LN	FIRSTNAME	IO	FATHER	MOM_SPOUSE	EVENT	EVENTDATE	CITY	COUNTY_PAR	ST	SOURCE
He	Amanda		Reuben	Jones	b	26 Dec 1837			GA	Parker Fam Bible
Ha	Amanda		Reuben	Jones	b	1838			GA	GA Carr 1860C p23
He	Amanda		Rueben	Jones	Orphan	1848		Carroll	GA	Min BkAA 1852-70
Hi	Amanda		Caleb Jr	Lydia Ann	b	1851		Twiggs	GA	
He	Amanda		Henry B	Stewart	b	1854			GA	GA Carr 1870C p28
Ha	Amanda			_Tompkins A	m	20 Dec 1863		Carroll	GA	37,000 MR
Ha	Amanda	C			m	18 Nov 1817			GA	GSLA Bible R
Ha	Amanda	C		_Bostick Abraham J	m	16 Oct 1842		Monroe	GA	
Ha	Amanda	M		_Chastain William J	m	08 Aug 1852		Floyd	GA	
Ha	Ambrose	P	Armstead	Petty_Mary L	b	1837			GA	GA Carr 1850C
He	Ambrose	P	Armstead	_Mary L	b in res Jn Cats	1837			GA	AL Cleb 1870C
He	America		Caleb Jr	Lydia Ann	b	1846		Twiggs	GA	1850C
Hi	America			_Granger Preston	m	05 Jul 1883		Appling	GA	
He	Andrew			_Rackley Kansas	m				GA	GA Gilm Annal of
He	Andrew				C	1840	Dist 700	Troup	GA	p352
He	Andrew	B	Presley Th	_Henderson Molly	m	18			GA	Ada mom
He	Andrew	Be		_Able Angeline	m A B				GA	TX Rusk Hist of
He	Andrew	Be	William M	Motlow_Able Angeline	b Sr	1807		Pendleton	SC	GA Cass 1850C #1373
He	Andrew	Be	William M	Motlow_Able Angeline	C p231	1830		Rabun	GA	TX Rusk t
He	Andrew	Be	Andrew Ber		b Jr t Rusk TX	1836		Cass	GA	Caldwell W in res
He	Andrew	Be	William M	Motlow_Able Angeline	C	1840		Gilmer	GA	p8
He	Andrew	Be			Ind Cher? L t	20 Mar 1844	Elijay	Gilmer	GA	Watkins AbnerBkFp24
He	Andrew	Be	William M	Motlow_Able Angeline	L f	10 Jul 1847		Cass	GA	Smith N H p102 Lot1
He	Andrew	J			War Cvl Conf CoE	1863			GA	30thInf NARS
Hi	Andrew	Ja	Thomas Jef	Cannaday_Sullivan Sarah	b as Jackson	1845		Lowndes	GA	1850C #792
Hi	Andrew	Ja	Thomas Jef	Cannady_Sullivan Sarah	b d12Feb1924	10 Jan 1846	Lake Park	Lowndes	GA	FL Lake Altoona Cem
He	Andrew	Sr		_Elizabeth	C	1850			GA	AL Cone p372
He	Aner		Elam		b	1849			GA	Twig 1850C
He	Angeline		George W S	Lambert_	b	1844			GA	GS NC Meck
Ha	Ann		Samuel	Sims	b				GA	So Kith&Kin p109
He	Ann			_Barnett Nemron	m	23 May 1814		Morgan	GA	
He	Ann		Lazarus	Narvel	b	1820			SC	GA Cass 1850C
Ha	Ann	El		_Lampkin Philip	m	15 Dec 1835		Clarke	GA	
Hi	Anna	B		Martha	b	1848			GA	Butt 1850C #398
He	Annery		Henry?	_Billingsley Walter/HA?	w of Henry see Ann	3 Feb 1849		Rabun	GA	SC Pick land in
Hi	Annie			_Brady John N	m	07 Apr 1887		Pierce	GA	
Hi	Anthony				C	1850	Milledge	Baldwin	GA	p94

LN	FIRSTNAME	IO	FATHER	MOM_SPOUSE	EVENT	EVENTDATE	CITY	COUNTY_PAR	ST	SOURCE
He	Aquilla		William	_Hopkins Lucinda	b Wiley?	1821			GA	GS NC Meck
He	Arcain		Archibald	Mary	b f	1847			GA	TN Hami 1860C p24
He	Arcane		Archibald	Mary	b f	1846			GA	GA Gord 1850C p51
He	Archibald		Lazarus	_Mary	RR hand b d1878 AL	1815			GA	GA Gord 1850C p51
He	Archibald				L	1842	Blue Ridge	Fannin	GA	
He	Archibald		Eli	Ledford	b	1845			GA	GA Unio 1850C p236
He	Archibald		Lazarus	Narvel_Mary	Assault	Nov 1850		Gordon	GA	Supr Court Min
He	Archibald		Lazarus	Narvel_Mary	Vs	14 May 1851		Gordon	GA	Holcomb E Supr Court
He	Archibald			_Shadwick Jincy A	m	30 Apr 1870		Fannin	GA	37,000 GA MR
He	Archibald			_Shelton Louisa	m	12 May 1872		Fannin	GA	37,000 GA MR
He	Archibald	Sr			Ind Cher? b	1776			VA	GA Unio 1850C p235
He	Arena		Henry W	_Johnson Joseph	m see Orena	02 Feb 1857		Tishomingo	MS	GA Walk f
Ha	Armstead			_ Petty Jane	b d1855?	1796			VA	GA Carr 1850C p7
Hi	Armstead				Minute Bk	06 Apr 1816	Mars Hill	Clarke	GA	Bapt Chur
Hi	Armstead				LL res	1820		Clarke	GA	
Hi	Armstead				LL	1820		Irwin	GA	#184 16
He	Armstead			_Petty Jane	m dau of Ambrose	18 Feb 1821		Morgan	GA	Loose mr GSLA
Hi	Armstead				L 490 Acr reg	02 Mar 1822		Irwin	GA	
Hi	Armstead				Member bf	Apr 1823	Mars Hill	Clarke	GA	Bapt Chur
He	Armstead				Tax Agnons Dist	1823	Sandy Cree	Morgan	GA	Gilbert adj
He	Armstead				Tax	1824	Watsons Di	Morgan	GA	
Hi	Armstead				Excluded f nonattend	May 1826	Mars Hill	Clarke	GA	Bapt Chur
He	Armstead				Tax Adairs Dist	1826	Sandy Cree	Morgan	GA	Jones adj
He	Armstead				Rest & dismissed	Feb 1829	Mars Hill	Clarke	GA	Bapt Chur
Ha	Armstead				Tax Crowleys Dist	1829		Morgan	GA	
He	Armstead				LL Cher res	1832		Campbell	GA	Lot116 Dist11 Sec1
He	Armstead				LL Cher	1832		Union	GA	
He	Armstead				C 40-50 Armsted	1840	Campbellto	Campbell	GA	1212001 110001 p39
Ha	Armstead	T		_Purdue Mary A	m	12 Sep 1849		Morgan	GA	37,000 MR
Hi	Asa		Caleb Sr	Margaret_Moore Jane	b	1796		Wilkes	GA	AL Butl 1850C p193
Hi	Asa				Tax	1818		Twiggs	GA	
He	Asa				LL	1821		Monroe	GA	96 3
He	Asa				LL Res	1821		Twiggs	GA	
Hi	Asa				b	1828			GA	GA Lown 1850C p167
Hi	Asa		Caleb Sr	_Moore Jane	w of Caleb	01 Mar 1845		Twiggs	GA	Misc deeds
Hi	Asa				C	1850	Div 84	Twiggs	GA	p177
Hi	Asa		Ed Asa	Moore_Sartor Sarah H	b	1824		Twiggs	GA	AL Butl 1850C p193

LN	FIRSTNAME	IO	FATHER	MOM_SPOUSE	EVENT	EVENTDATE	CITY	COUNTY_PAR	ST	SOURCE
He	Asa	Ed	Asa	Moore_Sartor Sarah	b d25Aug1900	22 Sep 1824		Twiggs	GA	
He	Augusta	L		Martha	b	1840			GA	GA Cass 1850C #384
Hi	Augustus		James Fulw	Hall	b	1843		Telfair	GA	
He	Augustus	Ed	James M	_Hutchinson Laura Jane	b Augustus Edwin	1847		Floyd	GA	
Ha	Augustus	Ed	James M	Martha E_Hutchinson Lau	b of dau Azzie Ophel	06 Nov 1876		Floyd	GA	
He	Austin	He	Oren O	_Lantrip Carrie	b Austin Henry	08 Aug 1855		Carroll	GA	Cartwright mom IGI
Ha	Azzie	Op	Augustus E	Hutchinson_Preskitt Dav	b d14Dec1956	06 Nov 1876		Floyd	GA	AL Birm d
Ha	Azzie	Op	Augustus E	_Preskitt David Oskar	m Azzie Ophelia	1896		Floyd	GA	
He	B	F			War Cvl POW d	12 Jul 1862	Macon		GA	Reg of Dis Sold v181
He	B	F			War Cvl POW d	12 Jul 1862	Macon		GA	COD War Cvl
Hi	Bartlett			_Alderman Margaret Ann	m	1847			FL	GA Pio of Wiregrass
He	Becky	A	John		b	1837			GA	GA Walk 1850C
Hi	Belle		William	_McLeod	b	1886		Coffee	GA	Haddock mom
He	Ben				Slave w of Henry	3 Feb 1849		Rabun	GA	
He	Benjamin		Henry W	Pinelope	b	1847		Walker	GA	1850C
He	Benjamin	T	William Ri	Blair	Ind Cher b	1838			GA	NC Cher 1850C p5
He	Berry		William M	Motlow_Angelina	C Andrew Berry	1850		Cass	GA	p196
Hi	Bithina			_Woolfork Jordon	m	19 Dec 1847		Thomas	GA	
He	Blanche		Hillyer L	Jackson	b	13 May 1905	Mineral Bl	Fannin	GA	IGI
He	Bob				Slave w of Henry	03 Feb 1849		Rabun	GA	
Hi	Bryant	F	Wiley Harg	_James Dicy	b	06 Mar 1890		Ware	GA	Booth mom IGI
He	Bug		Joseph Jr	_Cumley Julia	Ind Cher			Union	GA	Clark mom
Hi	Burwell	T	Bartlett		Pwr Atty t Pleasant	26 Feb 1844		Anson	NC	GA t Bk11 p282
He	C				C Chas F?	1840	Waldens	Pulaski	GA	p159
He	C				War Cvl Oath t US	1865		Fannin	GA	NW GA Hist&GS
Ha	C	A	Armstead	Petty	b	1844			GA	GA Carr 1850C
He	C	A			War Cvl Oath t US	1865		Fannin	GA	NW GA Hist&GS
Hi	Caleb		James L?	Obedience_Lydia Ann	b?	1810		Telfair	GA	
Hi	Caleb				C Calip	1840	Dist 785	Sumpter	GA	p170
Hi	Caleb				C	1850			GA	AL Butl p193
Hi	Caleb	Jr	Caleb Sr	Margaret	C	1840	Dist 355	Twiggs	GA	p386
Hi	Caleb	Jr	Caleb Sr	Margaret	w of Caleb Sr	01 Mar 1845		Twiggs	GA	Misc deeds
Hi	Caleb	Jr	Caleb Sr	Margaret	C	1850	Div 84	Twiggs	GA	p177
Hi	Caleb	Sr		_ Margaret	Militia	1793		Wilkes	GA	Fam Puz HHHH file
Hi	Caleb	Sr		_ Margaret	b of son Asa	1796		Wilkes	GA	AL Butl 1850C p193
He	Caleb	Sr			LL	1805		Washington	GA	P B
He	Caleb	Sr		_ Margaret	Tax	1818		Twiggs	GA	

LN	FIRSTNAME	IO	FATHER	MOM_SPOUSE	EVENT	EVENTDATE	CITY	COUNTY_PAR	ST	SOURCE
He	Caleb	Sr		_ Margaret	C Caleb	1830		Twiggs	GA	p62
He	Caleb	Sr		_ Margaret	C	1840	Dist 355	Twiggs	GA	p386
Hi	Caleb	Sr		_Margaret	w	01 Mar 1845		Twiggs	GA	Misc deeds
He	Callie	E	John	_England	Ind Cher? b	23 Feb 1869		Union	GA	Allison mom
He	Caroline		Charlie	_King Fi	Ind Cher			Union	GA	
He	Caroline			_Townsend Mark	m	20 Jan 1879		Paulding	GA	37,000 GA MR
He	Caroline	An		Dilday_ONeal Andy	Ind Cher? b of dau	1841			GA	TN Mari 1850C
He	Catherine			_Whitton William	m	13 Nov 1817		Clark	GA	Whitlow?
Ha	Catherine			_Peavy Daniel	m	19 Dec 1829		Morgan	GA	
Hi	Catherine		Jesse	Catherine_Price	b	1830			GA	AL Barb 1860C p177
Hi	Catherine		Jesse	_Price	b	1833			GA	AL Barb 1870C #1792
Ha	Catherine			_King William	Ind Cher m	03 Feb 1847		Washington	GA	37,000 MR
Ha	Catherine	E	Richard Th	_McCay Henry K	m	07 Dec 1841		Oglethorpe	GA	
He	Catherine	E	Richard Th	Wray_McCay Henry Kent	Res	1842	Americus	Sumter	GA	
He	Catherine	E	Richard Th	Wray_McCay Henry K Genl	d	1854	Atlanta	Fulton	GA	
Ha	Catherine	E			Estate	26 Aug 1856		Wilkes	GA	Ord Ofc Inf Court
He	Catherine	E	Richard Th	Wray_McCay Henry K Genl	War Cvl husb CSA	1863	Atlanta	Fulton	GA	
Hi	Caty		Robert Sr	_Holder John	m	01 Oct 1798		Fauquier	VA	GA Clar t
Hi	Caty			_ John Holder	Tax Scovalls Dist	1819	Bashers Cr	Clarke	GA	Crow adj
Hi	Caty			_ John Holder	Exec w of husb	26 Oct 1822		Clarke	GA	
He	Caty			_ John Holder	Tax Diches Dist	1830	Banberg Cr	Clarke	GA	Holder Tapley agt f
He	Caty			_ John Holder	Orphans of Tax	1830		Lee	GA	
He	Charity		Archibald		Ind Cher b	1820		Buncombe	NC	GA Unio 1850C p235
Hi	Charles				Tax Default 1793	1790		Burke	GA	GA Gen Gems p38 NGS
He	Charles				Tax	1794	Bickhams D	Warren	GA	
Hi	Charles				Tax	1795		Hancock	GA	
Ha	Charles				b Chas F Jr?	1815			NC	GA Pula 1850 MortSch
He	Charles				LL	1821		Dooly	GA	33 12
He	Charles				LL Res	1821		Rabun	GA	
Hi	Charles				C	1830		Hancock	GA	p156
He	Charles		Joseph Jr	_Swain Lissie	Ind Cher b Coon	1832				GA Unio 1850C p235
He	Charles				w	1834		Greene	GA	BkF p192
He	Charles			_Hammons Polly	m	02 Apr 1836		Rabun	GA	
Hi	Charles			_Mullis Rachel	m Chas F Jr?	18 May 1837		Pulaski	GA	Mullins
He	Charles				C	1840	Dist 735	Troup	GA	p369
He	Charles			_ Mary Dilday	Ind Cher? Disappeard	1845			GA	Hubbs Frostp708TNSLA
Ha	Charles				d Chas F Jr?	Jun 1849		Pulaski	GA	1850 Mort Sched

LN	FIRSTNAME	IO	FATHER	MOM_SPOUSE	EVENT	EVENTDATE	CITY	COUNTY_PAR	ST	SOURCE
Ha	Charles		Joseph Jr	_Swim Malissa	Ind Cher m	07 Feb 1858		Union	GA	Swain
He	Charles				War Cvl CoC	1863			GA	Smiths Legion NARS
He	Charles			_Conell Caroline	m	07 Jan 1866		Fannin	GA	
He	Charles	An	Thomas?	Dilday_Nancy Pearson	Ind Cher? b	1831	Ind Ter		GA	TN Mari 1870C p2653
He	Charles	An	Thomas?	Dilday_Pearson Nancy	Ind Cher? b Ind Ter	26 Jun 1831	Tunnel Hil	Gilmer	GA	Lit White Church Cem
He	Charles	An	Thomas?	_Pearson Nancy	Ind Cher bC Anderson	1831	Tunnel Hil	Gilmer	GA	TN Mari 1860C p62
He	Charles	An	Thomas?	Dilday_Pearson Nancy	Ind Cher sis C ONeal	1831	Tunnel Hil	Gilmer	GA	TN Mari 1850C p464
He	Charles	B	Sanford	Rachael	b	1859			GA	GA Carr 1870C p215
Hi	Charles	F	Charles F		b Jr	1806			NC	GA Pula t 1835
Hi	Charles	F	Charles F		Res Jr	1835		Pulaski	GA	NC Meck GS
Hi	Charles	F	William Os		Res Sr	1835		Pulaski	GA	NC Meck GS
Hi	Charles	H	William	Johnson	b	1850	Clayton	Barbour	AL	GA Fult Atlanta t
He	Charles	Jr			LL	1805		Hancock	GA	#1001 B
He	Charles	Jr			Tax	1812		Hancock	GA	#38 AIS #1
He	Charles	Jr	Charles Sr	Sally	b	1829			SC	GA Unio 1850C p235
He	Charles	Sr		_Sally	b	1785			SC	GA Unio 1850C p235
Hi	Charles	Sr			LL	1805		Hancock	GA	#1000 B-P
He	Charles	Sr			Tax	1812		Hancock	GA	#38 AIS#1
He	Charles	Sr		_ Sally	C	1840		Union	GA	p11
He	Charlotte		Daniel	_Cobb Alfred	m	11 Jan 1830		Haywood	NC	GA Unio 1851
Hi	Charlotte		Daniel	Pool_Cobb Alfred	Res	1851		Union	GA	#3991 Pen of Daniel
Ha	Cinderella	An		_Edwards John Crawford	m	20 Sep 1853		Jasper	GA	
He	Claiborne				War Rev Col LB	1776		Washington	GA	GA Fran
Hi	Claiborne				Admin f	26 Jan 1790		Liberty	GA	Kirkland Wm
Hi	Claiborne				w	1794		Liberty	GA	BkA p55
He	Claude	Po	Jay	King_Reeves Augusta	b	28 Nov 1898	Atlanta	Fulton	GA	IGI
He	Claude	Po	Jay	_Reeves Augusta	m	26 May 1918	Atlanta	Fulton	GA	IGI
Ha	Columbus	A		_Garner Matilda	m	06 Feb 1846		Coweta	GA	HS
Ha	Columbus	T			Tax	1829	Lumpkins D	Morgan	GA	
He	Coon		James M	Wiley_Swain	Ind Cher b Chas?			Union	GA	
He	Cordelia		John	Allison	Ind Cher b	07 Mar 1880		Union	GA	#28880
He	Cordelia		John	Allison	Ind Cher Appl	1909		Union	GA	#28880
Hi	Cordell		William	_Patrick Robert	b	1884		Coffee	GA	Haddock mom
He	Cornelia			_Henson Milton	m	1856		Towns	GA	1st MR
Ha	Cynthia	B		_Williams William S	m Cintha	07 Jun 1841		Morgan	GA	37,000 MR
He	Daniel		Allen	Blaylock	Ind Cher? b Dan	1837		Haywood	NC	GA Unio 1850C p206A
He	David			_Judy?	d	07 May 1821		Jasper	GA	Intestate R Austin

LN	FIRSTNAME	IO	FATHER	MOM_SPOUSE	EVENT	EVENTDATE	CITY	COUNTY_PAR	ST	SOURCE
Ha	David				b in Jn H res	1839			GA	Hall 1860C
He	David				C	1850	Div 12	Cass	GA	p151
He	David				War Cvl CoA Pvt	1863			GA	65thInf NARS
Hi	Delila		William Ri	Blair	Ind Cher b	1834			GA	NC Cher 1850C p5
He	Delila		William Ri	Blair	Ind Cher b	1834			GA	1851C Siler Roll
He	Delila		William Ri	Blair_Smith?	Ind Cher b	1835			GA	NC Cher 1860C
Hi	Delilah	An		_Drawdy Levi	m	1830			GA	Pio of Wiregrass
He	Della			_Williams Edwin J	m			Berrian	GA	
He	Dig		James M	Wiley	Ind Cher b			Union	GA	
Hi	Diley		Charles F		b	1818			NC	GA Pula t 1835
Hi	Diley		Charles F		Res	1835		Pulaski	GA	NC Meck GS
He	Doris		Everett	_Daniell	Res			Gilmer	GA	Family Puzzler #1037
He	Doris	Ma	Claude Pom	Reeves	b	06 Jul 1924	Atlanta	Fulton	GA	IGI
He	Dorman				C	1850	Coxes Div	Cobb	GA	p191
He	Doss		James M	_Lance Mary	Ind Cher			Union	GA	Wiley mom
He	E			_Chatham	m see Joel	11 Dec 1823		Franklin	GA	37,000 GA MR
Ha	E	L		_ Francis	b of son Iverson	19 Jan 1828			GA	Enoch Al?
He	E	P			C	1820		Richmond	GA	
He	E	T			Complaint owes money	03 Mar 1853		Gordon	GA	LDS Film#0424321
He	Eady		Allen	Blaylock	b Edy	1832		Haywood	NC	GA Unio 1850C p206
Ha	Edmond				Militia 1813-	1801		Morgan	GA	Coleman Capt DAR
Ha	Edmond				LL Res Ed	1805		Columbia	GA	B B
Ha	Edmond		Samuel?	_Jones Nancy	m	25 Feb 1806		Columbia	GA	37,000 MR
Ha	Edmond				Tax Colemans Dist	1810	Oconee Riv	Jackson	GA	Cowen adj
Ha	Edmond				Tax Colemans Dist	1812	Mulberry C	Jackson	GA	Gamble adj
Ha	Edmond				Tax Colemans Dist	1812	Sugar Cree	Morgan	GA	Meafre adj
Ha	Edmond				W	1815		Morgan	GA	WM A 34
He	Edmond		Archibald		Ind Cher? b	1840		Washington	TN	GA Unio 1850C p235
Hi	Edny	Ca		_Burch John Miles	m	28 Jan 1869		Pulaski	GA	
He	Edwin	L	George W S	Lambert_Nancy Morrison	b	1831		Coweta	GA	GS NC Meck
Ha	Edwin	L	George W S	_Morrison Nancy O	m	15 Sep 1853		Floyd	GA	37,000 MR
Hi	Elam				LL	1821		Monroe	GA	243 9
Hi	Elam				LL Res	1821		Twiggs	GA	
He	Elam				b	1830				GA Twig 1850C p176
Hi	Elam				b	1830				GA Lown 1850C p366
Hi	Elam				C	1830		Twiggs	GA	p81
Hi	Elam				LL Cher Res	1832		Twiggs	GA	Lot349 Dist1 Sec3

LN	FIRSTNAME	IO	FATHER	MOM_SPOUSE	EVENT	EVENTDATE	CITY	COUNTY_PAR	ST	SOURCE
He	Elam				C	1840		Twiggs	GA	
Hi	Elam		Caleb Sr	Margaret	w of Caleb	01 Mar 1845		Twiggs	GA	Misc deeds
He	Elender			_Reeves Samuel	m	11 Dec 1845		Coweta	GA	
He	Eli		Elisha	Smathers_Ledford Elizb	Ind Cher? b	1811		Macon	NC	GA Unio 1850C p236
Hi	Elias				LL	1827		Coweta	GA	1 8
Hi	Elias				LL Res	1827		Telfair	GA	
Hi	Elias		William	McDuffie_Lott Mary Jane	b	06 Dec 1849		Telfair	GA	
Hi	Elias	S			LL Cher Res	1832		Telfair	GA	Lot727 Dist3 Sec4
Hi	Elias	S			L t	26 Dec 1833	Ellijay	Gilmer	GA	Cochran E G BkH p309
Hi	Elisha		Phillip Sr	Brisco_Smathers Louisa	b of son Ephraim	1813			GA	NC Hayw 1850C
He	Elisha				C	1820		Hall	GA	?
He	Elisha				LL	1827		Carroll	GA	39 3
He	Elisha				LL Res	1827		Hall	GA	
He	Elisha				LL	1827		Lee	GA	239 12
He	Elisha			_Herrin Sarah	m	12 Jan 1838		Walton	GA	37,000 MR
He	Elisha			_Shephearde Martha J	m	20 Apr 1847		Walton	GA	37,000 MR
Ha	Eliza			_Sanders James	m	27 Mar 1839		Washington	GA	37,000 MR
He	Eliza	J	John		b	1835				GA Walk 1850C
Ha	Eliza	Ja	William C	Brantley	b	1861		Washington	GA	IGI
He	Elizabeth			Walkingstick_Tally Pryo	Ind Cher b	1755	Ind Ter	Buncomb	NC	GA Habe 1830C
Ha	Elizabeth		Samuel	Sims	b	1783			GA	So Kith&Kin p109
Ha	Elizabeth			_Williams William	m	14 Jun 1813		Morgan	GA	37,000 MR
Hi	Elizabeth			_Carter James	m	21 Aug 1816		Warren	GA	IGI .
Hi	Elizabeth		Robert Sr?	_ Whitton	Tax Garlingtons Dist	1819	Oconee	Clarke	GA	Garner adj
He	Elizabeth			Walkingstick_Tally Pryo	Ind Cher res	1821		Pendleton	SC	GA Lump t
Ha	Elizabeth		Reuben	Jones	b d1827	1823			GA	
Hi	Elizabeth				Mem of 1834-	1823	Bark Camp	Burke	GA	Church
He	Elizabeth		Joseph Sr	_Mathews William	Ind Cher Clm ofWm Ri	23 Apr 1828		Union	GA	Mathis BIA RG75
He	Elizabeth		Andrew Ber	Able	b	1828			SC	GA Cass 1850C #1373
He	Elizabeth		Lazarus	Narvel	b dau n law?	1830		Cass	GA	GA Cass 1850C #1527
He	Elizabeth		Lazarus	Narvel	b res of Mary J	1830		Cass	GA	AL Mars 1880C
He	Elizabeth			Walkingstick_Tally Prio	C Ind Cher	1830		Habersham	GA	under Tally
Ha	Elizabeth		Thomas	Evans_unm?	LW of Tms	02 May 1831		Newton	GA	Some GA Co Records
He	Elizabeth		Lazarus	Narvel	b res of Archibald	1832		Cass	GA	TN Hami 1860C p24
He	Elizabeth		James Ba	_Wells	Ind Cher b d1856	15 Aug 1832		Gilmer	GA	
He	Elizabeth			Walkingstick_Tally Pryo	Ind Cher of#16167res	1834		Gilmer	GA	Henson Henry gs
Ha	Elizabeth		Armstead	Petty_Haynes Hiram	b	1835			GA	GA Carr 1850C

LN	FIRSTNAME	IO	FATHER	MOM_SPOUSE	EVENT	EVENTDATE	CITY	COUNTY_PAR	ST	SOURCE
He	Elizabeth			Walkingstick_Tally Prio	Ind Cher of #940 res	1851- 1835		Lumpkin	GA	Tally Robt gs
He	Elizabeth			Walkingstick_Tally Prio	Ind Cher bro Henry	1835		Lumpkin	GA	Tally Robt #940
Ha	Elizabeth				w	1836		Newton	GA	Bk1 p85
Ha	Elizabeth		Thomas	Evans	LW	01 Jun 1836		Newton	GA	Some GA Co Records
He	Elizabeth		Allen	Blaylock	b	1836		Haywood	NC	GA Unio 1850C p206
Ha	Elizabeth		John M	Elizabeth	w of mom Elizb	09 Nov 1838		Wilkes	GA	
He	Elizabeth		George W S	Lambert_	b	1840			GA	NC Meck GS
Hi	Elizabeth		Richard Th	_Bradshaw William	m	20 Aug 1841		Oglethorpe	GA	
He	Elizabeth		Joseph Sr	_Mathis William	Ind Cher w of husb	29 May 1843	Blainsvill	Union	GA	Henson Nancy wit
He	Elizabeth			_Heath James	m 1864-	1850		Fannin	GA	
Hi	Elizabeth			_Ingram Jeremiah	m 1864-	1850		Fannin	GA	
He	Elizabeth		Joseph Sr	Scruggs_Mathis William	Ind Cher of#10393res	1851		Union	GA	GillespieSara gd rej
Ha	Elizabeth		Armstead	_Haynes Hiram	m	25 Aug 1853		Carroll	GA	37,000 MR
He	Elizabeth			_Scott David B	m	17 Mar 1858		Thomas	GA	
Ha	Elizabeth			_Beasly William	m	12 Oct 1876		Clarke	GA	37,000 MR
He	Elizabeth		Joseph Sr	Scruggs_Mathis William	Ind Cher of#18359res	1882		Union	GA	Bowers Danl gs rej
He	Elizabeth			Walkingstick_Tally Prio	Ind Cher of #3494	09 Jul 1908		Pickens	GA	Yather Dovea ggd rej
He	Elizabeth		Joseph Sr	Scruggs_Mathis William	Ind Cher of #18359	15 Jul 1908	Blairsvill	Union	GA	Bowers Danl gs rej
He	Elizabeth				Ind Cher Appl	1909			GA	#31861
He	Elizabeth			Walkingstick_Tally Prio	Ind Cher of #17531	1909	Ophir	Jasper	GA	McHan Arminda gd rej
He	Elizabeth			Walkingstick_Tally Prio	Ind Cher of #3496rej	1909	Ophir	Jasper	GA	Wigington Sarah ggd
He	Elizabeth		Joseph Sr	Scruggs_Mathis Wm	Ind Cher of #10393	1909		Union	GA	Carroll Jesse gs rej
Ha	Elizabeth	A		_Beck Lewis H	m	08 Apr 1841		Henry	GA	IGI
Ha	Elizabeth	A			m	23 Nov 1851			GA	GSLA Bible R
Ha	Elizabeth	An		_Gillespie Graves L	m	23 May 1860		Floyd	GA	
Ha	Elizabeth	F		_Phillips James L	m	07 Jan 1864		Floyd	GA	
Ha	Elizabeth	Je		_ Fortson Hailey	b	22 Jun 1819		Elbert	GA	IGI
Ha	Elizabeth	Je		_Fortson Haley	m	13 Jan 1842		Wilkes	GA	DAR
He	Elizabeth	M	Aaron	Mary_Merrell Franklin	b	1825		Appling	GA	
He	Elizabeth	M	Aaron	_Merrill Franklin	m	25 May 1842		Paulding	GA	37,000 GA MR
He	Ella			_Wood Thomas	m	28 May 1897		Townes	GA	
He	Ellen			_Driskell Washington	m	18				GA Gen Mag V26
He	Elmira		James	Costin_Byers John R	Ind Cher? b	1847		Forsyth	GA	1850C
He	Elmira		James	_Birse J R	Ind Cher? m Mirey	18 Nov 1866		Forsyth	GA	Byers
He	Emily		Aaron	_Rabun Thomas	m	03 Oct 1843		Carroll	GA	C145
Hi	Emily			_Ball George	m	02 Sep 1845		Morgan	GA	37,000 MR
Ha	Emily	Ja	Thomas Ken	_Simms James	b	1840		Heard	GA	?

LN	FIRSTNAME	IO	FATHER	MOM_SPOUSE	EVENT	EVENTDATE	CITY	COUNTY_PAR	ST	SOURCE
Ha	Emma			_Swan William J	m	12 Nov 1874		Carroll	GA	37,000 MR
Hi	Emma	Ja	James Fulw	Hall_Wilcox A J	b	07 Jan 1846		Telfair	GA	IGI
Hi	Emma	Ja	James Fulw	_Wilcox Andrew Jackson	m	1861		Telfair?	GA	GA Pio of Wiregrass
Hi	Emma	Su	Jacob Buck	Allen	b	25 Sep 1880	Cochran	Pulaski	GA	IGI
Ha	Enoch		William Sr	Crawford_Barber Cindere	b d29May1857	25 Sep 1792		Goochland	VA	GA Monr Hansen Cem
Hi	Enoch				Road hand f	1811		Clarke	GA	Ines Inf Court Min
Ha	Enoch		William Sr	_Barber Cinderella Ann	m	23 Feb 1813		Clarke	GA	VA Genealogist 17-28
Hi	Enoch				LL	1821		Henry	GA	12 12
Hi	Enoch		William Sr	Crawford_Barber Cindere	LL	1821		Monroe	GA	25 5 Fam Puzz
Hi	Enoch				LL Res	1821		Morgan	GA	
Ha	Enoch		William Sr	Crawford_Barber Cindere	C	1830		Monroe	GA	p213
Ha	Enoch		William Sr	Crawford_Barber Cindere	C	1840		Monroe	GA	p171
Ha	Enoch			_Catherine	m	30 Apr 1857			GA	GSLA Bible R
Ha	Enoch	Al			m	08 May 1827			GA	GSLA Bible R
Hi	Ephraim		Elisha	Smathers_Carpenter Anna	b	1813			GA	NC Hayw 1850C
He	Ephraim		Elisha	_Carpenter Anna	m Lucinda Ann?	13 May 1841		Macon	NC	GA Unio f?
Ha	Evaline			_Lanham James P	m	05 Sep 1866		Floyd	GA	
He	Evans			Mary	b	1827			GA	GA Talb 1850C#1184
He	Everett		William Sh	_Allred Violet	b	1898		Gilmer	GA	Rackley mom
Ha	F	A		_Smith John	m	15 Jun 1875		Carroll	GA	37,000 MR
Hi	F	H		_Copelin America	m	12 Jul 1877		Appling	GA	
Ha	Fanny			_Robinson Jesse	m	21 Oct 1831		Carroll	GA	
Hi	Fely		Charles F		Res Sely/Saly?	1835		Pulaski	GA	NC Meck GS
Ha	Fielding		Armstead	_Allewine Sarah	b	1831			GA	GA Carr 1850C
Ha	Fielding		Armstead	Petty_Allewine Sarah	d	08 Feb 1863			GA	
He	Fielding	E			War Cvl CoA Sgt	1863			GA	9thBn Art NARS
Hi	Frances		Charles F		Res	1835		Pulaski	GA	NC Meck GS
Hi	Frances			_Tripp John	m	21 Dec 1836		Pulaski	GA	Hunting f Bears
He	Frances		Elam		b	1846			GA	GA Twig 1850C
He	Frances		John		b	1846			GA	GA Walk 1850C
Hi	Frances	I		_Mullis Charlie I	m	18 Jan 1863		Pulaski	GA	
Ha	Frances	M	Tapley	Kilgare	b	1835		Morgan	GA	1850C p143
Ha	Francis				C	1840	N Oglethor	C. O. S.	GA	p18
Hi	Francis				C	1850	Millidge	Baldwin	GA	p966
He	Francis	J	Thomas Jef	Cannady_Mary L	b	1843		Lowndes	GA	1850C #792
Ha	Francis	M	Enoch	Barber_Tillery Elizabet	b d22Dec1900	18 May 1819		Morgan	GA	GA Monr Hansen Cem
Ha	Francis	M		_Brandon Mary M	m	07 Sep 1837		Jasper	GA	37,000 MR

LN	FIRSTNAME	IO	FATHER	MOM_SPOUSE	EVENT	EVENTDATE	CITY	COUNTY_PAR	ST	SOURCE
Ha	Francis	M	Enoch	Barber_Tillery Elizabet	C Frances	1840	Dist 504	Monroe	GA	p160
Ha	Francis	M	Enoch	_Tillery Elizabeth	m	21 Aug 1842		Monroe	GA	37,000 MR
Ha	Francis	M	Enoch	Barber_Tillery Elizabet	War Cvl Pvt	1863				GA Monr Hansen Cem
He	Frank		Charlie	Swain	Ind Cher			Union	GA	
He	Franklin		Caleb Jr	Lydia Ann	b	1845				GA Twig 1850C
He	Franklin		Henry B	Stewart	b	1861			GA	GA Carr 1870C p28
He	Franklin		James	Hobbs	Ind Cher? b	1875	Cedar Grov	Walker	GA	IGI
Ha	Franklin	M		_Short Mary B	m	09 Sep 1860		Morgan	GA	37,000 MR
He	Franklin	Ro	Littleton	_Smith Mary Louise	Ind Cher? b	1841			GA	Cain mom
Ha	Fred	Le		_Meacham Lynda Gayle	m			Troupe?	GA	GA Trou & her Peop
Ha	G	W			C	1840	Dist 859	Floyd	GA	p258
Ha	G	W			War Cvl Conf Roster	1863		Terrell	GA	CoE 5th Reg
He	Gabriel			Martha	b	1847			GA	GA Cass 1850C #384
Ha	Gaskey			b Ghasking	1803				GA	TN Hare 1850C 613
Hi	Gaskey			b Ghasking	1808				GA	TN Faye 1860C 224
He	Geneva		James	Wofford_Gravitt Wm Lee	Ind Cher? b	1873		Forsyth	GA	
He	Geneva		James	_Gravitt Wm Lee	Ind Cher? m	17 Jun 1897		Forsyth	GA	
He	George				b	1775				GA Walk 1840C p69
Ha	George				Tax	1807		Franklin	GA	#28
Hi	George				Vs	23 Jan 1810		Clarke	GA	Bond Inf Court Min
He	George		Allen	Blaylock	b	1829		Haywood	NC	GA Unio 1850C p206
Hi	George				C	1830		Taliaferro	GA	p364
He	George				C 60-70	1840		Walker	GA	000000001 p69
Ha	George			_Lester Mary	m Jn?	23 Sep 1845		Fayette	GA	37,000 MR?
Hi	George		William J	Elender	b	1847			GA	AL Covi 1850C p163
He	George	M		_McLeroy Rachael	m	07 Aug 1845		Fayette	GA	37,000 GA MR
He	George	W	Jesse Sr	Crawford_Lamberth Jerus	b Sr	1804			GA	GS NC Meck
Ha	George	W	Samuel	Sims	Orphan	03 Nov 1823		Morgan	GA	Aldridge Gaurd
Ha	George	W	Jesse Sr	_Lamberth Jerusa	m	08 May 1825		Fayette	GA	37,000 MR
Ha	George	W		_Turner Porthea	m	06 Oct 1825		Morgan	GA	37,000 MR
Ha	George	W	Samuel	Sims	Agent f Peggy Tax	1829	Hard Labor	Morgan	GA	Wade adj Lumpkins Di
Ha	George	W	Samuel	Sims	Tax Lumpkins Dist	1829	Hard Labor	Morgan	GA	Trimble adj
Ha	George	W	Jesse Sr	Crawford_Lambert Jerusa	C Sr	1830		Coweta	GA	p381
Ha	George	W			C	1830		Newton	GA	p42
Ha	George	W	Jesse Sr	Crawford_Lambert Jerusa	L Res Sr	1832		Coweta	GA	#253
Ha	George	W			LL Cher	1832		Floyd	GA	#249
Ha	George	W			Res	1832		Newton	GA	#249

LN	FIRSTNAME	IO	FATHER	MOM_SPOUSE	EVENT		EVENTDATE	CITY	COUNTY_PAR	ST	SOURCE
Ha	George	W			LL Cher		1832		Walker	GA	#253
Ha	George	W	Jesse Sr	Crawford_Lambert Jerusa	LL Res Sr		1838		Coweta	GA	p317
Ha	George	W		_Short Elizabeth	m		22 Apr 1838		Monroe	GA	37,000 MR
Ha	George	W		_Armenia	b		1845			GA	AR Scot 1870C
He	George	W	George W S	Lambert	b Jr		1846			GA	GS NC Meck
Ha	George	W			L t		05 Jan 1847		Cass	GA	Birrem J W M p184
He	George	W			L f J	Davis	08 May 1849		Cass	GA	AR t? BkI p11
Ha	George	W		_Sims Louisa	m		24 Apr 1870		Floyd	GA	37,000 MR
He	George	WC	William Ri	Blair	Ind Cher b		1841			GA	NC Cher 1850C p5
He	George	WC	William Ri	Blair	Ind Cher b		1841			GA	NC Cher 1860C
He	George	Wa	Thomas Jef	Cannaday_Lizzie	b		1839		Telfair	GA	GA Lown 1850C #792
He	George	Wa		_Tackett Delita	Ind Cher? m		17 Feb 1842		Fayettte	GA	MS Lee t
He	George	Wa	James	Costin_Pruitt Laura A 1	Ind Cher? b		1849		Forsyth	GA	1850C
He	George	Wa	James	Costen_Mann Martha 2	Ind Cher? b		10 Apr 1849		Forsyth	GA	MS Choc t
He	George	Wa	James	_Pruitt Laura A 1	Ind Cher? m		11 Apr 1872		Forsythe	GA	
He	Georgeanna		Archibald	Mary	Ind Cher? b		1854			GA	TN Hami 1860C p24
Hi	Georgia	An	Caleb Jr	Lydia Ann	b		1844			GA	
He	Germane		James	Hobbs	b		1871	Cedar Grov	Walker	GA	IGI
He	Green			_Smith Amanda	m		12 Jan 1880		Paulding	GA	37,000 GA MR
Ha	H	E			C		1830		Columbia	GA	p339
He	Hamilton				b		1828			GA	GA Murr 1850C
He	Haney			_Wheeler Robert M	m		12 May 1824		Monroe	GA	
He	Haney			_Roberts Samson W	m		19 Dec 1833		Walton	GA	
Hi	Hardy				C		1840		Early	GA	
He	Harriet			_Boon William	m		06 Mar 1827		Bibb	GA	
Hi	Harriet		Samuel	Hargroves	b		1832		Ware	GA	GA Clin Homerv res
Ha	Harrison	A		Francis	b H A		1830			GA	
He	Hemphill	H			Tax		1819		Franklin	GA	#66
Ha	Henderson			_Mainer Pinelope	m		24 Dec 1814		Morgan	GA	Mainor
He	Henderson				Tax		1817	Wrights Di	Morgan	GA	
Hi	Henderson				Tax		1818	Wrights Di	Morgan	GA	
He	Henrietta			_Burger Charles	m					GA	DAR Wills V1
He	Henry		James Barr	_Susan N	Ind Cher #16167 b		21 May 1823		Rabun	GA	Walkingstick Elizggm
He	Henry		James Barr	Tally_Hudman Mary Ann	Ind Cher b		1823		Rabun	GA	TX Pano 1850C p159
He	Henry				Tax		1826	Frosts Dis	Clarke	GA	Defaulter
He	Henry		James Barr	Tally_Susan N	Ind Cher res		1832		Gilmer	GA	#16167 rej
He	Henry			Walkingstick	Ind Cher sis Elizb		1835		Lumpkin	GA	Tally Robt #940

LN	FIRSTNAME	IO	FATHER	MOM_SPOUSE	EVENT	EVENTDATE	CITY	COUNTY_PAR	ST	SOURCE
He	Henry			_ Rachael	C	1840		Rabun	GA	p210
He	Henry			_Wood Mariah	Ind Cher? m RobtGile	25 Jul 1841		Union	GA	NC Bunc Herit of
He	Henry		John		b	1849				GA Walk 1850C
He	Henry			_Rachael	w t	03 Feb 1849		Rabun	GA	Loveless Jms
He	Henry			_ Rachael	w L t	03 Feb 1849	Chatooga R	Rabun	GA	Billingsley Jms
He	Henry			_ Rachael	w L t	03 Feb 1849	Lot 25	Rabun	GA	Billingsley H A
He	Henry			_ Rachael	L t Ann Billingsley	03 Feb 1849	Chatooga R	Pickens	SC	GA Rabu w of Henry
He	Henry			Walkingstick	Ind Cher visited sis	1851		Lumpkin	GA	Tally Robt #940
He	Henry		James	Costen	Ind Cher? b	1853		Forsyth	GA	MS d?
Ha	Henry				Heir Est of W	26 Aug 1856		Wilkes	GA	Ord Ofc Inf Court
Ha	Henry				Minor of	26 Aug 1856		Wilkes	GA	Adams F H Ord Ofc
He	Henry			_Humphrey Martha J	m	26 Sep 1858		Walton	GA	37,000 MR
He	Henry			_Corne Joannah	m	17 Oct 1878		Paulding	GA	37,0000 GA MR
He	Henry	B	Reuben	Jones_Stewart Sally	b H B	1821			GA	GA Carr 1860C p21
He	Henry	B	Reuben	Jones_Stewart Sarah	b d1897	1826			GA	GA Carr 1870C p28
He	Henry	B	Reuben	Jones_Sally Stewart	b	1828			GA	GA Carr 1880C
He	Henry	B	Reuben	Jones_Stewart Sally	b	20 Feb 1828			GA	Parker Fam Bible
He	Henry	B	Reuben	_Stewart Sarah	m	21 Jul 1847		Carroll	GA	37,000 MR
Ha	Henry	B	Reuben	Jones_Stewart Sally	Est of mom	Apr 1871		Carroll	GA	Min Bk
He	Henry	Br	Thomas Jef	_Moore Martha A	b Henry Briggs Sr	1842	Lake Park	Lowndes	GA	FL Clay 1850C #792
Ha	Henry	C			LL	1821		Houston	GA	222 6
Ha	Henry	C			LL Res	1821		Jackson	GA	
He	Henry	C			War Cvl CoH Corp	1863			GA	19th Cav NARS
He	Henry	Cl	Henry W	Pinelope	b?	1843		Walker	GA	MS Pren t
Ha	Henry	Ev	Thomas	Evans	LW of Tms	02 May 1831		Newton	GA	Some GA Co Records
Hi	Henry	Ho	James Henr	Bates	b	10 Mar 1911	Cochran	Bleckley	GA	IGI
He	Henry	M	Henry B	Stewart	b	1858			GA	GA Carr 1860C p21
He	Henry	W		_ Pinelope	b	1801			NC	GA Walk 1850C
He	Henry	W		_Pinelope	C 20-30 as H W	1840		Walker	GA	10001 1001 p89
He	Hiram	J	Henry W	Pinelope	b	1849		Walker	GA	1850C
He	Hiram	L		_Gravitt Nancy A	m	21 Dec 1852		Forsythe	GA	
Hi	Hoke	Sm	William Th	Ayers	b	12 Jun 1907	Chester	Dodge	GA	IGI
He	Howard			_Poole Prudence	m Hist of p488			Franklin	GA	NC Wayn?
He	Ida				Ind Cher Appl	1909			GA	#35190
He	Ida	F	John	_Erwin	Ind Cher? b	23 Feb 1877		Union	GA	Allison mom
Hi	Ira	Be	Wiley Harg	_Bennett Pansy	b Ira Bert	1894		Coffee	GA	Booth mom
Hi	Irena		William Ri	Blair_Ruddle	Ind Cher b as Lurena	1816			GA	NC Cher 1850C p5

LN	FIRSTNAME	IO	FATHER	MOM_SPOUSE	EVENT	EVENTDATE	CITY	COUNTY_PAR	ST	SOURCE
He	Isaac			_Kimball Mary	m	26 Oct 1820		Hall	GA	37,000 GA MR
He	Isaac				C	1820		Hall	GA	?
He	Isaac				LL Res	1827		Hall	GA	
He	Isaac				LL	1827		Troup	GA	225 8
He	Isaac				C	1830		Rabun	GA	p233
He	Isaac				C State	1834		Cobb	GA	5 white
He	Isaac				C	1840		Cobb	GA	p256
He	Isaac		Elisha	_Lowery Elizb	Ind Cher? m	30 Apr 1842		Macon	NC	GA Unio t
He	Isaac			_Strickland Casey F	m	20 Feb 1853		Cass	GA	
Hi	Isaac			_Poston Eliza	m	04 Oct 1860		Fannin	GA	37,000 GA MR
He	Isaac			_Cornett Rebecca	m	17 Nov 1875		Fannin	GA	37,000 GA MR
He	Isabelle			_Lankford John	m	28 May 1854		Paulding	GA	
Ha	Iverson	La	E L	_Barnes Mary J 1	b d13Nov1889	19 Jan 1828			GA	TX Libe t
Ha	Iverson	La	E L	_Litchfield Mary 2	b	19 Jan 1828			GA	see Enock Al?
He	J				Tax	1800		Franklin	GA	#25
Ha	J				Tax	1800		Franklin	GA	#32
Hi	J				Tax	1807		Franklin	GA	#27
He	J				Tax	1807		Franklin	GA	#88
He	J				Tax	1819		Franklin	GA	#55
He	J				Tax	1819		Franklin	GA	#150
He	J			_Owens Caroline	m	15 Jan 1831		Paulding	GA	BkI p69
Hi	J				C	1840		Pulaski	GA	
Ha	J	B			C	1840		Monroe	GA	p151 .
He	J	B			b War Cvl Oath t US	1844				GA NW Hist&GS
He	J	B			War Cvl Oath t US	1865		Fannin	GA	NW GA Hist&GS
Ha	J	B		_Shouse Carrie E	m	16 Jan 1868		Morgan	GA	
Ha	J	C		_Rebecca	Carpenter b	1812			GA	AL Covi 1860C p444
He	J	L			Deacon		Hunters Cr	Franklin	GA	Bapt Chur
Hi	J	Mo	James	Smith	b	03 Mar 1873		Coffee	GA	IGI
Ha	J	W			C Jn W?	1840	Capt Haris	Habersham	GA	p162
He	Jackson		Thomas Jef	Cannaday	b Andrew Jackson	1845			GA	GA Lown 1850C #792
He	Jacob		Eli	Ledford	Ind Cher? b	1849			GA	GA Unio 1850C p236
Hi	Jacob	Bu		Lamb_Allen	b Jacob Buchanan	27 May 1857		Pulaski	GA	IGI
He	James				War Rev grave loc			Franklin	GA	GA Step Hist of p20
He	James				LB t			Telfair	GA	Williamson Mcjc DAR
He	James		Charlie	_Lance Mary	Ind Cher			Union	GA	Swain mom
Ha	James				Res	12 Jun 1794		Oglethorpe	GA	GA GenGems p58 NGS

LN	FIRSTNAME	IO	FATHER	MOM_SPOUSE	EVENT	EVENTDATE	CITY	COUNTY_PAR	ST	SOURCE
Ha	James				War Rev CL Bounty	1796			VA	GA Roster of Rev
Hi	James				Tax	1801		Franklin	GA	#5
He	James				Tax	1801		Franklin	GA	#7
Ha	James			_Elizabeth	b	1802			GA	MS Scot 1860C p16
Hi	James				Tax 1805-	1802		Franklin	GA	#51
Hi	James				Tax	1802		Franklin	GA	#3
He	James				Tax	1802		Franklin	GA	#44
He	James		Jesse Sr	Crawford_Munkers Betsy?	b d post 1870	1803			GA	
He	James				Tax	1803		Franklin	GA	#16
He	James		Wash	_ Costin Sarah 1	Ind Cher b d1880	1803			NC	GA Fors 1850C p228
Hi	James		Charles F	_ Cook Margaret	b Jms Pickney? d1890	1804			NC	GA Pula t 1835
He	James				LL	1805		Franklin	GA	#611 B B
Hi	James				Tax Bartons Dist	1809	Sandy Cree	Baldwin	GA	Baley adj Hinston
Hi	James				Tax Bartons Dist	1809	Sandy Cree	Baldwin	GA	Hughey adj Hinston
Hi	James				Jury	Jun 1809		Clarke	GA	Inf Court Min
Ha	James				Tax	1809		Clarke	GA	
He	James				Tax slaves 2 21+	1810	Greenbrier	Clarke	GA	
Hi	James				Oversee Road	1811	Apalatchee	Clarke	GA	Inf Court Min
Hi	James				L f	16 Aug 1811		Clarke	GA	Suttles Isaac
Hi	James				Jury #19	30 Jan 1813		Clarke	GA	Inf Court Min
He	James			_Martha	b	1814			GA	AL Barb 1870C p185
He	James				LG 350 Acr	1814		Franklin	GA	SLA
Ha	James				Tax Parkers Dist	1817		Morgan	GA	Tapley Agent f
He	James		Lazarus?	_Martha	b ? mom Narvel	1817		Marlboro	SC	GA Cass
Ha	James				Tax	1818	Wrights Di	Morgan	GA	
Hi	James				Tax Dobbins Dist	1819	Apalatchee	Clarke	GA	Reeves adj
He	James				Tax	1819		Franklin	GA	#79
He	James				Tax	1819		Franklin	GA	#117
He	James				C 45+	1820	Athens	Clarke	GA	031101 32211 p127
Ha	James				C 26-45	1820		Morgan	GA	110110 00201
Hi	James				LL Res	1821		Clarke	GA	
Hi	James				LL	1821		Henry	GA	30 4
Hi	James				Tax	1822	Apalatchee	Clarke	GA	Jones adj
Hi	James				Tax	1824	Athens	Clarke	GA	
Ha	James				Tax Hughes Dist	1824	Wolf Creek	Clarke	GA	
Ha	James				Tax	1824	Tolberts	Morgan	GA	
Ha	James		Tapley	Kilgare	b	1826		Morgan	GA	1850C p143

41

LN	FIRSTNAME	IO	FATHER	MOM_SPOUSE	EVENT	EVENTDATE	CITY	COUNTY_PAR	ST	SOURCE
He	James		John W	Moore_Wiley Rebecca Ell	b d1864	1828			GA	AL Tall 1850C p405
He	James				Tax	1828	Applings D	Carroll	GA	
Ha	James				Tax	1828	Harris Dis	Clarke	GA	
Ha	James				Tax f	1828	Oconee	Clarke	GA	Garner Elijah
He	James				Tax Applings Dist	1828	Apalatchee	Clarke	GA	Tharasher adj 0poll
He	James		Jesse Sr	_Munkers Elizb	m	19 Sep 1829		Carroll	GA	Crawford mom
Ha	James				Tax	1829	Lynches Di	Carroll	GA	
Ha	James				Tax	1829	Applings D	Clarke	GA	
Ha	James				Tax Lynches Dist	1829	Apalatchee	Clarke	GA	Thrasher adj 0poll
Ha	James		Jesse Sr	Crawford_Munkers Elizab	C 20-30	1830		Carroll	GA	10001 10001 p215
Ha	James				Tax	1830	Smiths Dis	Carroll	GA	
Ha	James				Tax Smiths Dist	1830	Apalatchee	Clarke	GA	Thomas adj 0 poll
Ha	James				C	1830		Dekalb	GA	p50
Ha	James				Tax	1830	Smiths Dis	Lee	GA	
Ha	James		Armstead	Petty_Curry Harriet E	b	1832			GA	GA Carr 1850C
He	James		Armstead	Petty_Curry Harriet E	b d1911	1832			GA	AL Cleb 1870C
Ha	James		Jesse Sr	Crawford_Munkers Elizab	Res	1832		Carroll	GA	Cher LL
He	James				Res	1832		DeKaulb	GA	Cher LL
He	James				LL Cher	1832		Union	GA	#130
Ha	James				LL Cher	1832		Walker	GA	Lot846 Dist2 Sec4
Ha	James			_Freeman Wealthy	m	08 Feb 1833		Clarke	GA	37,000 MR
Hi	James		Charles F	Stewart	Res Jimmy	1835		Pulaski	GA	NC Meck GS
He	James				b dOct1850	1837			GA	GA Unio Mort Sch
Hi	James			_Dickerson Martha	m	20 May 1837		Putnam	GA	37,000 MR
He	James		Andrew Ber	Angelina	b	1838			GA	GA Cass 1850C #1373
Ha	James			_ Freeman Wealthy	C	1840	Dist 223	Clarke	GA	p233
He	James			_ Freeman Wealthy	LW of Jn Freeman	04 May 1840		Clarke	GA	GA Ogle L in
He	James				C	1840		Cobb	GA	
He	James		Wash	_Costin Sarah 1	C Ind Cher? d1880	1840		Forsyth	GA	Jms W? bro Jn M
Ha	James				C	1840	Dist 280	Morgan	GA	p231
Ha	James				C	1840	Dist 592	Pike	GA	p144
Hi	James				C	1840		Taliaferro	GA	
Ha	James				W	1842		Morgan	GA	BkC p72
He	James		Eli	Ledford	Ind Cher? b	1843			GA	GA Unio 1850C p236
He	James				L 2 Acr t	29 Oct 1847		Paulding	GA	Pace Jn p65
He	James			_Bathsby Catherine	Ind Cher? m	13 May 1847		Union	GA	Battbey
He	James				C	1850	Div 12	Cass	GA	p189

LN	FIRSTNAME	IO	FATHER	MOM_SPOUSE	EVENT	EVENTDATE	CITY	COUNTY_PAR	ST	SOURCE
He	James				C	1850	Div 12	Cass	GA	p204
He	James				C	1850	Dist 951	Paulding	GA	p103
Hi	James				C (2) Jms L&Jms Fulw	1850	Dist 437	Telfair	GA	p374
He	James				C	1850	Dist 85	Union	GA	p277
He	James				L 40 Acr f	30 Jan 1854		Paulding	GA	Candler Sam BkJ p464
He	James			_Hobbs Nancy Emma	Ind Cher? m	1855		Walker	GA	TN b IGI
Ha	James				War Cvl CoI 63Rgt	1863			GA	GA Vol V6 p464
He	James		Armstead	_Curry Eliza Harriet	Ind Cher wife m	28 Dec 1865		Carroll	GA	
He	James		Wash	_Wofford Louisa 2	Ind Cher m	29 Jun 1871		Forsythe	GA	
Ha	James			_Bonds Mattie	m Jim	01 Dec 1877		Clayton	GA	
Hi	James		Wiley Harg	Booth	b	1892		Ware	GA	IGI
He	James				Ind Cher Appl	1909			GA	#41486
He	James	B	Presley Th	_Keys Sarah Francis	Ind Cher m	18			GA	Ada mom
Ha	James	B		_Freeman Pamelia	m	25 Sep 1836		Monroe	GA	IGI
Hi	James	B		_Allen Elmira Dolly	m	30 Jul 1871		Pulaski	GA	Birch Fam ofGrBrit
He	James	Ba	William M	_Tally Elizabeth	Ind Cher wife m	25 Jun 1822		Pendleton	SC	GA Rabu t
He	James	Ba	William M	Motlow_Tally Elizabeth	Ind Cher res	1823		Rabun	GA	#16167 son Henry
He	James	Ba	William M	Motlow_Tally Elizabeth	C as Jms	1830		Rabun	GA	p232
He	James	Ba	William M	Motlow_Tally Elizabeth	Ind Cher 8 in res	Mar 1832	Elijay	Gilmer	GA	birth 15 Aug
He	James	Ba	William M	Motlow_Tally Elizabeth	Ind Cher res	1832		Gilmer	GA	#16167 son Henry
He	James	Ba	William M	Motlow_Tally Elizabeth	LL Cher Res	1832		Rabun	GA	Lot249 Dist14 Sec1
He	James	Ba	William M	Motlow_Tally Elizabeth	Ind Cher Emig Roll	Feb 1834	Elijay	Gilmer	GA	9 in res
Ha	James	C			b	1811			GA	CA Sutt 1850C p40
Ha	James	F		_Cox Victoria	m	13 Dec 1855		Morgan	GA	37,000 MR
Ha	James	FM	Reuben	Jones_Martha	b JFM	1842			GA	GA Carr 1880C
Ha	James	FM	Reuben	_Martha	b d1907	1842			GA	GA Carr 1860C p23
He	James	FM	Reuben	Jones_Martha	b	01 Jan 1842			GA	Parker Fam Bible
He	James	FM	Reuben	Jones_Martha	Orphan	1848		Carroll	GA	Min BkAA 1852-70
Hi	James	Fr	James Fulw	_Lott Nancy	Twin b Jms Franklin	02 Oct 1852		Telfair	GA	Hall mom
Hi	James	Fu	James L	Obedience_Hall Salena 1	b d22Jan1897	30 Mar 1816		Telfair	GA	GA Coff d
Hi	James	Fu	James L	Obedience_Hall Salena 1	b WarIndPenof Tms Je	1816		Telfair	GA	GA Coff bro res FL
He	James	Fu	James L	_Hall Salena 1	m	02 Jun 1840		Telfair	GA	37,000 MR
Hi	James	Fu	James L	Obedience_Hall Salena 1	Gaurd of Neph Albert	05 Mar 1845		Telfair	GA	
Hi	James	Fu	James L	Obedience_Douglas Eliz2	m	1857		Telfair	GA	Smith wid
Hi	James	Fu	James L	_Douglas Elizabeth Jane	b of dau Mary Ann	16 Feb 1864		Coffee	GA	IGI
Hi	James	Fu	James L	Obedience_Douglas Eliza	Wit Wid Pen of Tms J	21 Apr 1893		Coffee	GA	FL Lake Wid Pen#1110
Hi	James	Ga		_Dyess Caroline	m	1868		Ware	GA	Pio of Wiregrass

LN	FIRSTNAME	IO	FATHER	MOM_SPOUSE	EVENT	EVENTDATE	CITY	COUNTY_PAR	ST	SOURCE
He	James	H	Henry W	Pinelope	b	1838		Walker	GA	1850C
He	James	H			War Cvl CoG Sgt	1863			GA	28thInf NARS
He	James	H	Henry W?	_Duncan Sarah C	m	07 Mar 1868		Tishomingo	MS	GA Walk f
Ha	James	J			LL	1827		Muskogee	GA	62 23
Ha	James	Je	Thomas	Evans	LL Res	1827		Newton	GA	
Ha	James	Je	Thomas	Evans	C	1830		Newton	GA	p41
Hi	James	Jr			Tax	1819	Dobbins Di	Clarke	GA	
He	James	Jr			LL res	1820		Clarke	GA	
He	James	Jr			LL	1820		Early	GA	#184 26
Hi	James	Jr			Tax	1821	Fosters Di	Early	GA	
Hi	James	Jr			Tax	1823	Hughes Dis	Clarke	GA	
He	James	Jr			Tax	1827		Clarke	GA	
He	James	Jr	James Sr		b	1848				GA Paul 1850C
Hi	James	Jr	James Sr	Bird	b	1858		Telfair	GA	IGI
Ha	James	K	Thomas	Evans	LW of Tms	02 May 1831		Newton	GA	Some GA Co Records
Ha	James	K	Thomas	Evans	Trustee f sis Elizb	02 May 1831		Newton	GA	Some GA Co Records
Hi	James	K		_Ussery Lucy T	m	26 Sep 1876		Wilkinson	GA	
Hi	James	KP		_Joyner Mira	m Jms K Po	1867		Jefferson	GA	IGI
He	James	KP		_ Joyner Mira	b of son Jms S	01 Oct 1868		Pulaski	GA	IGI
Hi	James	L		_ Obedience	b d1853	1770			MD	GA Telf d
Hi	James	L		_ Obedience	b of son Tms Jeff	1803			SC	GA Lown 1850C #792
Hi	James	L		_ Obedience	C as Jms	1820		Telfair	GA	p448
Hi	James	L		_ Obedience	C State as Jms	1824		Telfair	GA	
Hi	James	L		_ Obedience	C as Jms	1830		Telfair	GA	p3
Hi	James	L		_ Obedience	C as Jms	1840		Telfair	GA	p 291
He	James	L		_Williams Susan F	m	26 Nov 1867		Walton	GA	37,000 MR
Ha	James	La	Stephen Da	Stewart	b	05 Dec 1892		Washington	GA	IGI
He	James	M	Joseph Jr	Clark_Wiley Sarah	Ind Cher b Jms	1823			TN	GA Murr 1850C #410
Ha	James	M	George W	_Martha E	b	1828		Coweta	GA	Lambert Jerusha mom
He	James	M	Joseph Jr	_Wiley Sarah	Ind Cher m	25 Aug 1850		Murray	GA	37,000 MR
He	James	M	Archibald	Mary J	b	1859			GA	TN Hami 1860C p24
He	James	Mi		_Sarah A	b of son Jms W	1800		Rutherford	NC	GA Fors mr of son
Ha	James	R			War Mex GA Vol	1846			GA	White Hist Collectio
Hi	James	S	James K Po	Joyner_Yarborough Sarah	b	01 Oct 1868		Pulaski	GA	IGI
Hi	James	S	James K Po	_Yarborough Sarah	m	1889		Pulaski	GA	IGI
Hi	James	Sr			Tax Dobbins Dist	1819	Wolf Creek	Clarke	GA	Jones adj
Ha	James	Sr			C James	1820		Morgan	GA	p376

LN	FIRSTNAME	IO	FATHER	MOM_SPOUSE	EVENT	EVENTDATE	CITY	COUNTY_PAR	ST	SOURCE
Hi	James	Sr			Tax	1821	Fosters Di	Clarke	GA	Jones adj
Hi	James	Sr			Tax Sorrels Dist	1823	Wildcat Cr	Clarke	GA	Jones adj
He	James	Sr			Tax Lumpkins Dist	1825	Apalatchee	Clarke	GA	Jones adj
He	James	Sr			Tax Lumpkins Dist	1826	Apalatchee	Clarke	GA	Thrasher adj
Hi	James	Sr			LL	1827		Carroll	GA	149 1
Hi	James	Sr			LL res	1827		Clarke	GA	
Ha	James	Sr			Tax Burchets Dist	1827	Apalatchee	Clarke	GA	Thrasher adj
Ha	James	Sr			JP	Nov 1828		Clarke	GA	
Hi	James	Sr	Samuel	Hargroves	b	1830		Appling	GA	
Hi	James	Sr			c	1830		Clarke	GA	,p306
Ha	James	Sr			LL Cher Res	1832		Clarke	GA	Lot916 Dist18 Sec2
Ha	James	Sr			LL Cher Res	1832		Jackson	GA	Lot808 Dist1 Sec4
Hi	James	Sr			LL Cher Res	1832		Telfair	GA	Lot604 Dist4 Sec3
He	James	Sr			Heirs L 100 Acr vs	17 May 1836	Conneross	Pickens	SC	GA GenMag #37 p271
He	James	Sr	Samuel	_Bird Sophronia	m	21 Jul 1853		Telfair	GA	Byrd 37,000 MR
Hi	James	Sr	Samuel	Hargroves_Bird Sophroni	d	1860	Homerville	Clinch	GA	
He	James	T		Martha	b	1839			GA	GA Cass 1850C #384
Hi	James	T		Martha	b	1845				GA Butt 1850C #398
He	James	T		_Stewart Marcella A	m	09 Aug 1849		Cass	GA	37,000 MR
He	James	W	James Mi	Sarah A_White Rebecca	b of bro Jn Miller	1805		Rutherford	NC	GA Fors mr
Hi	James	W	James Mi	_White Rebecca	m	08 Jan 1834		Forsythe	GA	37,000 MR
He	James	Wa		_Walkingstick Susan	Ind Cher Imig 5inres	Mar 1832	Elijay	Gilmer	GA	child died 25 Aug
He	James	Wa		_ Walkingstick Susan	Ind Cher Emig roll	Feb 1834	Elijay	Gilmer	GA	6 in res
Hi	James	Wa	Wiley Harg	_Tootte Bertie	b	08 Aug 1897		Clinch	GA	Booth mom
Ha	Jane		Reuben	Jones	b	18 Aug 1820		Morgan	GA	
He	Jane			_Martin John	m	19 Jun 1828		Monroe	GA	
Ha	Jane			_Silvey Jesse	m	07 Jan 1836		Campbell	GA	
Ha	Jane			_Wilson A I	m	01 Aug 1849		Morgan	GA	37,000 MR
He	Jay			_King	b of son Claude	28 Nov 1898	Atlanta	Fulton	GA	IGI
Ha	Jefferson		Thomas	Evans	LW of Tms	02 May 1831		Newton	GA	Some GA Co Records
Ha	Jefferson		Thomas	Evans	LW of sis Elizb	01 Jun 1836		Newton	GA	Some GA Co Records
He	Jennie		James M	_Lance James	Ind Cher			Union	GA	Wiley mom
He	Jenny		Jesse Sr	_Phelps Aquilla	m Jane	05 Dec 1807		Clarke	GA	BkA
Ha	Jesse				Tax	1802		Clarke	GA	
Hi	Jesse				Jury #12	Jun 1804		Clarke	GA	Inf Court Min
He	Jesse				LL	1805		Clarke	GA	#238-B
Hi	Jesse				Jury	20 Jan 1807		Clarke	GA	Inf Court Min

LN	FIRSTNAME	IO	FATHER	MOM_SPOUSE	EVENT	EVENTDATE	CITY	COUNTY_PAR	ST	SOURCE
He	Jesse				Tax Hills Dist	1808	Sandy Cree	Morgan	GA	Rogers adj
Hi	Jesse				Tax Middletons Dist	1809	Sandy Cree	Baldwin	GA	Rogers adj
He	Jesse				Tax Walkers Dist	1810	Sandy Cree	Baldwin	GA	Rogers adj
Hi	Jesse				Tax Jones Dist	1812	Sandy Cree	Morgan	GA	Rodgers R adj
He	Jesse				Tax	1817	Parkers Di	Morgan	GA	Reuben Agent f
He	Jesse				C	1820	Casity Car	Hall	GA	
Ha	Jesse				LL	1820		Irwin	GA	#475 6
Ha	Jesse				LL res	1820		Morgan	GA	
He	Jesse				Tax	1824	Cassity Ca	Hall	GA	AIS#1
Ha	Jesse				Tax	1824		Walton	GA	
He	Jesse				Tax Lumpkins Dist	1826	Sparks Dis	Clarke	GA	Single man
Ha	Jesse			_Daniel Elizabeth	m	10 Jun 1826		Morgan	GA	37,000 MR
Hi	Jesse				LL Res	1827		Clarke	GA	
Ha	Jesse				Tax	1827	Burchets D	Clarke	GA	
Hi	Jesse				LL	1827		Lee	GA	21 5
Ha	Jesse				LL	1827	Sparks Dis	Morgan	GA	Single man
Ha	Jesse				Tax	1828	Jones Dist	Lee	GA	
Ha	Jesse				Tax	1829	Applings D	Lee	GA	
Hi	Jesse			_ Catherine	b of dau	1830			GA	AL Barb 1860C p177
Ha	Jesse				Tax	1830	Smiths Dis	Clarke	GA	
Ha	Jesse			_ Daniel Elizabeth	C	1830		Morgan	GA	p272
He	Jesse				LL Cher Res	1832		Carroll	GA	Lot467 Dist11 Sec1
He	Jesse				Tax default	1832		Carroll	GA	
Ha	Jesse			_Wade Matilda	m	06 Dec 1832		Clarke	GA	37,000 MR
Ha	Jesse				LL Cher Res	1832		Coweta	GA	Lot665 Dist1 Sec4
Ha	Jesse				LL Cher Res	1832		Morgan	GA	Lot1237 Dist2 Sec2
He	Jesse				LL Cher	1832		Walker	GA	#467 Dist11 Sec1
He	Jesse				L f	1835		Carroll	GA	Miller Geo
Ha	Jesse				LL Res	1838	Hines	Coweta	GA	#99
He	Jesse				L Lot93 t	1839		Carroll	GA	Butler M BkC p468
He	Jesse			_ Wade Matilda?	C	1840	Dist 225	Clarke	GA	p200
He	Jesse				C	1840		Montgomery	GA	
Ha	Jesse				C	1840	Dist 285	Morgan	GA	p237
Hi	Jesse			_Faison Lewis	m	22 Mar 1884		Appling	GA	
He	Jesse	C	George W S	Lambert_Hart Susan A	b	1832			GA	GS NC Meck
Ha	Jesse	C	George W S	_Hart Susan A	m	20 May 1858		Floyd	GA	37,000 MR
He	Jesse	Jr	Jesse Sr	_Neil Polly 1	b	1808			GA	Crawford mom Meck GS

LN	FIRSTNAME	IO	FATHER	MOM_SPOUSE	EVENT	EVENTDATE	CITY	COUNTY_PAR	ST	SOURCE
He	Jesse	Jr	Jesse Sr	_Petty Eliz 2	m	07 Feb 1836		Morgan	GA	37,000 MR
Hi	Jesse	Ro	Wiley Harg	_Henderson Josie 1	b	1892		Clinch	GA	
Hi	Jesse	Ro	Wiley Harg	Booth_Henderson Josie 1	b	1893	Homerville	Clinch	GA	IGI
Hi	Jesse	Ro	Wiley Harg	_Corbitt Era C 2	m	1917	Homerville	Clinch	GA	IGI
Hi	Jesse	Sr		_Crawford Elizabeth 1	m dau of Reuben	28 Nov 1787		Fauquier	VA	GA Clar t
He	Jesse	Sr			Tax 50 Acr	1798	Wildcat Cr	Jackson	GA	Westbrook Fam Hist
Ha	Jesse	Sr			Tax	1800		Jackson	GA	
Hi	Jesse	Sr		_ Crawford Elizabeth	L 56 1/2 Acr	02 Dec 1802	Wildcat Cr	Clarke	GA	Cardin Jn Wm&Jn wit
He	Jesse	Sr		_ Crawford Elizabeth	Tax 50 Acr	1809		Jackson	GA	Westbrook Fam Hist
He	Jesse	Sr		_ Crawford Elizabeth	Tax	1811		Morgan	GA	Westbrook Fam Hist
Hi	Jesse	Sr		_ Crawford Elizabeth	War 1812 d1852	1812		Carroll	GA	#11625 Wid Pen 1875
Hi	Jesse	Sr		_ Crawford Elizabeth	War 1812 Butts Co	1812		Morgan	GA	Hoggs Rgmt #11625
He	Jesse	Sr			C	1820		Clarke	GA	
He	Jesse	Sr			C 45+ or p492?	1820		Walton	GA	120001 00101 p114
He	Jesse	Sr	William	Lambert_Walls Elizabeth	b	29 Apr 1828			GA	Westbrook Fam Hist
Ha	Jesse	Sr		_ Crawford Elizabeth	C 60-70 p204 or 167	1830		Fayette	GA	000010001 00000001
He	Jesse	Sr		_ Crawford Elizabeth 1	Mrs d res of	1840		Fayette	GA	Davis L Westbrook FH
He	Jesse	Sr		_Murphy Mary 2	m	1841		Morgan	GA	#11625 Wid Pen
Hi	Joan		Wiley Harg	_Smith H P MD	b	10 Feb 1894		Clinch	GA	Booth mom
He	Joanna			_Cockburn Jerimiah	m	27 Mar 1828		Franklin	GA	Hist Col DAR
Hi	Job				L	1784		Washington	GA	Hinton
He	Joe		Joseph Jr	Clark	Ind Cher b	1830			GA	GA Unio 1850C p241
Ha	Joel	Ta		_Durham Elizabeth	m Tapley?			Morgan	GA	Hist Col DAR V1 p83
He	Joel	Ta		_Chatham Eisu ?	m see E	11 Dec 1823		Franklin	GA	Hist Col DAR
He	John				Early Settler			Cherokee	GA	White Hist Coll p390
Hi	John				b	1777			NC	GA SavannahNewspaper
Hi	John				War Rev GA DAR V1	1784			GA	SC Grev
Hi	John				Admin & wit t	1792		Franklin	GA	Barr Jms DAR
Hi	John				LG 390 Acr	1800		Franklin	GA	
Ha	John				Tax 1801-	1800		Jackson	GA	
Hi	John				Wit L of Jesse	02 Dec 1801	Wildcat Cr	Clarke	GA	BkA p90
Hi	John				Tax	1801		Franklin	GA	#16
He	John				Tax	1801		Franklin	GA	#15
Hi	John				Dep Wit L of Jesse	11 Aug 1802	Wildcat Cr	Clarke	GA	BkA p90
Ha	John				Tax	1802		Clarke	GA	
Hi	John				Tax	1802		Franklin	GA	#32
Hi	John				Tax	1802		Franklin	GA	#37

47

LN	FIRSTNAME	IO	FATHER	MOM_SPOUSE	EVENT	EVENTDATE	CITY	COUNTY_PAR	ST	SOURCE
Hi	John				Tax	1802		Franklin	GA	#29
Hi	John				Tax	1802		Franklin	GA	#41
He	John				Tax	1802		Franklin	GA	#31
He	John				Tax	1802		Franklin	GA	#42
He	John				Tax	1802		Franklin	GA	#29
He	John				Tax	1802		Franklin	GA	#36
He	John				Tax	1803		Franklin	GA	#4
He	John				Tax	1803		Franklin	GA	#7
Ha	John				Jury #29 not called	Jun 1804		Clarke	GA	Inf Court Min
He	John				LL	1805		Clarke	GA	B B
Hi	John				LL	1805		Washington	GA	B 1 draw
Hi	John				LL	1805		Wilkes	GA	B 1 draw
Ha	John			_Swain Mary	LW	03 May 1806		Wilkes	GA	
Hi	John				Deserted US Artillry	18 Mar 1807	Savannah	Chatham	GA	Armistead Cap 1st Rg
Hi	John				Tax	1807		Franklin	GA	#14
Hi	John				Tax	1807		Franklin	GA	#25
Hi	John				LL	1807		Oglethorpe	GA	#124 16 W
He	John				Tax Lanes Dist	1808	Oconee	Clarke	GA	Randolph Adj
He	John				Tax	1808		Franklin	GA	#14
He	John				Tax	1808		Franklin	GA	#24
He	John				Tax	1808		Franklin	GA	#34
Ha	John			_Billups Maria	m	03 Apr 1808		Jackson	GA	
He	John				Tax	1808		Jones	GA	
He	John				Tax Lanes Dist	1808	Apalachee	Morgan	GA	Radford adj
Hi	John				Tax Lanes Dist	1809	Apalachee	Baldwin	GA	Radford adj
Hi	John				Deserted $50 reward	05 Jan 1809	Savannah	Chatham	GA	Newspaper age22 bNC
Hi	John				Carriagemaker Occupa	09 Jan 1809	Savannah	Chatham	GA	Newspaper
He	John				Tax	1809	Apalachee	Morgan	GA	
Hi	John				Tax Lanes Dist	1809	Apalachee	Wilkinson	GA	
He	John				Tax Lanes Dist (2)	1810	Apalatchee	Baldwin	GA	Heard adj
He	John				Tax Lanes Dist	1810	Oconee	Clarke	GA	Randle adj
He	John				Tax	1811		Jones	GA	
He	John				Tax	1811		Morgan	GA	
Ha	John			_ Swain? Mary	d	1813		Wilkes	GA	Intestate R Austin
Ha	John			_ Swain Mary	d Admin	05 Sep 1814		Jackson	GA	Montgomery H
Ha	John			_Pain Mary?	Est vs	05 Sep 1814		Jackson	GA	Paine Edw
Ha	John			_ Swain Mary	w Admin see Tms Jr	1814		Wilkes	GA	Harris Walton p101

LN	FIRSTNAME	IO	FATHER	MOM_SPOUSE	EVENT	EVENTDATE	CITY	COUNTY_PAR	ST	SOURCE
Ha	John			_ Swain Mary	Wid LW Prob	04 May 1814		Wilkes	GA	wife & poss child
He	John				b	1815			GA	GA Walk 1840C p69
Ha	John				Tax Wrights Dist	1817	Wolf Creek	Clarke	GA	McCalpin adj
Ha	John				Tax Wrights Dist	1817	Jacks Cree	Morgan	GA	Miles adj
Ha	John				Tax Wrights Dist	1817	Apalatchee	Morgan	GA	Phillips adj
Ha	John			_ Swain Mary	Wid LW	26 May 1817		Wilkes	GA	
He	John				Tax	1818		Twiggs	GA	GS Qt V11#3
Ha	John		Edward?		Settled?	1818		Washington	MS	GA Fran f
He	John				Tax	1819		Franklin	GA	#53
He	John				Tax	1819		Franklin	GA	#66
Ha	John			_ Mary Swain	Wid LW prob	04 Nov 1819		Wilkes	GA	
Hi	John				LL	1821		Henry	GA	150 1
Hi	John				LL Res	1821		Twiggs	GA	
He	John				Tax	1823	Hendersons	Morgan	GA	
He	John				Tax Stranges Dist	1824	Sandy Cree	Morgan	GA	Carroll adj
Ha	John			_Barrett Nancy	m	30 Jun 1825		Morgan	GA	37,000 MR
Ha	John				Tax	1826	Wrights Di	Clarke	GA	Defaulter
Hi	John				Tax	1827	Burchets D	Clarke	GA	
He	John			_Sims Betty Ann	m	17 Jun 1827		Clarke	GA	Loose mr GSLA
Ha	John				LL	1827		Coweta	GA	91 5
Hi	John				LL	1827		Lee	GA	229 24
He	John				Tax	1827		Morgan	GA	Single man
Ha	John				LL	1827	Christians	Morgan	GA	Single man
Hi	John				LL Res	1827		Telfair	GA	
Hi	John				Tax	1828	Jones Dist	Clarke	GA	
Ha	John				Tax	1829	Lynches Di	Muscogee	GA	
He	John			Mary	b	1830			GA	GA Talb 1850C #1184
Hi	John			_ Sims Betty Ann?	C 20-30	1830		Clarke	GA	00001 1001 p307
Ha	John			_ Sims Betty Ann?	Tax Lynches Dist	1830		Clarke	GA	
Ha	John			_ Barrett Nancy?	C	1830		Morgan	GA	p253
Ha	John		Thomas	Evans	LW of Tms Jn decd	02 May 1831		Newton	GA	Some GA Co Records
Ha	John				LL Cher Res	1832		Heard	GA	Lot813 Dist14 Sec1
He	John		Elam		b	1835				GA Twig 1850C
Hi	John				b	1835				GA Lown 1850C p167
He	John		Joseph Jr	Clark_Allison Roz Jane	Ind Cher b	1838		Union	GA	#28895
He	John		Joseph Jr	Clark_Allison Roz Jane	b	1838		Union	GA	1850C
Ha	John		John M	Elizabeth	w of Elizb mom	09 Nov 1838		Wilkes	GA	

49

LN	FIRSTNAME	IO	FATHER	MOM_SPOUSE	EVENT	EVENTDATE	CITY	COUNTY_PAR	ST	SOURCE
He	John		James	Costen_Bruce Rebecca	Ind Cher b	1840			GA	GA Fors 1850C
He	John				C	1840	Warren Dis	Bibb	GA	p94
He	John				C	1840	Dist 225	Clarke	GA	p199
He	John				C 20-30	1840		Walker	GA	00001 21001 p69
He	John				Tax 1 poll 1844-	1842		Carroll	GA	
Hi	John			_Lowe Martha G	m	04 Jan 1844		Houston	GA	Lane
Ha	John			_Lester Mary	m Geo?	23 Sep 1845		Fayette	GA	37,000 MR?
Hi	John		Caleb Sr	Margaret	w of Caleb	01 Mar 1845		Twiggs	GA	Misc deeds Jns Heirs
He	John		James		b	1846			GA	Paul 1850C
Ha	John				LG 250 Acr	1848		Hall	GA	Bkw5 p230
Ha	John			_Lewis Angeline F M	m	11 Feb 1848		Morgan	GA	37,000 MR
He	John				C	1850	Subd 33	Gilmer	GA	p400
Hi	John				C	1850	Div 59	Meriwether	GA	p365
Hi	John				C	1850	Dist 81	Thomas	GA	p18
Hi	John			_Lewis Sarah	m	21 Feb 1850		Thomas	GA	IGI
Hi	John				C	1850	Chickama	Walker	GA	p348
Ha	John			_Woodley Nancy A	m	17 Oct 1858		Carroll	GA	
He	John		James	_Bruce Rebecca	Ind Cher m	22 Aug 1858		Forsyth	GA	
Ha	John			_Brown Jane	m	26 Nov 1861		Fannin	GA	37,000 GA MR
He	John		James	Costen_Bruce Rebecca	War Cvl d	08 Mar 1862		Forsyth	GA	COD War Cvl
He	John				Ind Cher Appl	1909			GA	#34319
Ha	John	A	Thomas N	Peggy	Orphan GB Guard Jn N	06 Jul 1821		Morgan	GA	Intestate R Austin
Ha	John	A	Thomas N	Peggy	Orphan LL	1827	Jennings D	Morgan	GA	Billups R R by
Ha	John	A	John		b pre	1831		Newton	GA	Some GA Co Records
Ha	John	A		_Cartlidge Rebecca Ann	m	03 May 1842		Columbia	GA	
Ha	John	A			w	1844		Columbia	GA	BkX p70
Ha	John	Au	Thomas Jr	Maria	Orphan OM	02 Mar 1812		Jackson	GA	Intestate R Austin
Hi	John	B		_Willard Catherine	m	06 Aug 1839		Morgan	GA	37,000 MR
Ha	John	C			Tax Lumpkins Dist	1829	Indian Cre	Morgan	GA	
Ha	John	C			C	1830		Morgan	GA	p252
Ha	John	C			Tax	1830	Hames Dist	Morgan	GA	
Hi	John	C			C	1840		Merriweath	GA	p119
Ha	John	F		_Nancy	m	07 Nov 1834			GA	GSLA Bible R
Ha	John	F		_Shockley Elizabeth	m	19 Jul 1842		Monroe	GA	37,000 MR
Hi	John	F	Green	Lucinda	b	1855			GA	AL Coff 1870C #81
Hi	John	Fr	William	McDuffie_Lott Nancy	b see Elias	02 Oct 1843		Telfair	GA	IGI
He	John	G		_Mary	b	1823			VA	GA Carr 1850C #1285

LN	FIRSTNAME	IO	FATHER	MOM_SPOUSE	EVENT	EVENTDATE	CITY	COUNTY_PAR	ST	SOURCE
Ha	John	H			b C res Cyrus Yancy	1779			VA	GA Hall 1850C Dist38
Ha	John	H			b	1780			VA	GA Hall 1860C
He	John	H			Tax Wrights Dist	1818	Apalatchee	Morgan	GA	Phillips adj
He	John	H			Tax	1818	Wrights Di	Wayne	GA	
He	John	H			Tax	1818	Wrights Di	Wilkinson	GA	
Ha	John	H			C 50-60	1830		Hall	GA	11000001 1111001p117
He	John	H	George W S	Lambert	b	1836			GA	NC Meck GS
Ha	John	H			Guard of	03 Jan 1837		Hall	GA	Corley Elizb
Ha	John	H			Guard of	03 Jan 1837		Hall	GA	Manors Jn
Ha	John	H		_Williams Nancy	m	22 Jan 1837		Hall	GA	IGI
Ha	John	H		_ Williams Nancy?	C	1840		Hall	GA	
He	John	H	Andrew Ber	Angelina	b	1845			GA	GA Cass 1850C #1373
Ha	John	H			Surveyor county	1850		Hall	GA	1850C Dist38
Ha	John	H		_Morrison Martha	m	12 Oct 1876		Carroll	GA	37,000 MR
Ha	John	Je	Reuben	Jones_Vines Sarah A	b d1914	1840			GA	GA Carr 1860C p23
He	John	Je	Reuben	Jones_Vines Sarah A	b	1840			GA	GA Carr 1880C
He	John	Je	Reuben	Jones_Vines Sarah A	b	14 Mar 1840			GA	Parker Fam Bible
He	John	Je	Reuben	Jones_Vines Sarah A	Orphan	1848		Carroll	GA	Min BkAA 1852-70
He	John	Je	Reuben	Jones_Vines Sarah Arkan	War Cvl CoB 4th Sgt	16 Jun 1862		Carroll	GA	7thrgt Cal
He	John	Je	Reuben	Jones_Vines Sarah A	War Cvl CoB 4th Sgt	11 Jul 1864		Carroll	GA	10thRgt Cal
Ha	John	Je	Rueben	_Vines Sarah A	m	11 Mar 1869		Carroll	GA	37,000 MR
He	John	K		_Radford Betsy	m	17 Jul 1804		Oglethorpe	GA	37,000 GA MR
Hi	John	K		_ Radford Elizabeth	Exec LW of	07 Jan 1805		Clarke	GA	Radford H Some GA R
He	John	K		_ Radford Elizabeth	Tax agent f orphans	1808		Wilkinson	GA	Radford H of
Hi	John	K		_ Radford Elizabeth	Tax f Harry Radford	1809	Middle Riv	Clarke	GA	Randle adj
He	John	K		_ Radford Elizabeth	Tax f	1810	Apalatchee	Wilkinson	GA	Radford Harry
He	John	La	Archibald	Mary J_Bell Roxie Ann	b Jn Lazarus	1857		Gordon	GA	TN Hami 1860C p24
He	John	La	Archibald	_Bell Roxie Ann	b d14Jan1931	22 Jan 1857		Gordon	GA	TX Howa d
Ha	John	M			LL	1821		Monroe	GA	77 4
Ha	John	M			LL	1821		Monroe	GA	177 8
Ha	John	M	John	Mary	LL Res	1821		Wilkes	GA	
Ha	John	M	John	Mary	C	1830		Wilkes	GA	p307
He	John	M	Presley Th	Ada_Elmore M J	b	1847			GA	GA Cass 1850C #1372
He	John	M			C	1850	Dist 31		GA	p167
Ha	John	M			Heir Estate of W	26 Aug 1856		Wilkes	GA	Ord Ofc Inf Court
Ha	John	M			Est of Catherine	26 Aug 1856		Wilkes	GA	Ord Ofc Inf Court
Ha	John	M			Minor of	26 Aug 1856		Wilkes	GA	Adams F H

LN	FIRSTNAME	IO	FATHER	MOM_SPOUSE	EVENT	EVENTDATE	CITY	COUNTY_PAR	ST	SOURCE
He	John	M	Presley Th	_Elmore M J	m	23 Jan 1869		Gordon	GA	
He	John	Mi	James Mill	Sarah A_Ascew Elizabeth	b Jn Miller	1805		Rutherford	NC	GA Fors mr bro t Jms
Ha	John	Mi	James Mill	_Gordon Josephine	m	13 Aug 1835		Forsyth	GA	Francis mom
He	John	Mi	James Mill	_Ascew Elizabeth	m Jn Miller	24 Nov 1878		Forsyth	GA	
Ha	John	N			Gaurd Orphans of	06 Jul 1821		Morgan	GA	Tms N Guard Bonds
He	John	P			C	1830		Pike	GA	p117
Hi	John	P	Caleb Jr	Lydia Ann	b	1853		Twiggs	GA	
Hi	John	Q			War Cvl CoK d	11 May 1865	Finn Point		NJ	GA45th POW bur N
He	John	R	Henry B	Stewart	b	1850			GA	GA Carr 1860C p21
He	John	R		_Bailey Matilda A	m	01 Mar 1868		Carroll	GA	37000 GA MR
He	John	S	Andrew	_ Mardis Ann Eliza	War Cvl enl CoI 5MS	03 Aug 1861		Kemper	MS	GA POW taken
Hi	John	Sr		_ Rebecca	L 1791-	1787		Ninety six	SC	GA Fran BkB
Hi	John	Sr			LG 5000 Acr	31 Jul 1788		Franklin	GA	
Hi	John	Sr			LG 8 Acr	1788		Franklin	GA	
Hi	John	Sr			LG 8000 Acr	1788		Franklin	GA	
Hi	John	Sr			LG 500 Acr	1788		Franklin	GA	
He	John	Sr		_ Rebecca	L 330 Acr t Allison	01 Nov 1791		Franklin	GA	SC Nine of BkK
He	John	Sr		_ Rebecca	L t Dennis McFall	30 Oct 1791	Oconee	Franklin	GA	SC Nine
Hi	John	Sr		_ Rebecca	L 1794-	1791		Ninety six	SC	GA Fran BkC
He	John	Sr		_ Mary	L t	02 Apr 1794		Franklin	GA	McFall GA Pio V5#4
Hi	John	Sr		_Mary	L 700 Acr Wheeler	1794	Clark Cree	Wilkes	GA	Odear Wm adj
Hi	John	Sr		_ Rebecca	L 1798-	1794		Greenville	SC	GA Fran BkD
Hi	John	Sr		_ Rebecca	L t Josiah Kennedy	20 Nov 1796		Franklin	GA	SC Nine of
Ha	John	T		_Brand Mary	m	25 Dec 1854		Paulding	GA	Branel? BkI p161
Ha	John	W			Tax	1817	Tolberts D	Morgan	GA	
Ha	John	W			Tax Tolberts Dist	1818	Indian Cre	Morgan	GA	Mosley adj
He	John	W		_Barrett Harriet	m	18 Nov 1818		Morgan	GA	Barrott?
Ha	John	W			LL	1820		Early	GA	#107 18
Ha	John	W		_ Barrett Harriett?	LL Res	1820		Morgan	GA	
Ha	John	W		_ Barrett Harriett?	C	1820		Morgan	GA	p372
He	John	W			Tax	1823	Myers Dist	Morgan	GA	
He	John	W			Tax	1824	Myers Dist	Early	GA	
Ha	John	W			Tax	1824	Tolberts	Morgan	GA	
He	John	W			Tax Myers Dist	1824	Indian Cre	Morgan	GA	Brown adj
He	John	W		_ Moore Nelly	b of son Jms	1828			GA	AL Tall 1850C p405
Ha	John	W			Tax Lumpkins Dist	1829	Indian Cre	Morgan	GA	Brown adj
Ha	John	W			Tax Hames Dist	1830	Indian Cre	Morgan	GA	Brown adj

LN	FIRSTNAME	IO	FATHER	MOM_SPOUSE	EVENT	EVENTDATE	CITY	COUNTY_PAR	ST	SOURCE
Ha	John	W			LL Cher Res	1832		Morgan	GA	Lot621 Dist12 Sec1
Ha	John	W		_West Elizabeth	Ind Cher? m	04 Sep 1838	Clarksvill	Habersham	GA	
He	John	W			C	1840		Cherokee	GA	p167
He	John	W			C	1840	Dist 400	Morgan	GA	p247
He	John	W			C	1850	Dist 15	Cherokee	GA	p451
He	John	W			Sur m of	01 Aug 1853		Cherokee	GA	Pugh Jn Intestate R
Hi	John	We	James Fulw	_Melton Frances	b Jn Wesley	20 Aug 1870		Coffee	GA	Douglas mom
He	Johnathan		Elam		b	1832			GA	Twig 1850C
He	Johnathan	C	Joseph Jr	Clark	Ind Cher b Jr/Coot?	1840			GA	Unio 1850C
He	Joseph		William	Lambert_Nolan Susan	b	1819			GA	GS NC Meck
He	Joseph		William Ri	Blair_Warrick Salena	Ind Cher b	1819			GA	NC Cher 1860C p867
He	Joseph		William Ri	Blair_Warrick Salena	Ind Cher b	1820			GA	NC Cher 1850C p5
Ha	Joseph			_Susan	b	1827			GA	AL Covi 1860C #974
Ha	Joseph			_Elizabeth	b	1828			GA	MS Scot 1860C p16
Ha	Joseph				L Lot 127	1831		Carroll	GA	Harris Wm BkB p126
He	Joseph		James Sr		L vs Tms Vissage	17 May 1836	Conneross	Pickens	SC	GA Gen Mag #37 p271
He	Joseph		William	_Nolan Susan	m	1840			GA	NC Meck GS
He	Joseph		William Ri	_Worlix Sarah	Ind Cher? m	01 May 1842		Union	GA	37,000 GA MR
Hi	Joseph		William J	Elender	b	1845			GA	AL Covi p163
He	Joseph		Elam		b	1846			GA	Twig 1850C
Hi	Joseph				C	1850	Subd 33	Gilmer	GA	p409
Hi	Joseph			_Addison Polly Ann	m	26 Nov 1854		Franklin	GA	37,000 MR
He	Joseph	E	Orren O	Cartwright	b	28 Nov 1858		Carroll	GA	IGI
He	Joseph	EH	Thomas Jef	Cannaday_Jane H	b	Sep 1853	Lake Park	Lowndes	GA	1860C
Hi	Joseph	Ed	Jacob Buck	Allen	b	27 Aug 1882	Cochran	Pulaski	GA	IGI
He	Joseph	G			L	1848	Blue Ridge	Fannin	GA	
He	Joseph	Jr	Joseph Sr	Scruggs_Clark Nancy	Ind Cher b	1801		Pendleton	SC	GA Unio 1880C
He	Joseph	Jr	Joseph Sr	Scruggs_Clark Nancy	Ind Cher b	1806		Pendleton	SC	GA Unio 1850C p241
He	Joseph	Jr	Joseph Sr	Scruggs_Clark Nancy	Ind Cher bof son Jms	1823			TN	GA Murr 1850C Jms M
He	Joseph	Jr			LL	1827		Carroll	GA	52 5
He	Joseph	Jr	Joseph Sr	_Clark Nancy	C Ind Cher	1830		Habersham	GA	p48
He	Joseph	Jr	Joseph Sr	Scruggs_Clark Nancy	C Ind Cher State	1834		Union	GA	5m 4f
He	Joseph	Jr	Joseph Sr	Scruggs_Clark Nancy	C Ind Cher	1840		Union	GA	p12
He	Joseph	O	Samuel	Francis	b	1868			GA	Carr GA 1870C p31
Ha	Joseph	S	Tapley	Kilgare	b	1837		Morgan	GA	1850C p143
He	Joseph	Sr		_ Scruggs Rebecca	Ind Cher b	1765		Culpepper?	VA	GA Habe 1830C
He	Joseph	Sr		_ Scruggs Rebecca	C Ind Cher	1820		Habersham	GA	SC Pend f

LN	FIRSTNAME	IO	FATHER	MOM_SPOUSE	EVENT	EVENTDATE	CITY	COUNTY_PAR	ST	SOURCE
He	Joseph	Sr		_ Scruggs Rebecca	Ind Cher LL res	1827		Habersham	GA	
He	Joseph	Sr		_ Scruggs Rebecca	C Ind Cher 60-70 p27	1830		Habersham	GA	000010001 00010001
He	Joseph	Sr		_ Scruggs Rebecca	C Ind Cher State	1834		Union	GA	1m 1f
He	Joseph	Sr		_ Scruggs Rebecca	C Ind Cher	1840		Union	GA	p14
He	Josephine			_Garrison Bud	m				GA	
He	Josephine				Ind Cher Appl	1909			GA	#33177 aka Josie
Hi	Joshua	Mo	James Fulw	_Sullivan Alice	b Josh Monroe	03 Mar 1873		Coffee	GA	Douglas mom
Hi	Josiah	Fa	Elton Farr	Boone	b	14 Apr 1979	Brunswick	Glynn	GA	IGI
Hi	Juanita		William	Haddock	b	1885		Coffee	GA	IGI
He	Judith		William Ri	Blair	Ind Cher b	1830			GA	NC Cher 1860C
Hi	Judith		William Ri	Blair	Ind Cher b Judy	1830		Habersham	GA	NC Cher 1850C
He	Judy		William Ri	Blair_Peak James	Ind Cher of #9754 b	1830			GA	Peak Lovinia rej
He	Judy		William Ri	_Peak James	Ind Cher son Richd b	1830		Habersham	GA	AL Jack Pendergrass
He	Judy		William Ri	Blair_Peak James	Ind Cher wid back t	1846			GA	#9754
He	Julia	An	Elam		b	1834			GA	Twig 1850C
Hi	Julia	An			b	1837			GA	GA Lown 1850C p167
He	July	A	Henry W	Pinelope	b	1842		Walker	GA	1850C
He	Kate		Jesse Sr	_Lambert Allen	b	1807			GA	Crawford mom Meck GS
Ha	Katherine	G		_Sanford Asa	m	30 May 1830		Hall	GA	IGI
Hi	King		Charles F		Res	1835		Pulaski	GA	NC Meck GS
He	L				b War Cvl Oath t US	1810			GA	NW Hist&GS
He	L				C	1830		Jackson	GA	p371
Hi	L				C	1850	Elbert	Elbert	GA	p378
He	L				War Cvl Oath t US	1865		Fannin	GA	GA NW Hist&GS
He	L	C		_Wheeler Elizabeth	m	1856		Towns	GA	1st MR
Hi	L	C	Wiley Harg	_Barnard Ella	b Choochee	1900	Homerville	Clinch	GA	Booth mom
Hi	L	J	Jesse Robe	Corbitt	b	1920	Homerville	Clinch	GA	IGI
He	Lafayette		Caleb		b	1849			GA	Twig 1850C
He	Laura		John	Allison	Ind Cher b	30 Sep 1889		Union	GA	#28853 #24917
He	Laura		John	Allison	Ind Cher Final Roll	1909			GA	Dawes #24917
He	Laura	J	James	Martha	b	1848			GA	Cass 1850C
He	Lavina			_Nichols Henry	m	24 Dec 1840		Union	GA	
He	Lazarus		Edmond?	Lucy_Narvel Sarah	Shoemaker b	1784		Cheraws	SC	GA Cass 1850C #1527
Hi	Lazarus				Tax Hazrus	1807		Franklin	GA	#97
Hi	Lazarus				wit L BkB p32-22	02 Sep 1808		Franklin	GA	Hollingsworth
He	Lazarus			_ Cenny/Carry	War 1812 disch	1813		Washington	GA	Pen Appl 1851
Hi	Lazarus				Estray Sale	19 Dec 1817		Franklin	GA	Deed BkB p279-280

LN	FIRSTNAME	IO	FATHER	MOM_SPOUSE	EVENT	EVENTDATE	CITY	COUNTY_PAR	ST	SOURCE
He	Lazarus				Tax 1 poll	1818		Franklin	GA	#33
He	Lazarus				Tax	1819		Franklin	GA	#31
He	Lazarus				Tax	1819		Franklin	GA	#81
He	Lazarus				Tax	1819		Franklin	GA	#116
He	Lazarus				Tax	1819		Franklin	GA	#118
He	Lazarus				LL	1820		Appling	GA	#79 2
He	Lazarus				LL	1820		Appling	GA	#404 6
He	Lazarus				LL	1820		Early	GA	#131 14
He	Lazarus				LL Res	1820		Franklin	GA	
He	Lazarus				Tax Default	1820	Greens Dis	Franklin	GA	
He	Lazarus				C RS	1820		Franklin	GA	
He	Lazarus				Tax 1822-	1821	Dist 6	Appling	GA	
He	Lazarus				Tax 1822-	1821	Dist 14	Early	GA	Dist 23
He	Lazarus			_ Mary?	War Rev Pen Appl Lt	14 Sep 1832		Carroll	GA	#16412
Hi	Lazarus				LL Cher	1832		Cass	GA	#183
Hi	Lazarus				War Rev Res	1832		Franklin	GA	Cher LL #238
He	Lazarus				Res	1832		Jasper	GA	Cher LL
He	Lazarus				LL Cher	1832		Walker	GA	#238
Hi	Lazarus			Martha	b	1834			GA	Butt 1850C #398
He	Lazarus				Membr Prim 1837-	1834	Tallapoosa		GA	Baptist Chur
Ha	Lazarus			_Smith Matilda	m Lorazez	28 Jan 1834		Elbert	GA	IGI
He	Lazarus		Lazarus?	Mary	Buyer Est of Lazaraz	16 Mar 1835		Carroll	GA	Wills & Admin
He	Lazarus			_ Mary	Est sale	16 Mar 1835		Carroll	GA	Wills & Admin
He	Lazarus			_Mary	C wid State	1837		Paulding	GA	6 white
He	Lazarus				Rev Pen d last pymt	1839		Paulding	GA	#16412
Ha	Lazarus				C	1840	Dist 592	Pike	GA	Lazaraz p144
He	Lazarus		James	Martha	b	1847			GA	Cass 1850C
He	Lazarus				L	1848	Blue Ridge	Fannin	GA	
Hi	Leanna		Caleb Jr	Lydia Ann	b	1857		Twiggs	GA	
Hi	Leona		Asa	Moore	b				GA	AL Butl 1850C p193
Hi	Leonard	L	Caleb Jr	Lydia Ann	b	1851			GA	
Hi	Leonard	P	William	_Sykes Laura	b	22 Oct 1846		Telfair	GA	McDuffie mom
Hi	Levina			Martha	b	1839			GA	Butt 1850C #398
He	Levina		John		b Lovina	1845			GA	Walk 1850C
He	Levina		Joseph Jr	Clark_Daniel William	Ind Cher m Martha	10 Dec 1845		Union	GA	
Ha	Leviney				m	29 Sep 1847			GA	GSLA Bible R
He	Littleton		Josiah Jos	Hyde_Cain Amanda	Ind Cher b of son	1841			GA	Franklin Robt

LN	FIRSTNAME	IO	FATHER	MOM_SPOUSE	EVENT	EVENTDATE	CITY	COUNTY_PAR	ST	SOURCE
Hi	Loretta		William	_Sellars Peter	b	05 Aug 1858		Coffee	GA	McDuffie mom
He	Louden			_Robinson Nancy	m	08 Nov 1829		Greene	GA	37,000 GA MR
Hi	Louden				C Lowden	1830		Greene	GA	p274
Hi	Louden				C Lawder	1840		Sumter	GA	
Hi	Louisa		Asa	Moore	b			Twiggs	GA	AL Butl 1850C p193
Ha	Louisa		Thomas Ken	Moseley_Simms John D	LW of sis Elizb	02 May 1831		Newton	GA	Some GA Co Records
Ha	Louisa		Thomas Ken	_Simms John D	m	1848		Heard	GA	GA Gen Gleaning p361
Hi	Louisana		James Fulw	Douglas	b d1888	24 Sep 1875		Coffee	GA	IGI
Hi	Louise			_Weldon Johnny B	m	16 Jul 1838		Bleckley	GA	IGI
He	Loyde		Absolom	Ledford	b	1820		Haywood	NC	GA t
He	Loyde		Wiley Sr	_Harkins Millie	b d1907	1825		Haywood	NC	GA Gilm 1870C
He	Lucinda		John		Ind Cher? b	1839			TN	GA Walk 1850C
Hi	Lucretia		Caleb Sr	_Oglesby Ben	w of Caleb	01 Mar 1845		Twiggs	GA	Misc deeds
Hi	Lucy			_ Burris Allen	b d1885	10 Jul 1808		Montgomery	NC	GA Cher 1827 parents
Hi	Lucy	J	Martin M	Albritton	b	1857			GA	AL Barb 1860C
Ha	Ludza		Thomas N		Orphan Jn N Gaurd	06 Jul 1821		Morgan	GA	Intestate R Austin
He	Lulu		Sam	Francis	b	1866			GA	GA Carr 1870C p31
Hi	Luvicy			_Greer Elijah	m	05 May 1842		Pike	GA	
He	M	J		_Freeman Martha	m	1850		Gwinnett	GA	
Ha	M	S			Heir Est of W	26 Aug 1856		Wilkes	GA	Ord Ofc Inf Court
He	M	W		_ Margaret	b of dau Alice J	1847			GA	AL Barb 1860C #68
Ha	Mahala	N	Reuben	Jones_Odom	b	06 Jan 1826			GA	
He	Mahala	N	Reuben	_Odom Lewis	m	07 Jul 1842		Carroll	GA	
Ha	Mahala	N	Reuben	Jones_Odom	Est of Margaret	Apr 1871		Carroll	GA	Min BkB
He	Mahala	T	Robert Gil	Wood_Mathews Wm W	Ind Cher? b	Dec 1858		Dade	GA	TX Elli ED24 p21
He	Mahala	Te	Robert Gil	_Mathews W W	Ind Cher? b M TN	1859		Dade	GA	TN Mari 1860C p61
He	Mahala	Te	Robert Gil	Wood_Mathews W W	Ind Cher b Timmie	1860		Dade	GA	TN Fran 1870C p38
He	Malinda		Henry W	Pinelope	b	1845		Walker	GA	1850C
Hi	Malinda			_White Robert	m	1855		Pulaski	GA	
Hi	Malinda		Henry W	_Owens John H	m	01 Jan 1866		Tishamingo	MS	GA Walk f
He	Malinda		Henry W	Pinelope	d	1867		Prentiss	MS	GA Walk f
He	Mandy				Ind Cher Appl	1909			GA	#31489
He	Maniford		William M	Motley	d Winniford	09 Apr 1856		Polk	GA	1858 Lttr TXSLA
Hi	Mansfield				LL drew L	1832		Jackson	GA	Hinton
Hi	Margaret		Asa	Moore	b			Twiggs	GA	AL Butl 1850C p193
Ha	Margaret		Robert Sr	_ Presley Garner	Tax	1802		Clarke	GA	
Ha	Margaret		Robert Sr	_ Presley Garner	Tax	1805		Clarke	GA	

LN	FIRSTNAME	IO	FATHER	MOM_SPOUSE	EVENT	EVENTDATE	CITY	COUNTY_PAR	ST	SOURCE
Ha	Margaret		Robert Sr	_ Presley Garner	C under Garner	1820	Knights Di	Morgan	GA	
He	Margaret			_Perry Arthur	m	08 May 1827		Monroe	GA	
Ha	Margaret		Reuben	_Lambert	b mom Jones	03 Jan 1832		Carroll	GA	Min BkB 1871
Hi	Margaret		William Ri	Blair	Ind Cher bAmeliaAggi	1836			GA	NC Cher 1850C p5
Hi	Margaret		Robert Sr	_ Presley Garner	w of husb	14 Jan 1839		Clarke	GA	Whitten& Allied Fam
Hi	Margaret		Robert Sr	_ Presley Garner	w prob	04 Mar 1839		Clarke	GA	Whitten& Allied Fam
He	Margaret		James Fulw	_Beach W W	b	31 Oct 1858		Coffee	GA	Douglas mom
He	Margaret	A	Henry B	Stewart	b	1854		Carroll	GA	1860C p21
Ha	Margaret	A			Heir Est of W	26 Aug 1856		Wilkes	GA	Ord Ofc Inf Court
Ha	Margaret	A			Minor of	26 Aug 1856		Wilkes	GA	Adams F H Ord Ofc
Ha	Margaret	A			Est of Catherine	26 Aug 1856		Wilkes	GA	Ord Ofc Inf Court
Ha	Margaret	An		_Smith George Blakely	m	24 Nov 1859		Washington	GA	GA Gen Mag V3 #8
He	Margaretta	E	Caleb		b	1839			GA	GA Twig 1850C
Ha	Margie	Ma	George Dew	Finch	b	06 May 1930	Cave Sprin	Floyd	GA	IGI
Ha	Mariah			_Holloway Martin	m	19 Jan 1817		Clarke	GA	37,000 MR
He	Mariah		John G	Mary	b	1846			GA	GA Carr 1850C #1285
Hi	Marietta		James Fulw	Hall_Herrington Rowan	b Mary Etta	1849		Appling	GA	
Hi	Marjorie	An		_Black William W	m	22 May 1875		Appling	GA	
Ha	Martha				b	1808			GA	GA Hall 1860C
Ha	Martha			_Woodland Thomas	m	18 Mar 1829		Morgan	GA	37,000 MR
He	Martha		Thomas Jef	Cannaday	b	1837	Lake Park	Lowndes	GA	1850C #792
He	Martha		James		b	1840			GA	GA Cass 1850C
Ha	Martha		Armstead	Petty	b	1843			GA	GA Carr 1850C
He	Martha		Joseph Jr	_Daniel William	Ind Cher m akaLevina	10 Dec 1845		Union	GA	Clark mom
He	Martha		James		b	1846			GA	GA Paul 1850C
He	Martha		James	Hobbs	b	1868	Cedar Grov	Walker	GA	IGI
He	Martha			_Hearty John B	m	19 Sep 1874		Dooly	GA	
He	Martha			_Pool J C	m	09 Apr 1875		Carroll	GA	37,000 MR
He	Martha				Ind Cher Appl	1909			GA	#32153
He	Martha	A	James Fulw	_Cauley William	b	1840		Cass	GA	Hall mom Pio of Wire
He	Martha	An	Elam		b	1837		Twiggs	GA	1850C
Hi	Martha	An			b	1838			GA	GA Lown 1850C p167
Hi	Martha	An	Asa	_Liddle John	b	1838		Twiggs	GA	AL Butl 1850C p193
He	Martha	An	William	_Kirkland Z W	b	26 Nov 1859		Coffee	GA	McDuffie mom
Hi	Martha	E		_Evans Henry A	m	30 Jan 1859		Decatur	GA	
Ha	Martha	H	Joseph	_Rogers William A	Ind Cher m	13 Apr 1841		Monroe	GA	
He	Martha	J	Andrew Ber	Angelina	b	1847			GA	GA Cass 1850C #1373

LN	FIRSTNAME	IO	FATHER	MOM_SPOUSE	EVENT	EVENTDATE	CITY	COUNTY_PAR	ST	SOURCE
He	Martha	J	James	_Looney Abner	b	1868	Cedar Grov	Walker	GA	IGI
He	Martha	Ja	Orren O	_Hallonquist L Frank	b Mattie d1933	19 Mar 1852		Carroll	GA	Cartwright mom
Ha	Martha	M	William	Tinsley_Thomas G Wood	b	1812		Morgan	GA	Fam Puz #1015 p10
Ha	Martha	M	William	_Wood Thomas G	m	17 Jan 1829		Morgan	GA	Fam Puz #1015 p10
Ha	Martha	M		_Arrington Francis M	m	03 Dec 1865		Polk	GA	DAR V91
He	Martha	Ma	Charles?	_Daly Patrick	Ind Cher m	16 Apr 1841			GA	Frost Hubbs p722
He	Martin		Henry B	Stewart	b	1859			GA	GA Carr 1870C p28
Ha	Martin			_Pritchett Mary F	m	13 Mar 1880		Carroll	GA	37,000 MR
Hi	Martin	M	Needham	Lanney_Albritton Mary	b of dau Lucy	1857			GA	AL Barb 1860C #55
Ha	Mary		Samuel	Sims	b				GA	So Kith&Kin p109
Hi	Mary		Charles F		b	1810			NC	GA Pula t 1835
He	Mary			_Crowe Gray	m	1818			GA	DAR Bible R V4
Ha	Mary			_Britton James H	b	1826			GA	Francis mom
Hi	Mary			_West John	m	09 Nov 1828		Houston	GA	Hollingsworth GASLA
Ha	Mary		Reuben	Jones	b	30 Mar 1830			GA	
Hi	Mary			_Tillis Willoughby	m	1834				GA GenMag V27
Hi	Mary		Charles F		Res	1835		Pulaski	GA	NC Meck GS
Ha	Mary			_Whatley Wilson	m	10 Mar 1836		Morgan	GA	37,000 MR
He	Mary		Elam		b	1837				GA Twig 1850C
He	Mary			_Moore Daniel	m	26 Mar 1837		Talbot	GA	
He	Mary			_Henson Thomas	m	22 Jul 1843		Union	GA	37,000 MR
He	Mary		James	Martha	b	1848			GA	GA Cass 1850C #384
He	Mary		John G	Mary	b	1849				GA Carr 1850C #1285
He	Mary		Archibald	Mary	b	1852			GA	TN Hami 1860C p24
Ha	Mary		Samuel	Mary	b	31 Jan 1856		Talbot	GA	IGI
He	Mary			_Ammons John	m	03 Jan 1875		Clayton	GA	
He	Mary			_Owenby Thomas P	m	07 Feb 1876		Union	GA	IGI
Ha	Mary	A	Tapley	Kilgare	b	1833		Morgan	GA	1850C p143
He	Mary	A	James	Costin_Bruce Sml G	Ind Cher b	1837			NC	GA Fors 1850C
He	Mary	A	James	_Bruce Samuel G	Ind Cher m	30 May 1858		Forsyth	GA	
He	Mary	An	Caleb		b	1847				GA Twig 1850C
He	Mary	An	Thomas Jef	Cannady_Dees Leonard Br	b	15 May 1847	Lake Park	Lowndes	GA	1850C #792
Ha	Mary	An		_Williams Johnathan	m	29 Apr 1852		Morgan	GA	37,000 MR
He	Mary	An		_Black Alexander	m	23 Oct 1856		Randolph	GA	
He	Mary	An	James Fulw	_Wilcox Jeff Dr	b	16 Feb 1864		Coffee	GA	Douglas mom IGI
He	Mary	C	John		b	1843				GA Walk 1850C
He	Mary	E	Orren O	Cartwright	b	01 Nov 1849		Carroll	GA	IGI

LN	FIRSTNAME	IO	FATHER	MOM_SPOUSE	EVENT	EVENTDATE	CITY	COUNTY_PAR	ST	SOURCE
Ha	Mary	E			Heir Estate of W	26 Aug 1856		Wilkes	GA	Ord Ofc Inf Court
Ha	Mary	E			Est of Catherine	26 Aug 1856		Wilkes	GA	Ord Ofc Inf Court
Ha	Mary	E			Minor of	26 Aug 1856		Wilkes	GA	Adams F H Ord Ofc
He	Mary	E	James	Hobbs	b	1857	Cedar Grov	Walker	GA	IGI
He	Mary	El		_Bailey Jefferson F	b	01 Nov 1849		Carroll	GA	IGI
He	Mary	El	Oren Austi	Cartwright	b	09 Mar 1850		Bibb	GA	IGI
Hi	Mary	Et	James Fulw	_Harrington Roan	m Marietta	09 Aug 1871		Appling	GA	
He	Mary	F	Henry B	Stewart	b	1842			GA	GA Carr 1860C p21
Ha	Mary	F		_ Bryant William J	b C under Bryant	1848			GA	GA Carr 1880C #73
Ha	Mary	F		_Bryant William J	m	30 Sep 1867		Carroll	GA	37,000 MR
He	Mary	I			b	1845			GA	GA Cass 1850C #1527
He	Mary	J			b gd of Lazarus	1845		Cass	GA	1850C #1527
He	Mary	J	Lazarus	Narvel	b gd of Lazarus?	1846			GA	TN Hami 1860C p24
Hi	Mary	Ja	William	_Hall James Millender	b	1844		Telfair	GA	McDuffie mom IGI
Ha	Mary	Ja		_Bedgood James	m	21 Feb 1861		Washington	GA	IGI
He	Mary	L	John	Allison	Ind Cher b	29 Jun 1868		Union	GA	#28904
He	Mary	L	John	Allison	Ind Cher Appl	1909			GA	#28904
Ha	Mary	Lo		_Pitts William Harris	m	08 Jul 1848		Warren	GA	
He	Mary	Ma		_House Joseph David	m	1867		Habersham	GA	IGI
Ha	Mary	W		_Speer George W	m	29 Sep 1847		Monroe	GA	
Ha	Mary	W			m	03 Jan 1855			GA	GSLA Bible R
He	Mathew				Ind Cher Appl	1909			GA	#34320
He	Matilda			_Mitchell John	m	07 Jun 1806		Oglethorpe	GA	
He	Matilda			_Jones Alexander	m	29 Dec 1818		Hancock	GA	
He	Matilda	A		_Henson John R	m	01 Mar 1868		Carroll	GA	37,000 MR
Hi	Mattie			_Inman J L	m Mollie?	29 Nov 1899		Clinch	GA	
Hi	Melvin	C	William	Haddock	b	08 Aug 1888		Coffee	GA	
Ha	Michael				C	1830		Washington	GA	p255
Ha	Michael				LL Cher Res	1832		Washington	GA	Lot268 Dist1 Sec2
Ha	Michael				LL Cher Res	1832		Washington	GA	Lot1193 Dist4 Sec3
Ha	Michael				LG 27 Acr	1848		Washington	GA	BkW5 p285
Ha	Michael	Jr		_King Caroline	m	02 Jan 1850		Washington	GA	37,000 MR
He	Millie	J		_Nix James B	Ind Cher? m	04 Nov 1865		Union	GA	IGI
He	Milton			_Henson Cornelia	m	1856		Townesend	GA	1st MR
He	Mirabeau			Mary	b	1838			GA	GA Talb 1850C #1184
He	Mired		William C	Wood	b	1849				GA Unio 1850C
He	Mirem	Re	Orren O	Cartwright	b Mirem Rebecca	08 Apr 1860		Carroll	GA	TX Upsh t

LN	FIRSTNAME	IO	FATHER	MOM_SPOUSE	EVENT	EVENTDATE	CITY	COUNTY_PAR	ST	SOURCE
Hi	Missouri		William	_Mobley Milred J	b	1852		Coffee	GA	McDuffie mom
He	Missouri		Sanford		b	1857			GA	GA Carr 1870C p215
He	Mitch		Charlie	_Reece Jane	Ind Cher			Union	GA	Swain mom
Hi	Mollie		Wiley Harg	Booth_Inman James	b Mattie?	1874	Homerville	Clinch	GA	IGI
He	Mollie	E			Ind Cher of #153 rej	1909	Gillsville		GA	Adams Richard W
He	Moses		Henry B	Stewart	b	1866			GA	GA Carr 1870C p28
He	Moses			_Green Nancy	m	28 Jan 1868		Fannin	GA	
Ha	Nancy		Rueben	Jones	b	29 Nov 1818			GA	
Ha	Nancy			_Manis Reubin	m	31 Oct 1818		Morgan	GA	Mann
Hi	Nancy			_Robinson James	m	21 Dec 1828		Clarke	GA	
He	Nancy		Andrew Ber	Able	b	1832			GA	GA Cass 1850C #1373
Ha	Nancy			_Dennard Mitchell	m	19 May 1833		Elbert	GA	IGI
Ha	Nancy			_Bearden Richard	m	17 Sep 1835		Campbell	GA	
He	Nancy		James		b	1842		Paulding	GA	1850C
He	Nancy				Ind Cher? Wit w of	29 May 1843	Blainsvill	Union	GA	Mathis Wm
He	Nancy			_Owens E M	m	13 Apr 1848		Troupe	GA	Troup & her Peopl
Hi	Nancy			_Beale Jesse	m	13 Feb 1853		Morgan	GA	Loose mr GSLA
He	Nancy	A		_Clayton Levi R	m	21 Dec 1858		Forsyth	GA	
Hi	Nancy	A		_Clark J A	m	25 May 1869		Clinch	GA	
Ha	Nancy	A		_Watson William M	m	08 Nov 1877		Hall	GA	IGI
He	Nancy	An	Presley Th	_White	m	18			GA	Ada mom
He	Nancy	An	James	Hobbs	b	1864	Cedar Grov	Walker	GA	IGI
Ha	Nancy	El	George Was	Tackett	Ind Cher b	24 May 1854		Coweta	GA	IGI
Hi	Nancy	J		_Berry Thomas G	m	07 May 1856		Randolph	GA	GA Gen Mag
He	Nancy	J	James Fulw	Douglas_Odom J M	b	17 Oct 1860		Coffee	GA	
Hi	Nancy	J	James Fulw	_Odom J M	m	25 Mar 1877		Coffee	GA	IGI
He	Nancy	Ja	James	_Tatum Robert P	Ind Cher? b	1864	Cedar Grov	Walker	GA	IGI
He	Nancy	Ja	John	_Hamby	Ind Cher? b	06 Apr 1871		Union	GA	Allison mom
He	Nancy	M	Henry W	Pinelope	b	1840		Walker	GA	1850C
He	Nancy	M	Henry W?	_Owens A F	m	18 Jan 1866		Tishomingo	MS	GA Walk f
He	Napoleon		Sanford	Rachael	b	1861		Carroll	GA	1870Cp215
Hi	Nathan				c	1840		Houston	GA	
Hi	Nathan			_Bell Sandarilla	m Mathan	14 Jun 1846		Randolph	GA	
Ha	Nathaniel	O		Athan	b	12 Aug 1872		Stewart	GA	IGI
He	Neal		.		Tax	1805		Franklin	GA	p6
He	Newton			_Garner Haney	m	27 Jan 1817		Clarke	GA	37,000 GA MR
Hi	Newton				Tax	1819	Garlington	Clarke	GA	

LN	FIRSTNAME	IO	FATHER	MOM_SPOUSE	EVENT	EVENTDATE	CITY	COUNTY_PAR	ST	SOURCE
Ha	Newton				LL Res	1820		Clarke	GA	
Hi	Newton				C	1820	Athens	Clarke	GA	p143
Ha	Newton				LL	1820		Early	GA	#99 6
He	Newton				Tax	1821	Garlington	Clarke	GA	
He	Newton				Tax	1822		Clarke	GA	
He	Newton				Tax	1823	McCrees Di	Early	GA	
Hi	Newton				Tax	1824	Athens	Clarke	GA	
Hi	Newton				Tax	1824	Hughes Dis	Early	GA	
He	Newton				Tax	1825	Lumpkins D	Early	GA	
Hi	Newton				Tax	1826	Greers Dis	Early	GA	
He	Newton				Tax	1827	Marseys Di	Early	GA	
He	Newton				Tax	1828	Applings D	Early	GA	
Ha	Newton				C	1830		Oglethorpe	GA	p95
Hi	Newton				C	1840		Oglethorpe	GA	
He	Newton				C	1850	Puryears	Clarke	GA	p47
Ha	Nicey			_Coley John	m Vicey	20 Jun 1824		Habersham	GA	Coleman? DAR V166
He	Nicey	An		_Camp William T	m Nancy Ann?	22 Jun 1844		Fayette	GA	Hunting for Bears
He	O	A			JP #858	03 Jun 1839		Paulding	GA	Hist of p100
He	O	A			L 40 Acr BkK p2	20 Sep 1849		Paulding	GA	Chance Isaac t
He	O	A			C	1850	Div 11	Carroll	GA	p69
Ha	O	A			War Cvl enl	1863		Carroll	GA	GSLA
Ha	O	O			b	1805				GA Pauld 1840C p108
Ha	O	O			C 30-40	1840	Dist 858	Paulding	GA	000001 00132001 p108
He	Oliver	Mi	William Re	Smith	b	22 Jan 1885	Kingston	Bartow	GA	IGI
He	Orena		Henry W	Pinelope	b see Arena	1839		Walker	GA	1850C
He	Orren				GA Vol Cher removal	02 Jun 1838		Paulding	GA	Witchers Co WAC p210
He	Orren	A			Tax 1847-	1844		Walker	GA	GA Paul Carr
He	Orren	Au	Orren O	Cartwright	b Orren Austin	08 Aug 1855		Carroll	GA	IGI
He	Orren	O	Aaron	Mary_Cartwright Martha	Admin est of Aaron	1835		Carroll	GA	
He	Orren	O	Aaron	_Cartwright Martha	m as O O	24 Dec 1846		Carroll	GA	37,000 MR
He	Orren	O			Tax	1847		Carroll	GA	GA Walk Paul L
He	Orren	O	Aaron	Mary_Cartwright Martha	L Pwr of Atty	1854		Gordon	GA	BkF p528
Hi	Patsy			_Yeates John	m	21 Aug 1817		Laurens	GA	Yates Hist Col DAR
He	Peggy		Jesse Sr	_Davis Lewis	b	1820			GA	
He	Peggy		Jesse Sr	Crawford_Davis Lewis	C under Davis	1840		Fayette	GA	
He	Permelia			_Moss Thomas B	m	04 Dec 1849	Lexington	Oglethorpe	GA	
Hi	Phillip				Tax Default 1793-	1790		Burke	GA	GA Gen Gems p38 NGS

LN	FIRSTNAME	IO	FATHER	MOM_SPOUSE	EVENT	EVENTDATE	CITY	COUNTY_PAR	ST	SOURCE
Hi	Phillip				LL	1805		Jefferson	GA	B 1 draw
Hi	Phillip	Jr	Phillip Sr		LL	1807		Burke	GA	#45 7 B
Ha	Polly			_Strickland	m	04 Feb 1813		Morgan	GA	
He	Polly	An	Joseph Jr	Clark	Ind Cher b	1835		Union	GA	see Rebecca An
He	Polly	E	John		b	1844				GA Gilm 1850C
He	Presley	Th	William M	_Ada	Ind Cher b	1812		Pendleton	SC	GA Cass 1850C #1372
He	Presley	Th	William M	Motley_Ada	Ind Cher b	22 Apr 1815		Rabun	GA	1858 Lttr
He	Presley	Th	William M	Motley_Ada	Ind Cher d	1888		Gordon	GA	
He	Randall				L	1838	Blue Ridge	Fannin	GA	
Ha	Rebecca		Thomas	_Rogers David	m	11 Jan 1815		Jackson	GA	Hollingsworth GASLA
Ha	Rebecca		Thomas	Evans_Rogers David	LW of Tms	02 May 1831		Newton	GA	Some GA Co Records
Ha	Rebecca		Thomas	Evans_Rogers David	LW of sis Elizb	01 Jun 1836		Newton	GA	Some GA Co Records
He	Rebecca		William Ri	_Starrit Preston	Ind Cher m	16 Feb 1839		Union	GA	
He	Rebecca			_Camp T Pascal	m	06 May 1849		Coweta	GA	Hunting for Bears
He	Rebecca	A	Aaron	Mary_Fulbright Leonard	b	1813			GA	
He	Rebecca	A	Aaron	Mary_Fulbright Leonard	Res 1837-	1834		Paulding	GA	C State
He	Rebecca	A	Aaron	_Fulbright Leonard	m	28 Jan 1836		Carroll	GA	37,000 GA MR
Ha	Rebecca	A		_Roper Charles F	m	09 Oct 1866		Forsythe	GA	
Ha	Rebecca	Al	George Tho	_Avant Hardy H	Ind Cher m see Alice	06 Jun 1855		Washington	GA	OK t
He	Rebecca	An	Joseph Jr	Clark	Ind Cher b Polly Ann	1835				GA Unio 1850C p241
He	Rebecca	An	Joseph Jr	Clark	Ind Cher Appl	1909			GA	#28902
He	Rebecca	B	Robert Gil	Wood_Dobbins Joseph	Ind Cher? b	Aug 1857		Dade	GA	TN Mari mr
He	Rebecca	B	Robert Gil	Wood_Dobbins Joseph	Ind Cher? b d1916	18 Aug 1857		Dade	GA	TN Mari Pleasant Cem
He	Rebecca	B	Robert Gil	Wood_Dobbins Joseph	Ind Cher? b	1858		Dade	GA	TN Mari 1860C p61
He	Rebecca	B	Robert Gil	Wood_Dobbins Joseph	Ind Cher? b	1858		Dade	GA	TN Fran 1870C p38
He	Reuben				Tax	1817	Parkers Di	Morgan	GA	
He	Reuben				Tax	1817	Parkers Di	Morgan	GA	Agent f Jesse
He	Reuben				Tax Parkers Dist	1818	Hard Labor	Morgan	GA	Jones adj & agent f
He	Reuben		Jesse Sr	_Jones Margaret	m	16 Jan 1818		Morgan	GA	37,000 MR
Ha	Reuben				LL	1820		Early	GA	#25 5
Ha	Reuben				LL res	1820		Morgan	GA	
He	Reuben		Jesse Sr	Crawford_Jones Peggy	L f	08 Jul 1826		Fayette	GA	McNeil Jms
He	Reuben		Jesse Sr	Crawford_Jones Peggy	L t	08 Dec 1827		Fayette	GA	Westbrook Moses
Ha	Reuben				C	1830		Coweta	GA	p381
Ha	Reuben				LL Cher Res	1832		Campbell	GA	Lot558 Dist1 Sec2
Ha	Reuben		Jesse Sr	Crawford_Jones Margaret	C 40-50	1840	Dist 729	Carroll	GA	3010101 2301001 p53
He	Reuben				C	1840		Coweta	GA	p354

LN	FIRSTNAME	IO	FATHER	MOM_SPOUSE	EVENT	EVENTDATE	CITY	COUNTY_PAR	ST	SOURCE
He	Reuben		Jesse Sr	Crawford_Jones Margaret	Tax Slave 1 21+	1842		Carroll	GA	Meck NC GS
He	Reuben				Tax Slave 2 21+	1844		Carroll	GA	
Hi	Reuben		Jesse Sr	Crawford_Peggy Jones	d	1848		Carroll	GA	Min BkAA 1852-1870
Ha	Reuben		Jesse Sr	Crawford_Peggy Jones	L Lot 101 t	1848		Carroll	GA	Odom BkF p587
Ha	Reuben		Jesse Sr	Crawford_Peggy Jones	Bur Jones Cem	1848		Douglas	GA	GA Carr
He	Reuben	A			LL Cher Res	1832		Warren	GA	Lot695 Dist4 Sec3
Ha	Reuben	Cr	Reuben	Jones_Caldonia Bearden	b	14 May 1834		Fayette	GA	
He	Reuben	Cr	Reuben	_Bearden Caldonia 1	m	1851		Carroll	GA	
Ha	Reuben	Cr	Reuben	Jones_Bearden Caldonia	Est of mom	Apr 1871		Carroll	GA	Min BkB
He	Reuben	Cr	Reuben	_Wilder Nancy 2	m	1874		Carroll	GA	
He	Rhoda		James M	_Allison James	Ind Cher Rody			Union	GA	Wilies mom
Hi	Rhoda		James Fulw	Hall_Carter John J	b	1854		Coffee	GA	
Hi	Rhoda		James Fulw	_Carter John J	m	24 Jan 1872	Baxley	Appling	GA	IGI
He	Richard				b	1785				GA Hall 1830C p133
Ha	Richard				LL	1821		Monroe	GA	194 1
Ha	Richard				Tax	1824	Myers Dist	Monroe	GA	
He	Richard				C 40-50	1830		Hall	GA	1110001 110001 p133
Ha	Richard				Tax Hames Dist	1830	Hard Labor	Morgan	GA	Perkins adj
He	Richard				C	1840		Montgomery	GA	
Ha	Richard				C	1840		Morgan	GA	
Ha	Richard	Th		_Wray Elizabeth Sophia	m	04 Jul 1810		Oglethorpe	GA	37,000 MR
Ha	Richard	Th		_ Wray Elizabeth	C	1820		Oglethorpe	GA	p175
Ha	Richard	Th		_ Wray Elizabeth	Tax	1824		Oglethorpe	GA	
Ha	Richard	Th			LL	1827		Muskogee	GA	55 18
Ha	Richard	Th			LL res	1827		Oglethorpe	GA	
Ha	Richard	Th		_ Wray Elizabeth	C	1830		Oglethorpe	GA	p99
He	Richard	W	Samuel	Sims_Loyd Sarah	b?	1810			GA	So Kith&Kin p109
Ha	Richard	W	Samuel	Sims_Loyd Sarah	LL Res	1821		Morgan	GA	
Ha	Richard	W	Samuel	_Loyd Sarah	m	15 Jul 1824		Morgan	GA	37,000 MR
Ha	Richard	W	Samuel	Sims_Loyd Sarah	Tax Adairs Dist	1826	Hard Labor	Morgan	GA	Wade adj
Ha	Richard	W	Samuel	Sims_Loyd Sarah	C	1830		Morgan	GA	p252
Ha	Richard	W	Samuel	Sims_Loyd Sarah	Tax Agent f Peggy	1830		Morgan	GA	
He	Richard	W	Samuel	Sims_Loyd Sarah	C	1840	Dist 400	Morgan	GA	p247
He	Riley	W			War Cvl CoC Pvt	1863			GA	19thBat Cav NARS
He	Rittes	S	Aaron	_Bird Franklin	m	01 Jun 1847		Carroll	GA	Mary mom C225
He	Robert			_Chambers Lucretia	m Lavidia?	15 Sep 1831		Morgan	GA	Loose mr GSLA
He	Robert				C Roben	1840		Coweta	GA	p354

LN	FIRSTNAME	IO	FATHER	MOM_SPOUSE	EVENT	EVENTDATE	CITY	COUNTY_PAR	ST	SOURCE
Ha	Robert				C	1840	Dist 367	Putnam	GA	p187
Ha	Robert				b in Jn H res	1842			GA	Hall 1860C
He	Robert	Gi		_Wood Mahaley	Ind Cher m akaHenry?	1841		Union?	GA	dau of Andrew
He	Robert	Gi		Dilday_Wood Mahaley	Ind Cher bofdauMahal	Dec 1858		Dade	GA	TN Mari 1860C p61
Hi	Robert	W			b C res of Green	1850			GA	AL Coff 1870C #81
He	Robinson				b pre Robin/Robt?	1755			GA	Ogle 1800C p10
He	Robinson				C Slaves 3 45+	1800	Colberts D	Oglethorpe	GA	11001 11010 p10
He	Roderick	P			War Cvl CoB Pvt	1863			GA	15thCav NARS
Ha	Ruby			_Rodgers Chesley	m	26 Feb 1838		Walton	GA	Hunting f Bears
He	Rufus		James	Martha	b	1836			NC	GA Cass 1850C #384
He	Rufus	P		_Nelson Emma J M	m	05 May 1863		Newton	GA	
He	S				Adj L of Sml	1817	Crooked Cr	Jackson	GA	Tolberts Tax Dist
He	S	M			C	1840		Carroll	GA	p96
He	S	P		_Sanders Thomas A	m	22 Jul 1867		Fannin	GA	
Hi	Saley		Charles F		Res Fely/Sely?	1835		Pulaski	GA	NC Meck GS
Hi	Salina		James Fulw	_Moody Daniel	Twin b	02 Oct 1852		Telfair	GA	Hall mom
He	Sally			_Scroggins Millinton	m	18 Jan 1800		Oglethorpe	GA	
Ha	Sally		Jesse Sr	_Lambert Edwin	m d1868 Sarah	14 Dec 1809		Morgan	GA	Crawford mom
Ha	Sally		Reuben	Jones	b d1922	08 Apr 1822			GA	GS NC Meck
He	Sally		Sam	Francis	b Sallie	1869			GA	GA Carr 1870c p31
Ha	Samuel			_Sims Peggy 2	War Rev b	1758			GA	DAR
Hi	Samuel			_ Peggy Sims	L Adj Wm Sims	1784		Richmond	GA	GA GenGems p92 NGS
He	Samuel				War Rev	1784		Washington	GA	GA Sold of Rev
Ha	Samuel			_ Peggy Sims	LG 500 Acr	1785	Spirit Cre	Richmond	GA	BkFFF p714
Ha	Samuel			_ Sims Peggy	Orig LG #1189	1785	Spirit Cre	Richmond	GA	Tax f Wm 1830
Ha	Samuel			_ Peggy Sims	Sur f	07 Jul 1788		Richmond	GA	Kindar Peter Intesta
He	Samuel				LG 12 Acr	1799		Richmond	GA	
Ha	Samuel				LG 500 Acr	1801		Richmond	GA	BkD p181
Ha	Samuel				LL Res	1805		Columbia	GA	B B
Hi	Samuel		James L	Obedience_Hargrove Marg	b	1805		Telfair	GA	IGI
Ha	Samuel				Tax Brantlies Dist	1808	Crooked Cr	Jackson	GA	
Ha	Samuel				Tax Brantlies Dist	1808	Hard Labor	Morgan	GA	Copeland adj
Ha	Samuel			_ Rice Ann 1	Tax Brantlies Dist	1808	Spirit Cre	Richmond	GA	Conery adj
Ha	Samuel			_Rice Ann 1	m	12 Sep 1809		Columbia	GA	Some Heads of GA Fam
Ha	Samuel				Tax Brantlies Dist	1812	Crooked Cr	Jackson	GA	Thomas Hanson adj
Ha	Samuel				Tax Brantlies Dist	1812	Hard Labor	Morgan	GA	Copeland adj
Ha	Samuel			_ Rice Ann 1	Tax Brantlies Dist	1812	Spirit Cre	Richmond	GA	

LN	FIRSTNAME	IO	FATHER	MOM_SPOUSE	EVENT	EVENTDATE	CITY	COUNTY_PAR	ST	SOURCE
Ha	Samuel			_Patillo Elizabeth	m	21 Apr 1813		Morgan	GA	IGI
Ha	Samuel			_ Sims Margaret 2	d	1817			GA	So Kith&Kin pp109
Ha	Samuel				Tax Tolberts Dist	1817	Crooked Cr	Jackson	GA	Hanson S adj
Ha	Samuel				Tax Tolberts Dist	1817	Indian Cre	Morgan	GA	? adj
Ha	Samuel				Tax Tolberts Dist	1817	Indian Cre	Morgan	GA	Browning adj
Ha	Samuel				Tax Tolberts Dist	1817	Indian Cre	Morgan	GA	Mosley adj
Ha	Samuel				Tax	1817	Tolberts D	Richmond	GA	
Ha	Samuel				Tax Tolberts Dist	1818	Indian Cre	Morgan	GA	Fomboy adj
Ha	Samuel				Tax Tolberts Dist	1818	Spirit Cre	Richmond	GA	McCoy adj
Ha	Samuel				LL	1820		Early	GA	#415 28
Hi	Samuel				LL	1820		Irwin	GA	#111 9
He	Samuel				C Slaves 6 16-26	1820		Jackson	GA	000100 10200 p623
Ha	Samuel				LL Res	1820		Jackson	GA	
Ha	Samuel				C 26-45	1820	Tolberts	Morgan	GA	p370
Hi	Samuel				LL Res	1820		Telfair	GA	
Ha	Samuel				C	1820		Walton	GA	p492
He	Samuel				C	1820		Wilkes	GA	
Ha	Samuel			_ Sims Peggy 2	War Rev w Prob	27 Aug 1821		Morgan	GA	
He	Samuel			_ Sims Peggy 2	Wid Tax exempt	1823	Hard Labor	Morgan	GA	Trimble adj
He	Samuel			_ Sims Peggy 2	Wid Tax exempt	1823	Indian Cre	Morgan	GA	Brown adj
He	Samuel				C state	1824		Jackson	GA	AIS#2
He	Samuel				Tax	1824	Tolberts	Morgan	GA	
Ha	Samuel			_ Sims Peggy 2	Wid Tax exempt	1824	Hard Labor	Morgan	GA	Trimble adj
Ha	Samuel			_ Sims Peggy 2	Wid Tax exempt	1824	Indian Cre	Morgan	GA	Browning adj
Hi	Samuel		James L	_Hargrove Margret	m	16 Sep 1824		Telfair	GA	37,000 MR
Ha	Samuel				Tax	1824		Walton	GA	
Ha	Samuel			_ Sims Peggy 2	Wid Tax Adairs Dist	1826	Hard Labor	Morgan	GA	Wade adj
Hi	Samuel		James L	Obedience_Hargroves Mar	C	1830		Appling	GA	p12
He	Samuel				C	1830		Henry	GA	p238
He	Samuel				C	1830		Talbot	GA	p326
Ha	Samuel		Thomas	Evans	LW of Tms	02 May 1831		Newton	GA	Some GA Co Records
He	Samuel			_Francis	b	1834			GA	GA Carr 1870C p31
Hi	Samuel		James L	Obedience_Hargrove Marg	d	1835	Homerville	Ware	GA	GA Clin now
Ha	Samuel		Thomas	Evans	LW of sis Elizb	01 Jun 1836		Newton	GA	Some GA Co Records
He	Samuel			Mary	b	1840			GA	GA Talb 1850C #1184
He	Samuel				C	1840		Heard	GA	
He	Samuel				C	1840		Henry	GA	p337

LN	FIRSTNAME	IO	FATHER	MOM_SPOUSE	EVENT	EVENTDATE	CITY	COUNTY_PAR	ST	SOURCE
He	Samuel				c	1840		Talbot	GA	p195
Hi	Samuel		Green	Lucinda	b	1853			GA	AL Coff 1870C #81
Ha	Samuel	S			Tax	1817	Tolberts D	Morgan	GA	
Ha	Samuel	Sr			Tax Tolberts Dist	1817	Hard Labor	Morgan	GA	Copeland adj
Ha	Samuel	Sr			Tax Tolberts Dist	1818	Hard Labor	Morgan	GA	Copeland adj
He	Samuel	T			c	1840		Montgomery	GA	
Ha	Samuel	T			c	1840	Dist 400	Morgan	GA	p247
Ha	Samuel	T		_Cotten Elmira	m	06 Oct 1841		Upson	GA	37,000 GA MR
He	Samuel	T	Andrew Ber	Angelina	b	1842			GA	GA Cass 1850C #1373
He	Sanford				b	1829			GA	Carr 1850C p7
He	Sanford			_Bearden Nancy	m	09 Jul 1856		Carroll	GA	37,000 MR
Ha	Sanford			_Story R H	m	26 Dec 1869		Carroll	GA	37,000 GA MR
Ha	Sanford		Reuben	Jones	Est of mom	Apr 1871		Carroll	GA	Min BkB
Ha	Sanford	Ha	Armstead	Petty_Nancy C White	b Sanford Harold Sr	26 Aug 1823		Morgan	GA	
He	Sanford	Ha	Armstead	Petty_White Nancy	b d15May1892	1823		Morgan	GA	AL Cleb 1870C
He	Sanford	Ha	Armstead	_White Nancy C	b Sr	1823		Morgan	GA	AL Rand 1860C
Ha	Sanford	Jr	Sanford Sr	Mary	b	1850		Carroll	GA	1860C #1507
Ha	Sanford	Sr		_ Mary	b	1810			GA	Carr 1860C #1507
He	Sanford	Sr		_Rachael Emily	b	1810	4th Dist		GA	GA Carr 1880C #144
Ha	Sanford	Sr		_ Rachael Emily	b	1810			VA	GA Carr 1870C p215
Ha	Sarah			_Jackson Lucas	m	10 Feb 1822		Hancock	GA	
He	Sarah		Aaron	_Ramsey Wade Hampto	m	22 Dec 1831		Franklin	GA	Hist Col DAR
He	Sarah		Aaron	Mary_Ramsey Wade Hampto	d	1834		Franklin	GA	
He	Sarah		Aaron	Mary_Ramsey Wade Hampto	Widower m post	1834		Franklin	GA	Crump Clary
Ha	Sarah		John M	Elizabeth	w of Elizb mom	09 Nov 1838		Wilkes	GA	
He	Sarah			Martha	b	1844			GA	GA Cass 1850C #384
He	Sarah			_Ferguson James F	Ind Cher? m	15 Jul 1849		Lumpkin	GA	
Hi	Sarah			_Sellers William	m	28 Nov 1850		Twiggs	GA	IGI
He	Sarah			_Smith Green Jackson	m	08 Jan 1852		Pulaski	GA	IGI
He	Sarah		Henry B	Stewart	b	1869			GA	GA Carr 1870C p28
He	Sarah		William Ri	_Thompson	Ind Cher of #117	11 Jul 1908	Blue Ridge		GA	Thompson Mary A rej
He	Sarah				Ind Cher Appl	1909			GA	#34321
He	Sarah	A	James	Martha	b	1838				GA Cass 1850C
He	Sarah	An	Elam		b	1839				GA Twig 1850C
He	Sarah	An		_Canten Charles Jr	m	31 Aug 1845		Forsyth	GA	?
He	Sarah	An		_Blanton Charles	m	31 Aug 1846		Forsyth	GA	?
He	Sarah	E	James	Hobbs	b	1861	Cedar Grov	Walker	GA	IGI

LN	FIRSTNAME	IO	FATHER	MOM_SPOUSE	EVENT	EVENTDATE	CITY	COUNTY_PAR	ST	SOURCE
Ha	Sarah	J	Armstead	Petty	b	1839			GA	GA Carr 1850C
He	Sarah	Ja	James	Costin_Harrison Leroy	Ind Cher b	1844			GA	GA Fors 1850C p228
He	Sarah	Ja	James	_Harrison Leroy	Ind Cher m	06 Nov 1866		Forsyth	GA	
He	Shadrack				C State	1834		Lumpkin	GA	5 white
He	Silas			_Whitton Mary Ann	m aka Wm Silas?	21 Dec 1826		Clarke	GA	Loose mr GSLA
Ha	Silas				Tax	1828	Harris Dis	Clarke	GA	
Ha	Silas				Tax aka Wm Silas?	1830	Smith Dist	Clarke	GA	
Ha	Silas				LL Cher Res	1832		Clarke	GA	Lot342 Dist20 Sec3
He	Silas				C	1840		Montgomery	GA	
Ha	Silas				C aka Wm Silas?	1840	Dist 280	Morgan	GA	p231
Ha	Simon				War Rev Loyalist	01 Aug 1779			GA	SC Royalist deserted
He	Solomon			_ Hall Fanny	b res of Thompson	1792			SC	GA Cass 1850C p192
Ha	Solomon				LL Cher Res	1832		Pulaski	GA	Lot810 Dist20 Sec3
He	Solomon				L t	20 Mar 1848		Gordon	GA	Ransom Ed
He	Solomon			_Curtis Catherine	m	08 May 1884		Fannin	GA	37,000 GA MR
He	Solomon	C			War Cvl CoF Pvt1865-	1861			GA	4thInf NARS
Ha	Stephen	Da	William C	Brantley_Stewart Leona	b	02 Jul 1863		Washington	GA	IGI
Ha	Stephen	Da	William C	_Stewart Leona	m	24 Jan 1892		Laurens	GA	IGI
He	Susan		Aaron	_ Whisenhunt Arthur	b	1823		Appling	GA	
Ha	Susan			_Curry Johnson A	m	07 Apr 1838		Carroll	GA	37,000 MR
He	Susan			_Rainwater James	Ind Cher? m	25 Jan 1846		Cherokee	GA	37,000 MR
He	Susan		Aaron	_Wisenhunt Arthur	m	30 Dec 1847		Carroll	GA	37,000 MR
Ha	Susan			_Robertson Calvin L	m	03 Jan 1855		Morgan	GA	37,000 MR
Ha	Susan	A	Thomas Ken	Moseley	b	02 Jan 1837		Heard	GA	IGI
Hi	Susan	A		_Butler George E	m	14 Jan 1874		Thomas	GA	IGI
He	Susanna		William	Lambert	b	1822			GA	Meck NC GS
Ha	Susanna			_Finch Robert W	m	11 Aug 1836		Carroll	GA	37,000 MR
He	Sut			_Jackson Serena	m	13 Jun 1869		Burke	GA	
Hi	Sylvanius				C	1820		Lincoln	GA	p162
Hi	Sylvanius				C State	1824		Lincoln	GA	
He	T	A			L Lot 159 t	01 Dec 1842		Bartow	GA	Reed Geo p482
Hi	T	H		_Carter Americus	m	02 Jun 1878		Ware	GA	
He	T	P		_Mahoney S	m	08 Oct 1846		Union	GA	37,000 GA MR
Hi	Tabitha		James L	_Smith Joshua	b	1817		Telfair	GA	Obedience mom
Hi	Tabitha	Ja	James Sr	_Godwin Bryant	b	1858		Coffee	GA	Bird mom IGI
Ha	Tally		Thomas N	Peggy	Orph Jn N Gaurd	06 Jul 1821		Morgan	GA	Intestate R Austin
He	Tapley				Tax	1809		Clarke	GA	

LN	FIRSTNAME	IO	FATHER	MOM_SPOUSE	EVENT	EVENTDATE	CITY	COUNTY_PAR	ST	SOURCE
Hi	Tapley				Tax	1810	Trammels	Clarke	GA	
Hi	Tapley				Tax Jones Dist	1812	Sandy Cree	Wilkinson	GA	Tarpley
He	Tapley				Debt t	Jan 1813		Clarke	GA	Strong W InfCourtMin
Ha	Tapley				Tax Parkers Dist	1817	Sandy Cree	Morgan	GA	Greer adj
Ha	Tapley				Tax	1817	Parkers Di	Morgan	GA	Agent f James
He	Tapley			_Freeman Mariah	m	18 Feb 1818		Clarke	GA	GA Co R by Lucas
Ha	Tapley				Tax Parkers Dist	1818	Sandy Cree	Morgan	GA	Greer adj
Ha	Tapley				LL	1820		Appling	GA	#61 8
Ha	Tapley				LL Res	1820		Morgan	GA	
Ha	Tapley				C 16-26	1820	Leonards D	Morgan	GA	221400 13011
He	Tapley				Tax	1823	Hendersons	Morgan	GA	
Hi	Tapley				Tax	1824	Wrights Di	Clarke	GA	
Ha	Tapley				Tax	1824	Stranges D	Morgan	GA	
He	Tapley				Tax Lumpkins Dist	1825	Greenbrier	Clarke	GA	Jones adj
He	Tapley				Tax Wrights Dist	1826		Clarke	GA	
Hi	Tapley				LL Res	1827	Sparks Dis	Clarke	GA	Single man
Ha	Tapley				Tax	1827	Burchets D	Clarke	GA	Defaulter Tarpley
Ha	Tapley				LL	1827	Sparks Dis	Morgan	GA	Single man
Hi	Tapley				LL	1827		Muskogee	GA	98 2
Hi	Tapley				Tax	1828	Jones Dist	Muscogee	GA	Tarpley
Ha	Tapley				Tax	1829	Lynches Di	Muscogee	GA	Tarpley
Hi	Tapley				C 40-50 Tarpley	1830		Clarke	GA	3000001 030101 p307
Ha	Tapley				Tax	1830	Lynches Di	Muscogee	GA	Tarpley
He	Tapley				C	1840	Dist 261	Clarke	GA	Tarpley p232
Hi	Tapley	Ol	Robert Sr	_ Holder Elizabeth	w of Robt Sr	29 Mar 1802		Fauquier	VA	GA Clar t
Ha	Tapley	Ol	Robert Sr	_ Holder Elizabeth	Wid LL	1827	Jennings D	Morgan	GA	Tarpley
Ha	Tapley	Ol	Robert Sr	_ Holder Elizabeth	Orphans of LL	1827		Morgan	GA	Tarpley
Ha	Tapley	Sr	Tapley Old	Holder_Kilgare Mariah	b Tarpey	1796			VA	GA Morg 1850C p143
He	Tapley	Sr	Tapley Old	_Kilgare Mariah	m	14 Dec 1817		Clarke	GA	
Ha	Tapley	Sr	Tapley Old	Holder_Kilgare Mariah	C	1840		Morgan	GA	Tarpley
He	Tapley	Sr	Tapley Old	Holder_Kilgare Mariah	C	1860	Center	Cherokee	AL	GA Morg Mariah res
He	Tennessee		Robert Gil	Woods_Mathews W W	Ind Cher b	1859		Dade	GA	TN Mari see Mahala
He	Terrell				Ind Cher Emig Roll	24 Mar 1832	Ellijay	Gilmer	GA	9 reds in res
He	Thaddeus				War Cvl CoH Pvt1865-	1861			GA	6thInf NARS
Hi	Theresa	Ma	James	Douglas	b Theresa Mae	06 Feb 1863		Coffee	GA	IGI
He	Thomas		Charlie	_Lance Louisa	Ind Cher			Union	GA	Swain mom
He	Thomas				C	1800	Lees Dist	Oglethorpe	GA	

LN	FIRSTNAME	IO	FATHER	MOM_SPOUSE	EVENT	EVENTDATE	CITY	COUNTY_PAR	ST	SOURCE
Hi	Thomas				LL Tms W Sr?	1805		Hancock	GA	B B
He	Thomas				LL	1807		Hancock	GA	#273 19 W
He	Thomas				Tax	1812		Hancock	GA	#38 AIS#1
He	Thomas		Lazarus?	Mary?	RR hand b res of Arc	1818			GA	GA Gord 1850C p51
Ha	Thomas				C	1820		Walton	GA	p492
Ha	Thomas		Thomas N	Peggy	Orphan Jn N Gaurd	06 Jul 1821		Morgan	GA	Intestate R Austin
Ha	Thomas				C	1830		Coweta	GA	p381
Ha	Thomas		Jesse Sr	Crawford?	C	1830		Fayette	GA	p202
Ha	Thomas				C	1830		Newton	GA	p211
Ha	Thomas				C	1830		Newton	GA	p30
Ha	Thomas				C	1830		Newton	GA	p41
Ha	Thomas			_Thompson Fanny	m	03 Jan 1830		Newton	GA	37,000 MR
Ha	Thomas				LL Cher Res	1832		Jackson	GA	
Ha	Thomas				LL Cher	1832		Murray	GA	#259
Ha	Thomas				Res	1832		Newton	GA	Cher LL
Ha	Thomas				LL Cher	1832		Walker	GA	#132
Ha	Thomas				Res	1832		Walton	GA	#259 Cher LL
He	Thomas				L f A Copeland	1837		Walker	GA	NC Tryo GS
He	Thomas				L f M P Dill	1837		Walker	GA	NC Tryo V7 #4 p173
He	Thomas				L f M P Dill	1837		Walker	GA	NC Ruth f
He	Thomas				L f M P Dill	1837		Walker	GA	SC Spar f
He	Thomas				L f A Copeland	1837		Walker	GA	SC Spar f
Ha	Thomas				LL Cher	1838	7th Dist	Newton	GA	#131 Sec 3
Ha	Thomas				LL Cher Res	1838		Walton	GA	#259
Ha	Thomas				C	1840	Dist 549	Fayette	GA	p233
He	Thomas				C Tms R?	1840		Heard	GA	
Ha	Thomas		Tapley	Kilgare	b	1840		Morgan	GA	1850C p143
He	Thomas			_Henson Mary	m	22 Jul 1843		Union	GA	37,000 GA MR
He	Thomas				L	1849	Blue Ridge	Fannin	GA	
He	Thomas	A	John		b	1849		Gilmer	GA	1850C
Ha	Thomas	C			Tax Wm Agent f	1830		Morgan	GA	
Ha	Thomas	C		_Turner Mary S	m	13 Feb 1833		Newton	GA	37,000 MR
He	Thomas	C		_ Turner Mary S	C	1840		Newton	GA	p28
He	Thomas	F		_Starke Jane E	m	10 Aug 1848		Walton	GA	37,000 MR
Ha	Thomas	H		_Addison Rebecca	War Rev m Sr	21 Mar 1778		Prince Geo	MD	GA Fran t
Ha	Thomas	H		_ Addison Rebecca	L f Leonard Marbury	04 Nov 1798		Franklin	GA	MD PGeo of 5750 Acr
Ha	Thomas	H	Thomas H S	_Maria	d Jr	02 Mar 1812		Jackson	GA	Harris Test Ord Min

LN	FIRSTNAME	IO	FATHER	MOM_SPOUSE	EVENT	EVENTDATE	CITY	COUNTY_PAR	ST	SOURCE
Ha	Thomas	H	Thomas H S	Addison_Maria	d Lttr of Admin Sr	02 Mar 1812		Jackson	GA	Rogers Test Ord Min
Ha	Thomas	H		_ Addison Rebecca	Lttr of Admin f Jr	02 Mar 1812		Jackson	GA	Ord Min
Ha	Thomas	H		_ Addison Rebecca	C RS Slaves 5 45+	1820		Jackson	GA	001101 00101 p616
Hi	Thomas	He	James Fulw	_Graham America Mrs	b Tms Helvin	1855		Coffee	GA	Hall mom
He	Thomas	J	George W S	Lambert	b	1829			GA	GS NC Meck
Ha	Thomas	J		_Smith Elizabeth F	m	06 Aug 1854		Floyd	GA	37,000 MR
He	Thomas	Je	James L	_Cannady Elizabeth 1	b Sr	1803			SC	GA Lown 1850C #792
Hi	Thomas	Je	James L	Obedience_Cannady Elizb	C	1830		Telfair	GA	10001 0001 p4
Hi	Thomas	Je	James L	Obedience_Cannday Elizb	d of wife Elizb	1831		Telfair	GA	Eddington wid?
Hi	Thomas	Je	James L	_Cannady Eliza J 2	m sis of 1st wife	13 Apr 1835		Telfair	GA	Hist Col DAR
Hi	Thomas	Je	James L	Obedience_Cannady Eliza	War Ind Pvt Co2RegE	16 Jun 1837	Mineral Sp		GA	Fl Lake #1110
He	Thomas	Je	James L	Obedience_Cannady Eliza	War Indian enl Pvt	16 Jun 1837	Ft Reed	?	GA	Wid Pen #1110 1892
Hi	Thomas	Je	James L	Obedience_Cannady Eliza	C Sr	1840		Lowndes	GA	
He	Thomas	Je	Thomas Jef	Cannaday_Bundy Louisa A	b Jr	1850		Lowndes	GA	1850C #792
Hi	Thomas	Je	Thomas Jef	Cannady_Bundy Louisa An	b Jr age 42 1892	1850		Lowndes	GA	Wid Pen Appl of Tms
Hi	Thomas	Je	Thomas Jef	Cannaday_Bundy Louisa A	b Jr d15Apr1918	26 Aug 1851		Lowndes	GA	FL Lake Altoona Cem
Ha	Thomas	Ke	Thomas W	Boswell_Gracie Mosely	b	1799		Columbia	GA	Some Heads of GA Fam
Ha	Thomas	Ke			b Tms Kendrick	09 Aug 1808		Hancock	GA	NC?
Ha	Thomas	Ke	Thomas W	_Mosely Gracie	m	07 Feb 1828		Morgan	GA	37,000 MR
Ha	Thomas	Ke			C	1830		Coweta	GA	p384
Ha	Thomas	Ke	Thomas W	Boswell_Grace Mosley	b of dau Susan A	02 Jan 1837		Heard	GA	IGI
Ha	Thomas	Ke	Thomas W	Boswell_Moseley Grace	LL Cher	1838	4th Dist	Heard	GA	#224 Sec4
Ha	Thomas	Ke	Thomas W	Boswell_Moseley Grace	C	1840		Heard	GA	
Ha	Thomas	Ke			d	05 May 1892		Columbia	GA	
He	Thomas	N	James M	_Carroll Sallie	Ind Cher			Union	GA	Wilies mom
Ha	Thomas	N		_ Peggy	LL RS	1820		Appling	GA	#173 5 reverted
Ha	Thomas	N		_ Peggy	War Rev LL Res	1820		Jackson	GA	#73 5
Ha	Thomas	N		_Peggy	War Rev d GB	06 Jul 1821		Morgan	GA	Intestate R Austin
Ha	Thomas	N		_ Peggy	Orphans LL	1827		Lee	GA	159 24
Ha	Thomas	N		_ Peggy	Wid LL RS	1827		Morgan	GA	
Ha	Thomas	N		_ Peggy	Orphans LL Res	1827		Morgan	GA	
Ha	Thomas	N		_ Peggy	Wid LL RS	1827		Muskogee	GA	92 13
Ha	Thomas	N		_ Peggy	Wid LL Cher	1838		Morgan	GA	DAR p238
He	Thomas	N	John	_Carrie	Ind Cher b	23 Oct 1882		Union	GA	#28881
He	Thomas	N	John	Allison_Carrie	Ind Cher Appl	1909			GA	#28881
Ha	Thomas	Ol		_ Evans Mary	War Rev res	10 Sep 1785		Richmond	GA	GA Gen Gems p81 NGS
Ha	Thomas	Ol			L 200 Acr w of	10 Sep 1785		Richmond	GA	Garnet Jn

LN	FIRSTNAME	IO	FATHER	MOM_SPOUSE	EVENT	EVENTDATE	CITY	COUNTY_PAR	ST	SOURCE
Ha	Thomas	Ol		_Evans Elizabeth	m	20 Feb 1788		Richmond	GA	GA Newt t
Ha	Thomas	Ol			Test w of	08 Mar 1788		Richmond	GA	Walker David p81
Ha	Thomas	Ol		_ Elizabeth Evans	w	1831		Newton	GA	Bk1 p45
Ha	Thomas	Ol		_ Elizabeth Evans	LW	02 May 1831		Newton	GA	Some GA Co Records
Ha	Thomas	R			Res	1832		Heard	GA	#68
Ha	Thomas	R			LL Cher	1832		Murray	GA	#68
Ha	Thomas	Si		_Morgan Amanda	b	1832			GA	Francis mom
Ha	Thomas	V			C	1830		Coweta	GA	p384
Ha	Thomas	W	Thomas Old	_Boswell Sarah	m	20 Jul 1803		Columbia	GA	37,000 MR
Ha	Thomas	W			LL Res Tms W	1805		Columbia	GA	B B
Ha	Thomas	W	Thomas Old	Evans_Boswell Sarah	d no Newton 1811	1811		Morgan	GA	Some Heads of GA Fam
Ha	Thomas	W	Thomas Old	Evans_Boswell Sarah	Wid Tax Tolberts Dis	1817	Indian Cre	Morgan	GA	Finley adj Sarah adx
Ha	Thomas	W	Thomas Old	Evans_Boswell Sarah	Wid Tax Tolberts Dis	1818	Indian Cre	Morgan	GA	Fombrey adj
Ha	Thomas	W		_Glaze Sarah	m	16 Aug 1859		Floyd	GA	37,000 MR
He	Thompson	M	William M	Motley_Reed Martha	b of dau Winnifred	1822			SC	GA Cass 1850C
He	Thompson	M	William M	Motley_Reed Martha L	C	1830		Rabun	GA	p233
He	Thompson	M	William M	Motley_Reed Martha L	Res	1832		Rabun	GA	Cher LL
He	Thompson	M	William M	Motley_Reed Martha L	LL Cher	1832		Union	GA	#270
He	Thompson	M	William M	Motley_Reed Martha L	L t State of GA	01 Apr 1839		Cass	GA	Lot159 16 3 T M
He	Thompson	M	William M	Motley_Reed Martha L	L see T A t	02 Apr 1847		Cass	GA	Reed Geo BkG p482
He	Thompson	M	William M	Motley_Reed Martha L	C	1850	Div 12	Cass	GA	p193
He	Thompson	M			Grand Jury	Mar 1856		Gordon	GA	LDS Film#0424321
He	Thompson	M	William M	Motley_Martha L Reed	d	Jul 1873		Gordon	GA	aka TM
He	Tilmon		Elam		b	1839			GA	GA Twig 1850C
Hi	Tilmon				b	1841			GA	GA Lown 1850C p167
Hi	Tilmon	G	Asa	Moore	b	1841			GA	AL Butl 1850C p193
Hi	Timothy				LL Cher Res	1832		Wilkes	GA	Lot18 Dist3 Sec2
Hi	Victoria		James Fulw	_Andrews A A 1	b	01 Mar 1866		Coffee	GA	Douglas mom
Hi	Victoria		James Fulw	_Thompson Henry 2	b	01 Mar 1866		Coffee	GA	
He	Virgil		Andrew Ber	Angelina	b	1831			GA	GA Cass 1850C #1373
He	Virgil			_Masters Mary Ann	m	16 Apr 1856		Whitfield	GA	
Hi	Virgil		Joshua Mon	_Padgett Alice	b?	1895		Coffee	GA	
Ha	Virginia		Thomas H J	Maria	Orphan OM	02 Mar 1812		Jackson	GA	Intestate R Austin
He	Virginia		Tapley Sr	Kilgare	b	1842			GA	AL Cher 1860C
Ha	Virginia		Tapley Sr	Kilgare	b	1842		Morgan	GA	1850C p143
Ha	W				C Wm?	1840	Dist 596	Monroe	GA	p171
Ha	W			_Catherine?	Dist of Est	26 Aug 1856		Wilkes	GA	Ord Ofc Inf Court

LN	FIRSTNAME	IO	FATHER	MOM_SPOUSE	EVENT	EVENTDATE	CITY	COUNTY_PAR	ST	SOURCE
He	W	A			War Cvl res 1865-	1861		Carroll	GA	#27 GSLA
Ha	W	D	Armstead	Petty	b	1846			GA	GA Carr 1850C
He	W	H		_Wood Lucindy	m	1856		Townesend	GA	1st MR
Ha	W	M			Admin Est of W	26 Aug 1856		Wilkes	GA	Ord Ofc Inf Court
Ha	W	M			Adm Est of Catherine	26 Aug 1856		Wilkes	GA	Ord Ofc Inf Court
He	W	T			War Cvl CoA Pvt1865-	1861			GA	2nd Bn Art NARS
Ha	W	Th			LL Res	1805		Columbia	GA	B B
He	Wallace			_Chandler Francis H	Ind Cher? m Wm?	01 Jun 1865		Carroll	GA	AR t?
Hi	Walter	Fu	James Fulw	_Williams Rena	b	25 Oct 1880		Coffee	GA	Douglas mom
Hi	Walter	L	Wiley Harg	_Kilpatrick Bonnie	b	13 May 1881		Clinch	GA	
Hi	Warren	L	James Fulw	_Wilson Alice Mrs	b	28 Jan 1878		Coffee	GA	Smith mom
He	Wash				Ind Cher b of son	1803			NC	GA Fors 1850C Jms
He	Wesley	Ti		_Garrison Permelia Obed	m				GA	
Hi	Wiley	Ha	James Sr	Bird_Booth Caroline Pri	b	1856		Coffee	GA	
Hi	Wiley	Ha	James Sr	_Booth Caroline Priscil	m	28 Dec 1876		Clinch	GA	
Hi	Wilkes	W	James Fulw	_Newborn Eliza	b	01 Jan 1847		Telfair	GA	Hall mom IGI
He	William			_Reynolds Margaret	m				GA	
He	William				Mortality Sched b	1772			VA	GA Cher 1860
He	William				War Rev Loyalist GA	24 Dec 1781	Savannah		GA	#52 Loy Sou Camp
He	William				LG 200 Acr Ind Ter	05 May 1785	Tugallo Rv	Franklin	GA	SC Pend LG V40 p67
Hi	William				Petition t fortify	13 Oct 1787	Ft Wood	Burke	GA	Gen Gems p6
Hi	William				LG 300 Acr	1790		Washington	GA	
Hi	William				Slave Owner (1)	01 Oct 1798		Burke	GA	GA Gen Gems p47 NGS
Ha	William		Robert?		Tax	1799		Jackson	GA	
Ha	William			_Shipman Lucinda	m	18			GA	
Ha	William		Robert?		Tax 1801-	1800		Jackson	GA	
He	William				C	1800	Colberts	Oglethorpe	GA	
Hi	William		Robert?		wit L of Jesse	02 Dec 1801	Wildcat Cr	Clarke	GA	BkA p90
Ha	William				Militia 1813-	1801		Morgan	GA	Coleman Capt DAR
Hi	William				Dep wit L of Jesse	11 Aug 1802	Wildcat Cr	Clarke	GA	BkA p90
Ha	William				Tax	1802		Clarke	GA	
Hi	William				LG 44 Acr	1803		Burke	GA	
He	William				LG 28 Acr	1803		Burke	GA	
Hi	William				LG 350 Acr	1803		Montgomery	GA	
Ha	William				Jury #1	Jun 1804		Clarke	GA	Inf Court Min
Hi	William				LL	1805		Burke	GA	#54 B-B
Hi	William				LL	1805		Clarke	GA	#274 P-B

LN	FIRSTNAME	IO	FATHER	MOM_SPOUSE	EVENT	EVENTDATE	CITY	COUNTY_PAR	ST	SOURCE
He	William		Robert?		L 84 Acr f J Garner	17 Apr 1805	Wildcat Cr	Clarke	GA	Kilgore adj BkB p237
Ha	William				LL Res	1805		Columbia	GA	B B
Ha	William			_Tinsley Peggy	m	26 Mar 1805		Columbia	GA	37,000 MR
He	William				LL	1805		Hancock	GA	#978 B B
Hi	William				Reimb f gaurd duty	Jan 1806		Clarke	GA	Inf Court Min
He	William		Jesse Sr	Crawford_Lambert Sarah	b d09Apr1866	1806		Jackson	GA	Meck NC GS
Ha	William		Samuel?		LL	1807		Columbia	GA	#149 7 W
He	William		John		Tax	1809		Clarke	GA	
Ha	William		Samuel		Tax Cunninghams Dist	1809	Spirit Cre	Richmond	GA	
Ha	William				Tax Cunninghams Dist	1809		Wilkinson	GA	
Hi	William				Tax	1810	Trammels	Clarke	GA	
He	William		Aaron	_ Ramsey Nancy	b	1810		Franklin	GA	
Ha	William				Tax Walkers Dist	1810	Spirit Cre	Wilkinson	GA	
He	William			_Millie	b	1812			GA	AL Lawr 1860C #274
Ha	William			_ Tinsley Margaret	Res ca	1812		Morgan	GA	Fam Puz #1015 p10
Ha	William				Tax Brantlies Dist	1812	Hard Labor	Morgan	GA	Lane adj
Ha	William		Samuel		Tax Brantlies Dist	1812	Spirit Cre	Richmond	GA	Walker adj
Ha	William				Tax	1812	Brantlies	Wilkinson	GA	
Ha	William				Tax Tolberts Dist	1817	Hard Labor	Morgan	GA	Lane Wm adj
Ha	William		Samuel		Tax Tolberts Dist	1817	Spirit Cre	Richmond	GA	Walker adj
He	William				Tax	1818		Franklin	GA	#21
Ha	William				Tax Tolberts Dist	1818	Hard Labor	Morgan	GA	Lane adj
He	William		Jesse Sr	_Lambert Polly	m dau of Edwin	06 Apr 1818		Morgan	GA	37,000 MR
Ha	William		Samuel		Tax Tolberts Dist	1818	Spirit Cre	Richmond	GA	Crawford adj
He	William		Jesse Sr	Crawford_Lambert Polly	b of son Joseph	1819			GA	GS NC Meck
Hi	William		John		Tax Dobbins Dist	1819	Wolf Creek	Clarke	GA	Jones adj
Hi	William				Tax Dobbins Dist	1819	Apalatchee	Clarke	GA	Jones adj
He	William				C	1820		Clarke	GA	
Ha	William				Dr Res LL	1820		Columbia	GA	
Ha	William				LL	1820		Early	GA	#234 5
Ha	William				C	1820		Morgan	GA	p370
Ha	William				C	1820		Walton	GA	p508
Hi	William				Tax Fosters Dist	1821	Wolf Creek	Clarke	GA	Jones adj
He	William				LL	1821		Houston	GA	5 8
He	William				LL Res	1821		Walton	GA	
Hi	William				Tax	1822	Apalatchee	Clarke	GA	Smith adj
Hi	William		James L	Obedience_McDuffie Nanc	b d29Sep1904	09 Jun 1822		Telfair	GA	

LN	FIRSTNAME	IO	FATHER	MOM_SPOUSE	EVENT	EVENTDATE	CITY	COUNTY_PAR	ST	SOURCE
Hi	William		James L	Obedience_McDuffie Nanc	b	1822		Telfair	GA	1850C p374
Hi	William		James L	Obedience_McDuffie Nanc	b WarIndPenof Tms Je	1822		Telfair	GA	GA Coff bro res FL
Ha	William				Tax Myers Dist	1823	Hard Labor	Morgan	GA	Pames adj
Ha	William		Samuel		Tax Myers Dist	1823	Spirit Cre	Richmond	GA	Walker adj
Hi	William				C	1824		Baldwin	GA	AIS#2
Ha	William				Tax Myers Dist	1824	Hard Labor	Morgan	GA	Lane adj
Ha	William		Samuel		Tax Myers Dist	1824	Spencer Cr	Richmond	GA	McCoy adj
Ha	William				Tax Davenports Dist	1825	Apalatchee	Clarke	GA	Jackson adj
He	William				Ind Cher? b	1826			GA	GA Union 1850C
He	William				Tax 1 poll	1826		Franklin	GA	Paid by agent Aaron
Ha	William				Tax Adairs Dist	1826	Hard Labor	Morgan	GA	Aldridge adj
Ha	William		Samuel		Tax Adairs Dist	1826	Spencer Cr	Richmond	GA	
Ha	William			_Dunn Marthy	m	11 Dec 1827		Fayette	GA	37,000 GA MR
Ha	William				Tax Lumpkins Dist	1829	Atapugy Cr	Decatur	GA	Bellah adj
Ha	William				Tax Lumpkins Dist	1829	Atapugy Cr	Decatur	GA	Bonner Orig LG
He	William				War Rev LL	07 May 1829		Glynn	GA	#151
Ha	William				Tax Lumpkins Dist	1829	Hard Labor	Morgan	GA	Lane adj
Ha	William		Samuel		Tax Lumpkins Dist	1829	Spirit Cre	Richmond	GA	S Hanson Orig grant
He	William			_Precious	Ind Cher? b	1830			GA	TN Monr 1870C p170
He	William			_ Precious	Ind Cher? b	1830			GA	TN Monr 1850C #1648
Ha	William				C 30-40	1830		Carroll	GA	230001 01001 p215
He	William				C	1830		Columbia	GA	p339
Ha	William				Tax	1830	Alapeque C	Decatur	GA	Calway orig LG
Ha	William				C	1830		Fayette	GA	p202
He	William				Tax poll 1832-	1830		Franklin	GA	Aaron paid
Hi	William				C Ind Cher Wm Rich?	1830		Habersham	GA	p66
He	William				C Slave 1 60-70 p79	1830		Hall	GA	010100001 01010001
Ha	William				C	1830		Morgan	GA	p252
Ha	William				Tax Hames Dist	1830	Hard Labor	Morgan	GA	Lane adj
Ha	William				Tax Hames Dist	1830	Hard Labor	Morgan	GA	Welborne P Orig LG
Ha	William				Tax Agent f Tms C	1830		Morgan	GA	
Ha	William		Samuel		Tax Orig LG to Sml	1830	Spirit Cre	Richmond	GA	McCoy adj
Ha	William		Thomas	Evans	LW of Tms	02 May 1831		Newton	GA	Some GA Co R
Ha	William				Res	1832		Carroll	GA	Cher LL
He	William				Tax 2 polls	1832		Carroll	GA	
He	William				L	1832		Carroll	GA	Hardy Jms f
He	William				Tax 2poll 10 1/2Acr	1832		Carroll	GA	

LN	FIRSTNAME	IO	FATHER	MOM_SPOUSE	EVENT	EVENTDATE	CITY	COUNTY_PAR	ST	SOURCE
Ha	William				Res	1832		Columbia	GA	#41
Ha	William				LL Cher Res	1832		Columbus	GA	Lot1189Dist18Sec3
Ha	William				LL Cher	1832		Murray	GA	#41
Hi	William				LL Cher Res	1832		Twiggs	GA	Lot360 Dist14 Sec1
Ha	William				LL Cher	1832		Walker	GA	Lot796 Dist2 Sec2
Ha	William				LL Cher	1832		Walker	GA	Lot490 Dist14 Sec1
He	William		Aaron	_Ramsey Nancy	m	26 Apr 1833		Franklin	GA	Hist Col DAR
He	William				L Lot#119	Mar 1835		Carroll	GA	Tiner Wiley f BkC p2
He	William				Appraiser f Aaron	1835		Carroll	GA	
He	William				L	1836		Carroll	GA	Hardy Jms f 119-D
Ha	William				w	1836		Morgan	GA	BkC p28
He	William				C State	1837		Paulding	GA	
Ha	William				L Lot8 Dis10	1839		Carroll	GA	Hix Jn f BkC p487
He	William		Aaron	Mary_Ramsey Nancy	d	1839		Franklin	GA	
Ha	William		Aaron	Mary_Ramsey Nancy	Wid m	17 Sep 1839		Franklin	GA	Scoggins David
He	William				L Lot#113	Mar 1840		Carroll	GA	Young K f BkD p44
He	William				C	1840		Carroll	GA	p215
He	William				L	1840		Carroll	GA	113 D-11
He	William				C p17 60-70	1840		Cherokee	GA	000010001 000100001
He	William				C	1840		Cobb	GA	
Ha	William				C	1840	Dist 2	Columbia	GA	p290
Hi	William				C	1840		Pike	GA	
He	William				C	1840		Richmond	GA	
He	William				C	1840		Twiggs	GA	
Hi	William				C	1840		Walton	GA	
Hi	William				C	1840		Washington	GA	
Hi	William		James L	_McDuffie Nancy 1	m	1842		Telfair	GA	IGI
He	William		James		Ind Cher? b	1843		Forsyth	GA	1850C
He	William			_Hardyman Eliza Ann	m	30 Jul 1844		Cherokee	GA	37,000 MR
Hi	William		Caleb Sr	Margaret	w of Caleb	01 Mar 1845		Twiggs	GA	Misc deeds
He	William			Martha	b	1846			GA	GA Cass 1850C #384
He	William		Archibald	Mary	b	1849		Gordon	GA	1850C p51
He	William				C	1850		Cass	GA	p150
He	William				C	1850		Cherokee	GA	p417
He	William				C	1850		Twiggs	GA	p175
Hi	William				C	1850	Div 91	Washington	GA	p205
He	William		Charles	_Reece Mary	Ind Cher b post	1858		Union	GA	Swain mom

LN	FIRSTNAME	IO	FATHER	MOM_SPOUSE	EVENT	EVENTDATE	CITY	COUNTY_PAR	ST	SOURCE
He	William				d	May 1859		Cherokee	GA	1860 Mort Sched
Hi	William			_ McDuffie Nancy	b of dau Almira	1859		Coffee	GA	IGI
He	William		Daniel		War Cvl 1865-	1861			GA	CoC 145thInf
He	William			_Holcombe Melinda	b of son Jms	10 Feb 1878		Carroll	GA	IGI
Hi	William		James L	_Haddock Nancy 2	m	1883		Telfair	GA	IGI
Hi	William		James L	Obedience_Haddock Nancy	Wit Wid Pen of Tms J	21 Apr 1893		Coffee	GA	FL Lake Wid Pen#1110
He	William	A	Armstead	Petty	b				GA	AL Rand 1860C
He	William	A			War Cvl CoA 38th	09 Sep 1861			GA	TN Dyer 1890C-25-5
He	William	B	George W S	Lambert	b	1838			GA	NC Meck GS
Hi	William	Ba	William Th	Starr	b Wm Baxley	19 Nov 1897	Chester	Twiggs	GA	IGI
Hi	William	Ba	William Th	_Lord Lillie Mae	b	28 Jun 1921	Crawford	Oglethorpe	GA	IGI
He	William	C	Presley Th	_Grogan Mary C	m	18			GA	Ada mom
He	William	C	Joseph Jr	Clark_Wood Polly Ann	Ind Cher Wm b	1824			GA	GA Unio 1850C p241
He	William	C	Joseph Jr	_Wood Polly Ann	Ind Cher m	23 Apr 1848		Union	GA	37,000 MR
He	William	C	Joseph Jr	Clark_Wood Polly	Ind Cher of #117 res	1851	Blue Ridge	Union	GA	Thompson Mary gd
Ha	William	C		_Brantley Ann Elizabeth	m	15 Feb 1860		Washington	GA	IGI
Hi	William	C	James Fulw	_Ashley Victoria	b	10 Apr 1868		Coffee	GA	Douglas mom
He	William	C	Joseph Jr	Clark_Wood Polly Ann	Ind Cher of #117	11 Jul 1908	Blue Ridge	Union	GA	Thompson Mary A
Ha	William	Cr	Enoch	Barber_Martha G	b d08Dec1893	02 Sep 1813		Clarke	GA	GA Monr Hansen Cem
Hi	William	Cr	Enoch	_Spear Mary	m	10 Mar 1836		Monroe	GA	37,000 GA MR
Ha	William	Fa		_Odom Delila 1	b	08 Feb 1834			GA	Frances mom
Ha	William	Fa		_Cogburn E A 2	b	08 Feb 1834			GA	Frances mom
He	William	H			C State	1834		Cass	GA	2 whites
He	William	H	John		b	1842			GA	GA Gilm 1850C
Ha	William	Ha	Jesse Jr	Petty_Taylor Martha Ama	Ind Cherb d23Apr1917	13 Jan 1849		Morgan	GA	TX Shel d
Hi	William	I	Wiley Harg	_Mattox Wilma	b	1893			GA	
He	William	J	James	_Bruce Sarah	Ind Cher b Bill	1843			GA	GA Fors 1850C
He	William	J	Caleb Jr		b	1843			GA	GA Twig 1850C
Hi	William	J		_ Elender	b of son Joseph	1845			GA	AL Covi 1850C p163
He	William	Je	Orren O	Cartwright	b Wm Jefferson	07 Dec 1857	Temple	Carroll	GA	IGI
He	William	Jr		_ Millie	b	1810			GA	TN Lawr 1880C
He	William	Jr			LL Res drew1820	1832		Hall	GA	
He	William	M			b	1805			GA	GA Cass 1840C
He	William	M	William H	_Motlow Drucilla	War 1812	1812			TN	GA t?
He	William	M			C	1840	Dist 952	Carroll	GA	p96
He	William	M			C 30-40	1840		Cass	GA	000001 0011
He	William	M	Tapley Jr	Kilgare	b	1844			GA	AL Cher 1860C

LN	FIRSTNAME	IO	FATHER	MOM_SPOUSE	EVENT	EVENTDATE	CITY	COUNTY_PAR	ST	SOURCE
Ha	William	M	Tapley Jr	Kilgare	b	1844		Morgan	GA	1850C p143
He	William	M		_ Motlow Drucilla	C wid	1850	Div 12	Cass	GA	p193
He	William	Ne	William M	Motley_Moore Louisa	C	1830		Rabun	GA	p231
He	William	Ne	William M	Motley_Moore Louisa A	LL Cher Res	1832		Rabun	GA	Lot320 Dist17 Sec3
He	William	Ne	William M	Motley_Moore Louisa A	C State	1837		Paulding	GA	3 white
He	William	Ne	William M	Motley_Moore Louis A	L Lot320 t	17 May 1839		Bartow	GA	Lynch Tms p387
Ha	William	Ne	William M	Motley_Moore Louisa A	L t	05 Jan 1847		Cass	GA	Lynch Tms BkG p387
He	William	Ri	Joseph Sr	Scruggs_Blair Margaret	Ind Cher crop destr	1824	Frogtown	Habersham	GA	NARS BIA RG75
He	William	Ri	Joseph Sr	Scruggs_Blair Margaret	Ind Cher Nation Oath	07 Oct 1830	Ind Ter		GA	6 children WAC p36
He	William	Ri	Joseph Sr	Scruggs_Blair Margaret	C Ind Cher as Wm	1830		Habersham	GA	p66
He	William	Ri	Joseph Sr	Scruggs_Blair Margaret	Ind Cher Nation Lic	1831			GA	6 children WAC p63
He	William	Ri	Joseph Sr	Scruggs_Blair Margaret	Ind Cher Emig Roll	13 Mar 1832	Frogtown	Lumpkin	GA	10 red 4 black n res
He	William	Ri	Joseph Sr	Scruggs_Blair Margaret	Ind Cher Imig t	13 Mar 1832	Frogtown	Lumpkin	GA	AR BIA Clm 04Dec1844
He	William	Ri	Joseph Sr	Scruggs_Blair Margaret	Ind Cher Imig Draft	Mar 1832	Frogtown	Lumpkin	GA	10 red 4 black inres
He	William	Ri	Joseph Sr	Scruggs_Blair Margaret	Ind Cher Clm#56 p27	Mar 1837	Mill Creek	Union	GA	NARS BIA RG75
He	William	Ri	James	Hobbs	Ind Cher? b	05 Jul 1859	Cedar Grov	Walker	GA	IGI
Ha	William	S			Gaurd of Henry M S?	26 Aug 1856		Wilkes	GA	Ord Ofc Inf Court
Ha	William	S			Est of Catherine	26 Aug 1856		Wilkes	GA	Ord Ofc Inf Court
He	William	Sh	Loyde	_Rackley Jane	b Wm Sherman	1867		Gilmer	GA	GA Gilm 1870C
Hi	William	Si		_ Whitton Mary Ann	m Silas	21 Dec 1826		Clarke	GA	Whitten&Allied Fam
Ha	William	Sr	John	Pace_Crawford Ann	b	1770		Goochland	VA	GA Monr Hansen Cem
Ha	William	Sr	John	_Byrd Ann or Crawford	b	1770		Henrico	VA	GA t? VA Gen 17-28
He	William	Sr		_ McDonald Harriet	Wid b	1798			GA	MS Leak 1850C p26
Hi	William	Sr	John	_Crawford Ann	C	1830		Monroe	GA	p220
He	William	Sr			C	1840		Cherokee	GA	p177
Ha	William	Sr	John	Pace_Crawford/Byrd Ann	C	1840	Dist 496	Monroe	GA	VA Henr of ? p182
Ha	William	Sr	John	Pace_Crawford Ann	d	Mar 1842			GA	Monr Hansen Cem
Ha	William	Sr	John	Pace_Byrd/Crawford Ann	w	1842		Monroe	GA	BkA p188
He	William	T	Andrew Ber	Able_Coat	Ind Cher? b	1841			GA	GA Cass 1850C #1373
Hi	William	Th		_Starr Mattie	Ind Cher bof son WmB	19 Nov 1897	Chester	Twiggs	GA	IGI
Ha	William	W	Reuben	Jones	b	1836			GA	GA Carr 1860C p23
Ha	William	W	Reuben	Jones	b	14 May 1836			GA	
He	William	Wa	John	Allison	Ind Cher b	19 Apr 1876		Union	GA	#28901
He	William	Wa	John	Allison	Ind Cher Appl	1909			GA	#28901
He	Winifred		Thompson M	Reed	b	1822		Cass	GA	1850C
He	Winifred		William M	Motley	d	09 Apr 1856		Polk	GA	1858 lttr
Hi	Winifred		William	McDuffie	b	1859		Coffee	GA	

LN	FIRSTNAME	IO	FATHER	MOM_SPOUSE	EVENT	EVENTDATE	CITY	COUNTY_PAR	ST	SOURCE
He	Zaretta				Ind Cher Appl	1909			GA	#28895
He	Zora			_Turner J Lon	m	20 Dec 1931	Choestoe	Union	GA	IGI
Ha	Zora	E	John	Allison	Ind Cher b	28 May 1886		Union	GA	#28854
He	Zora	E	John	Allison	Ind Cher Appl	1909			GA	#28854

MISSISSIPPI

LN	FIRSTNAME	IO	FATHER	MOM_SPOUSE	EVENT	EVENTDATE	CITY	COUNTY_PAR	ST	SOURCE
He				_White Susannah	w of	21 Feb 1803		Claiborne	MS	White Tms p72
He				_Mary	Wid b nres Satefield	1804			SC	MS Kemp 1870C #398
He				_ Mary	Wid b	1806			SC	MS Kemp 1860C #578
He				_ Mary	Wid b	1808			SC	MS Kemp 1850C #496
Ha				_Mary	C wid	1830		Wilkinson	MS	
Hi				_Elizabeth	Wid w 1900-	1834		Clarke	MS	Bk1 p105
Hi				_Elizabeth	C wid male 50-60	1840		Kemper	MS	10000001 110120001p7
Hi				_Nancy	C wid	1840		Pike	MS	p161
He				_ Elizabeth	Wid tax	1841		Kemper	MS	AIS#4
Hi				_ Nancy	Wid tax	1841		Pike	MS	AIS#4
He				_ Mary	Wid L 80 Acr	06 Feb 1843		Kemper	MS	S18T11R14 E1/2NE1/4
He				_Mary	Wid L 80Acr	06 Feb 1843		Kemper	MS	S19T11R14 E1/2 NE1/4
He				_ Elizabeth	Wid tax	1845		Kemper	MS	AIS#4
Hi				_Gathings Lucy	w of Sampson Gathing	1845		Monroe	MS	AL Bald Lucy of
Hi				_ Nancy	Wid tax	1845		Pike	MS	AIS#4
He				_ Mary	Wid L 80Acr Patented	17 Aug 1847		Kemper	MS	S18T11R14 E1/2 NE1/4
He				_ Mary	Wid L 80Acr Patented	17 Aug 1847		Kemper	MS	S19T11R14 E1/2 NE1/4
He	A	A		_M T	d of son Loyd dy			Kemper	MS	Henson Cem
He	A	A		_Callie C	d of wife	06 Apr 1882		Kemper	MS	Henson Cem
He	A	A		_Fulton M T	m	15 Jan 1885		Neshoba	MS	IGI
Hi	A	C		_Knowles Malissa	m	16 Dec 1867		Lee	MS	IGI
Ha	A	E		_Harper W L	m	24 Dec 1885		Yazoo	MS	IGI
He	A	J		_Harwell Rachel	m	02 Dec 1874		Lauderdale	MS	IGI
He	A	M			C	1840		Yalobusha	MS	p304
He	A	M			Tax	1841		Yalobusha	MS	AIS#4
He	A	M			Tax	1845		Yalobusha	MS	AIS#4
He	Aaron		Wright	Elizabeth	b	1844			MS	MS Leak 1850C p26
Hi	Aaron			_Clark Nancy	m	05 Sep 1866		Leake	MS	IGI
He	Adaline		Lazarus	Ceny/Carry_Lawler Riley	b C under Lawler	1820		Tuscaloosa	AL	MS Choc 1860C #1478
Ha	Adaline			_Collier Alvatus	m	06 Sep 1881		Leake	MS	IGI
He	Adeline		Edward D	_Clark Archiblad	b	1857			MS	MS Kemp 1870C #251
He	Alex			_Clemons Ann	m	05 Mar 1875		Kemper	MS	IGI
He	Alexander		Andrew	Sarah E	b	1858		Kemper	MS	1860C #401
He	Alexander		Andrew	Sarah E	b d1903	30 Jun 1859		Kemper	MS	Henson Cem
Hi	Alexander	H		_Broadway Elizabeth	m	07 Nov 1854		Marshall	MS	IGI
He	Alfred		James	Costen_Adams Elizabeth	Ind Cher? b d1932	17 Apr 1852		Forsyth	GA	MS d
He	Alfred		James	_Adams Elizabeth 1	m	26 Nov 1873			MS	

LN	FIRSTNAME	IO	FATHER	MOM_SPOUSE	EVENT	EVENTDATE	CITY	COUNTY_PAR	ST	SOURCE
He	Alfred		James	_Scrivner Callie 2	m	14 Jan 1886		Choctaw	MS	
He	Alfred		James	_Tanksley Lou Ella 3	m	19 Feb 1905		Choctaw	MS	
Hi	Alonzo			_Wesson Bammie	m	09 May 1886		Lee	MS	IGI
He	Amanda	J	James J	Elizabeth	b d1856	09 Feb 1833	Fredonia	Panola	MS	Meth Church Cem
Hi	Amitus			_Hannah Callinus	m	01 Jan 1879		Leflore	MS	IGI
He	Anderson				L 41 Acr Patented	15 Mar 1854		Kemper	MS	S20T11R14 SE1/4NE1/4
He	Andrew		William?	_Sophia	Dr b	1818			MS	MS Leak p26
He	Andrew		Richard?	Frances_Sarah E 3	b	1818	Greenville		SC	MS Kemp 1860C #401
He	Andrew			_Sarah E 3	b	1819			SC	MS Kemp 1850C #485
He	Andrew			_ Sarah E 3	b d02Mar1891	15 Aug 1820			SC	MS Kemp Henson Cem
Hi	Andrew				C 15-20	1840		Kemper	MS	00010 0001 p18
He	Andrew			_ 1?	L 164.57 Acr	15 Jun 1840		Kemper	MS	S294T11R14 NW 1/4
He	Andrew			_ 1?	Tax	1841		Kemper	MS	AIS#4
He	Andrew			_ 1?	Tax	1842		Kemper	MS	
He	Andrew			_ 1?	Tax	1845		Kemper	MS	AIS#4
He	Andrew			_Gray Mary W 2	m	15 Oct 1845	DeKalb	Kemper	MS	
He	Andrew			_McSweeny Sopia	m	09 Apr 1850		Madison	MS	IGI
He	Andrew			_ Sarah E 3	L 41 Acr	21 Sep 1853		Kemper	MS	S20T11R14 SE1/4NE1/4
He	Andrew				L 39.87 Acr	23 Jan 1854		Kemper	MS	S304T11R14NE1/4NE1/4
He	Andrew				L 39.87 Acr Patented	23 Jan 1854		Kemper	MS	S304T11R14NE1/4NE1/4
He	Andrew				L 79.76 Acr	05 Dec 1854		Kemper	MS	N1/2 NE1/4 30/11/14
He	Andrew			_ Sarah E	War Cvl Conf CoA	1863			MS	26th Inf NARS
Ha	Andrew			_Gremer Mary	m	11 Aug 1879		DeSoto	MS	IGI
Ha	Andrew	J		_Winborn Donnie	m	13 Nov 1878		Tippah	MS	IGI
He	Andrew	Ja			War Cvl Pvt CoI d	04 Jan 1865	Oak Woods		IL	MS 3rd POW bur N
He	Andy	E	Andrew	Sarah E	b f Andy Eveline	1856		Kemper	MS	1860C &Henson Cem
He	Angeline		Wright	Elizabeth	b	1838		Bibb	AL	MS Leak 1850C p26
He	Angeline			_Allen James M	m	20 Sep 1860		Leake	MS	IGI
Ha	Ann			_Wesson Douglas	m	06 Jan 1876		Noxubee	MS	IGI
He	Ann			_Clayton F J	m Annie	26 Feb 1879		Tippah	MS	IGI
Ha	Ann	M		_Mann J H	m Annie M	25 Dec 1879		Leake	MS	IGI
Hy	Ann	Ma		_Muir James Gustavus	m	24 Nov 1836		Warren	MS	IGI
He	Anna	C	John L	Jane L	b	1835			MS	AR Newt 1850C p11
He	Anna	Ja	Joseph Cal	_Ray Rufus Sr	m	mom Clark 1894		Meridian	MS	TX Fish t
He	Araminta	M	John L	Jane L	b	1838			MS	AR Newt 1850C p11
He	Arena		Henry W	_Johnson Joseph	m see Orena	02 Feb 1857		Tishomingo	MS	GA Walk f
He	Arthur			_Dunn Melona	m	31 Dec 1840		Carroll	MS	IGI

LN	FIRSTNAME	IO	FATHER	MOM_SPOUSE	EVENT	EVENTDATE	CITY	COUNTY_PAR	ST	SOURCE
He	Arthur				c	1850	Sou Div	Carroll	MS	p236
He	Barbara		J D	Clarisa	b	1843			AL	MS Tish 1850C p83B
Hi	Bartley	M		_Boykins Mary J Leanna?	b Jms? d1920	02 Jun 1846			AL	MS d
Hi	Brooks			Hinson_Liles Obedience	Lttr f dau Elizb	1855		Anson	NC	MS Carr Eliz in
He	Burrell			_Bizer Harriet	m	20 Aug 1874		Panola	MS	IGI
He	C	F		_Muse Mollie	m	09 Nov 1884		Prentiss	MS	IGI
Ha	C	Is		_Hannah A J	m	07 May 1879		Leflore	MS	IGI
Ha	Caleb				War Cvl vet	1863				MS Mars 1890C
Ha	Callie			_Brown R D	m	25 Dec 1876		Newton	MS	IGI
Hi	Callie	L		_Vann John M	m	06 Dec 1868		Clarke	MS	IGI
He	Calvin		J	Lavinia	b in res Lowry	1848			MS	MS Tish 1850C p22
Ha	Catherine			_Simmons Charles	m	03 Jul 1866		Lafayette	MS	IGI
Ha	Charles				c	1840		Lafayette	MS	p178
Ha	Charles				Tax	1841		Lafayette	MS	AIS#4
Ha	Charles				Tax	1845		Lafayette	MS	AIS#4
He	Charles				c	1850		Noxubee	MS	p214
He	Charles			_McCoy Mary Elizabeth	b of dau Annie Mae	1862			MS	
He	Charles	A	William M	Margaret	b	1859		Kemper	MS	1860C #396
He	Charles	Es		_Jacobs Martha Dollie	m	01 Feb 1881		Alcorn	MS	IGI
Hi	Charles	F		_Middleton Elizabeth	m	06 Mar 1873		Warren	MS	IGI
He	Clarissa		J D	Clarisa	Twin b	1835			NC	MS Tish 1850C p83B
Ha	D	J		_Miles A R	m	25 Apr 1878		Lafayette	MS	IGI
He	David	C	John L	Jane L	b	1840			MS	AR Newt 1850C p11
Ha	Dora			_Brown Charlie S	m	08 Jan 1882		Newton	MS	IGI
He	Dora	B			Ward of J M Henson	07 Jan 1870		Tuscaloosa	AL	MS Monr res
He	Dora	Bl		_Snowed W P	b Dora Blanche d1874	1847				MS Goodspeeds Hist
He	E				Tax Ebenezer?	1839		Kemper	MS	
He	E	D			b	1830			SC	MS Kemp 1860C #577
He	E	N		_Annie	b d19Jun1905	17 Sep 1862		Kemper	MS	Henson Cem
Hi	E	S		_Davis J L	m	29 Oct 1880		Carroll	MS	IGI
He	Easter		Thomas	Mary	b	1836			SC	MS Noxu 1850C p215
He	Easter			_Norton Wade H	m	09 May 1855		Noxubee	MS	IGI
He	Eben	L	E N	Annie	b d02May1898	24 Feb 1898		Kemper	MS	Henson Cem
He	Ebenezer			Mary	b Ebin	1828			SC	MS Kemp 1850C #496
Hi	Ebenezer				C 21-45	1837		Kemper	MS	2M-18 3F-16 1F16+
He	Ebenezer				C 30-40	1840		Kemper	MS	011001 211001 p18
He	Ebenezer				Tax	1841		Kemper	MS	AIS#4

LN	FIRSTNAME	IO	FATHER	MOM_SPOUSE	EVENT	EVENTDATE	CITY	COUNTY_PAR	ST	SOURCE
He	Ebenezer				Tax	1842		Kemper	MS	
He	Ebenezer				Tax	1845		Kemper	MS	AIS#4
He	Ed			_McLauren Callie	b			Kemper	MS	
He	Edward			_Mary M	b	1829			SC	MS Kemp 1860C #395
He	Edward			_ Mary M	War Cvl killed 1865-	1861		Kemper	MS	COD War Cvl Shiloh
He	Edward	He			C Slave 1 45+	1837		Kemper	MS	4F-16
He	Eli	Jr	Eli Sr	Eady_James Elizabeth	War Cvl Conf dischar	1864	Macon		MS	C of Conf Sold 1907
Hi	Eli	M	William Sr	Cook_Tursey Biggers	War Cvl 36Reg CoE	1863			NC	MS t?
He	Eliza		Thomas	Mary	b	1828			SC	MS Noxu 1850C p215
He	Eliza	J		_Denney Benjamin J	m	13 Jul 1873		Yalobusha	MS	IGI
Hi	Elizabeth		Brooks	_Streater	lttr t Brooks f	1855		Carroll	MS	NC Anso Brooks in
He	Elizabeth			_Johnson Joe	m	09 Sep 1886		Leake	MS	IGI
He	Ella			_Hyneman B F	m	15 Nov 1877		Alcorn	MS	IGI
Hi	Ella	Ja		_Sandifer Peter H	m	21 Dec 1887		Pike	MS	IGI
Hi	Emily			_Buckley B G	m	10 Mar 1872		Yazoo	MS	IGI
He	Emma			_Hyneman W I	m	06 Jan 1866		Tishomingo	MS	IGI
Hi	Esther			_Bolen Thomas	m	22 Jan 1874		Lee	MS	IGI
Ha	Esther			_Dogan Martin	m	04 Jan 1875		Leake	MS	IGI
He	Etta		Hadly	Avery_Hutchinson Allen	b d bf1889?	1838			AL	MS t
He	Etta		Hadley	_Hutchinson Allen	m	07 Jan 1869		Lowndes	MS	IGI
He	Evaline		Andrew	Sarah E	b Andy E? d1883	23 Dec 1856		Kemper	MS	
He	Everett	E	William Ma	Little	b d27Jun1890	30 Aug 1889				MS Kemp bur Bluff Sp
He	Fannie		John Luthe	Hester	b	1841		Tishomingo	MS	
Hi	Fannie	E		_Thrasher J F	m	06 Dec 1874		Sunflower	MS	IGI
He	Fanny			_Moore Green	m	21 Dec 1878		Lowndes	MS	IGI
He	Frances			Mary	b f Francis	1835			SC	MS Kemp 1850C #496
He	Frances		E D		b	1855		Kemper	MS	1860C #577
He	Frances		Andrew	Sarah E	b f	1858		Kemper	MS	1860C #401
He	Frances		Andrew	Sarah E	b	1860		Kemper	MS	Henson Cem
Hi	Frances			_Allen William	m	14 Oct 1866		Leake	MS	IGI
He	Frances	Ja	Edward	_Clark Alexander Jn	b	1855		Kemper	MS	1870C #251
He	Frances	Ja	Edward	Mary M_Clark Alexander	b	1855		Kemper	MS	1860C #395
He	Francis		John	Elizabeth	b	1818			SC	MS Noxu 1850C p215
He	Francis		Wright	Elizabeth	b	1834		Bibb	AL	MS Leak 1850C p26
He	Francis		Andrew	Sarah E	b see Geo Francis	1844		Kemper	MS	1850C #485
Ha	Francis	M		_Cooper Martha	m	04 Dec 1865		Yazoo	MS	IGI
Ha	G	E		_Bowles Georgia Ann	m	31 Aug 1882		Lafayette	MS	IGI

LN	FIRSTNAME	IO	FATHER	MOM_SPOUSE	EVENT	EVENTDATE	CITY	COUNTY_PAR	ST	SOURCE
Ha	G	W		_Humphries Julia A	m	30 Jan 1879		Lafayette	MS	IGI
Hi	G	W		_Strickland Merandy	m	09 Apr 1885		Leake	MS	IGI
He	George			_Rimes Levinia	m	10 Aug 1867		Hinds	MS	IGI
Ha	George			_Slater Adeline	m	24 Aug 1879		DeSoto	MS	IGI
He	George	Fr	Andrew	Sarah E	b Francis d young	1844		Kemper	MS	Henson Cem
He	George	H		_Burpass Ethelinda J	m	08 Sep 1858		Tishomingo	MS	IGI
He	George	M		_Curtis Charity	m	19 Feb 1852		Tishomingo	MS	IGI
He	George	Ra		_Howell Lura	m	08 Mar 1919	Charleston	Tallahatch	MS	IGI
He	George	Wa		_Tackett Delita	Ind Cher? m	17 Feb 1842		Fayettte	GA	MS Lee t
He	George	Wa	James	Costen_Mann Martha 2	Ind Cher? b	10 Apr 1849		Forsyth	GA	MS Choc t
Ha	George	Wa		_ Tackett Delilah	b of dau Nancy	24 May 1851	Tupelo	Lee	MS	IGI
He	George	Wa	James	_Mann Martha 2	Ind Cher? m d1906	26 Feb 1888		Choctaw	MS	
Hi	Georgie			_Nixon John R	m	19 Feb 1884		Washington	MS	IGI
He	H			_Dunn Margaret L	m	16 Jan 1867		Yalobusha	MS	IGI
Ha	H	Cl		_Luckett O A	m Henry Clay?	25 Dec 1879		Leake	MS	IGI
He	H	F		_Spurgeon M C	m	20 Dec 1878		Lafayette	MS	IGI
Ha	H	H		_Hill M E	m	26 Apr 1866		Leake	MS	IGI
Hi	H	Re		_Newton Lorenzo D	m	06 Jan 1881	Charleston	Tallahatch	MS	IGI
He	Harriet	An	William	McDonald_Redus Jms C	b	26 Jul 1828		Jefferson	MS	Fam R Rev Sold p192
He	Harriet	An	William	_Redus James C	m	10 Jul 1849		Leake	MS	TX Mr d1905
He	Harry			_Jones Nancy	m	17 Aug 1867		Oktibbeha	MS	IGI
He	Henry		J D	Clarisa	b	1832			NC	MS Tish 1850C p838
He	Henry		James	Costen	Ind Cher? b	1853		Forsyth	GA	MS d?.
Ha	Henry			_Johnson Tilda	m	20 Mar 1867		DeSoto	MS	IGI
Ha	Henry			_Ashley Mary	m	04 Mar 1869		Yalobusha	MS	IGI
He	Henry			_Russell Alice	m	05 Apr 1879		Carroll	MS	IGI
Ha	Henry			_Desmuke Martha	m	02 Nov 1881		Leake	MS	IGI
He	Henry			_Miller Frances	m	24 Dec 1885		LeFlore	MS	IGI
Ha	Henry			_Boyd Emma L	m	15 May 1889		Leake	MS	IGI
He	Henry	Cl	Henry W	Pinelope	b?	1843		Walker	GA	MS Pren t
He	Henry	T		_Johnson Etha	m	24 Dec 1879		Prentiss	MS	IGI
He	Henry	W		_Pinelope	b	1801			NC	MS Pren Boonville d
Ha	Hilda			_Andrews Oliver	m	06 Dec 1884		Jackson	MS	IGI
He	Hiram	W		_Brinkley Missouri	m	11 Sep 1879		Marshall	MS	IGI
He	Houston				War Cvl CoK Pvt	1863			MS	40thInf NARS
He	Hulda		John	Elizabeth	b	1828			SC	MS Noxu 1850C p215
Hi	Huse			_Shannon Adeline	m	13 Dec 1877		Tallahatch	MS	IGI

LN	FIRSTNAME	IO	FATHER	MOM_SPOUSE	EVENT	EVENTDATE	CITY	COUNTY_PAR	ST	SOURCE
Hi	Huse			_Thomas Adeline	m	13 Dec 1877		Tallahatch	MS	IGI
Ha	Ida			_Adams Guffin	m	23 Mar 1870		Noxubee	MS	IGI
Hi	Isham				C	1840		Pike	MS	p162
Hi	Isham				Tax	1841		Pike	MS	AIS#4
Hi	Isham				Tax	1845		Pike	MS	AIS#4
Hi	J			_Lowry? Lavinia	Cabinet Maker b	1817			TN	MS Tish 1850C p22
He	J	D		_Clarisa	b	1806			NC	MS Tish 1850C p83B
He	J	D		_ Clarisa	b of son Joshua	1838			AL	MS Tish 1850C p83B
He	J	G		_Sullivant Caroline	m	26 Nov 1860		Tallahatch	MS	IGI
He	J	H		_Mills Frances N	m	20 Nov 1873		Leake	MS	IGI
Ha	J	J		_Staten Nancy	m	09 Aug 1877		Tallahatch	MS	IGI
Ha	J	J		_Pilcher F E	m	06 Aug 1881		Pontotoc	MS	IGI
Ha	J	J		_Richardson Alice B	m	24 Dec 1884		Yazoo	MS	IGI
He	J	L			C Jn Luther?	1840		Tishomingo	MS	p232
He	J	L			Tax Jn Luther?	1841		Tishomingo	MS	AIS#4
He	J	L			Tax Jn Luther?	1845		Tishomingo	MS	AIS#4
Hi	J	L			C	1850		Tishomingo	MS	p22
He	J	L		_Wallace M P	m	07 Apr 1880		Lafayette	MS	IGI
He	J	M			gaurd of Dora B	07 Jan 1870		Tuscaloosa	AL	MS Monr ward res
He	J	P		_Horney Eliza Jane	m	13 Jan 1880		Alcorn	MS	IGI
He	J	R		_Spurgeon Martha J	m	16 Jan 1872		Yalobusha	MS	IGI
Hi	J	R		_Williams M C	m	26 Jan 1881		Leake	MS	IGI
Ha	J	T		_Joiner Lizzie	m	11 Jan 1872		Lee	MS	IGI
Ha	J	T		_Morrow N J	m	18 Dec 1873		Lafayette	MS	IGI
Hi	J	T		_Henry M E	m	17 Jan 1884		Newton	MS	IGI
Ha	J	W		_Watsen Elizabeth	m	25 Nov 1880		Lafayette	MS	IGI
Hi	Jack			_Gary Mary	m	25 Jul 1867		Clarke	MS	IGI
Ha	James			_Elizabeth	b	1802			GA	MS Scot 1860C p16
Hi	James			_Thompson Sarah	m	17 Mar 1818		Amite	MS	IGI
Hi	James				C 26-45	1820		Amite	MS	0002300 002300 p38
He	James		John G		b	1845		Lauderdale	MS	1850C IGI
Hi	James			_Walker Mary E	m	20 Jan 1853		Amite	MS	IGI
He	James		Edward D	_Wright Hallie	b	1859			MS	MS Kemp 1870C #251
He	James		Edward D	Mary M_Wright Hallie	b	1860		Kemper	MS	1860C #577
He	James				War Cvl Vet	1863				MS Adam 1890C #6
Ha	James			_Etheridge Mary	m	30 Apr 1870		Noxubee	MS	IGI
He	James			_Patterson Mary	m Jim	11 Aug 1870		Warren	MS	IGI

LN	FIRSTNAME	IO	FATHER	MOM_SPOUSE	EVENT	EVENTDATE	CITY	COUNTY_PAR	ST	SOURCE
Hi	James			_Walker Virginia L	m	02 May 1872		Amite	MS	IGI
Ha	James			_Swendenburg Mat	m	12 Dec 1874		Panola	MS	IGI
He	James			_Barnes Luisa	m	09 Mar 1876		Coahoma	MS	IGI
He	James			_Blackburne Josephine H	m	14 Dec 1876		Warren	MS	IGI
Hi	James	A			War Cvl CoC muster	16 May 1862	Columbus	Lowndes	MS	AL Wilc f 42nd Inf
He	James	An	E N	Annie	b d20Feb1893	17 Nov 1892		Kemper	MS	Henson Cem
He	James	E	William M	Margaret	b	1856		Kemper	MS	1860C #396
He	James	H			War Cvl CoK Pvt	1863			MS	17thInf NARS
He	James	H	Henry W?	_Duncan Sarah C	m	07 Mar 1868		Tishomingo	MS	GA Walk f
He	James	J		_ Elizabeth	b of dau Amanda J	09 Feb 1833	Fredonia	Panola	MS	Meth Church Cem
He	James	J		_ Elizabeth	C	1840		Panola	MS	p133
He	James	J		_ Elizabeth	Tax	1841		Panola	MS	AIS#4
He	James	J		_ Elizabeth	Tax	1845		Panola	MS	AIS#4
He	James	Jo	James Josh	_Halmark Catherine 1	Ind Cher m Josh	24 Sep 1876	Goldsburg	Howell	MO	MS t?
He	James	Ma	Andrew	Sarah E_Yarbrough M E	b	1843		Kemper	MS	1850C #485
He	James	Ma	Andrew	Sarah E_Yarbrough M E	b Jms Marshall	1848		Kemper	MS	1860C #401
He	James	Ma	Andrew	_Yarbrough M E	m	22 Aug 1871		Williamson	TX	MS Kemp b
Hi	James	Pe		_Luter Mary Ann	m	28 May 1849		Warren	MS	IGI
Ha	James	W		_Wilson Mary	m dau of Jms	22 Oct 1836		Monroe	MS	IGI
Hi	James	W		_Noles Emiline	m	07 Mar 1868		Lee	MS	IGI
Ha	James	W		_Watson Maggie	m	31 Aug 1873		Lafayette	MS	IGI
Ha	Jane			_Gray Isham	m	04 Jan 1878		Leake	MS	IGI
He	Jane			_Gardner Moses	m	17 Sep 1879		Greene	MS	IGI .
Ha	Jane			_Smith William	m	06 Feb 1885		Yazoo	MS	IGI
Hi	Jane	M		_Fauver William	m	21 Apr 1838		Jefferson	MS	IGI
Hi	Jennette			_Heath D F	m	29 Jan 1868		Tallahatch	MS	IGI
He	Jenny			_Ficklin William	m	04 Apr 1870		Leake	MS	IGI
He	Jesse	C			Tax	1842		Kemper	MS	
He	Jesse	C			War Cvl AWOL	Jul 1862	Iuka	Tishomingo	MS	NARS
He	Jesse	C			War Cvl AWOL surrend	13 Apr 1865	Iuka	Tishomingo	MS	NARS
Ha	Jesse	C		_White Sarah Ann	m	03 Feb 1867		Yazoo	MS	IGI
He	Jesse	Ch	Jesse Chat	Boon_Amanda Long	War Cvl deserted	1863		Jackson	IL	MS?
Ha	Joanah			_Cooper Lewis	m	13 Jan 1876		Oktibbeha	MS	IGI
He	Joanie	F	William M	Margaret	b	1853		Kemper	MS	1860C #396
He	John			_Elizabeth	b	1773			SC	MS Noxu 1850C p215
Hi	John				Tax	1810	MS Ter	Wayne	MS	NPN AIS
Hi	John				Admin f	1810	MS Ter	Wayne	MS	Sullivant Owen f

LN	FIRSTNAME	IO	FATHER	MOM_SPOUSE	EVENT	EVENTDATE	CITY	COUNTY_PAR	ST	SOURCE
He	John				L	1811	MS Ter	Baldwin	MS	
Hi	John			_Elizabeth	b	1816			KY	MS Tish 1850C p120
Ha	John		Edward?		Settled?	1818		Washington	MS	GA Fran f
He	John			_ Elizabeth	b of son Francis	1818			SC	MS Noxu 1850C p215
He	John				b resof Calvin Grist	1833			MS	MS Noxu 1850C p214
He	John		J D	Clarisa	Twin b	1835			NC	MS Tish 1850C p838
Hi	John				C	1840		DeSoto	MS	p107
He	John			_ Elizabeth?	C	1840		Noxubee	MS	p97
Hi	John				C	1840		Yazoo	MS	p325
Hi	John				Tax	1841		DeSoto	MS	AIS#4
He	John			_ Elizabeth?	Tax	1841		Noxubee	MS	AIS#4
Hi	John				Tax	1841		Yazoo	MS	AIS#4
Hi	John				Tax	1845		DeSoto	MS	AIS#4
He	John			_ Elizabeth?	Tax	1845		Noxubee	MS	AIS#4
Hi	John				Tax	1845		Yazoo	MS	AIS#4
He	John		Wright	Elizabeth	b	1847			MS	MS Leak 1850C p26
Hi	John			_Grizzard Elizabeth	m	01 Dec 1850		Yazoo	MS	IGI
Hi	John			_Woodruff Mary	m	20 Jul 1852		Yazoo	MS	IGI
He	John			_Donahoo Elizabeth	m	16 Jun 1855		Tishomingo	MS	IGI
He	John			_Rite Fanny	m	06 Sep 1869		Lee	MS	IGI
Ha	John	A		_Billingslea Sarah H	m	09 Jun 1853		Madison	MS	IGI
Ha	John	A		_Coates Julia E S	m	30 Aug 1855		Leake	MS	IGI
He	John	Al	E N	Annie	b d19Jun1905	30 Sep 1895		Kemper	MS	Henson Cem
He	John	G			b of dau Parthenia	1848		Lauderdale	MS	1850C IGI
Ha	John	J		_Smith Emily A	m	05 Jan 1853		Yazoo	MS	IGI
He	John	L		_ Jane L	b of dau Anna C	1835			MS	AR Newt 1850C p11
He	John	Lu		_Kinningham Mary Jane 2	b of dau Lucy KY	04 Jul 1856		Tishomingo	MS	IGI
He	John	Lu		_Alexander E H Mrs 3	m	01 Feb 1877		Prentiss	MS	IGI
He	John	M		_Snowden Cora	m	29 Oct 1857		Monroe	MS	IGI
He	John	S	Andrew	_ Mardis Anna Elisa	b	1840		Kemper	MS	1850C #485
He	John	S	Andrew	_ Mardis Ann Eliza	b d28Oct1920	07 Oct 1840		Kemper	MS	TX Fisher d
He	John	S	Andrew	_Mardis Ann Eliza	b	1842		Kemper	MS	1860C #401
He	John	S	Andrew	_ Mardis Ann Eliza	War Cvl enl CoI 5MS	03 Aug 1861		Kemper	MS	GA POW taken
He	John	T	Lazarus	_Harriet E	b mom Ceny/Carry	1828			AL	MS Choc 1850C# 148
He	John	W		_ Merritt Opelia Angeln	b d1884	1844			AL	MS Monr t
He	John	W		_Merritt Ophelia Angeli	m	14 Dec 1865		Monroe	MS	IGI
Hi	John	W		_Griffin Sallie C	m	27 Oct 1881		Amite	MS	IGI

LN	FIRSTNAME	IO	FATHER	MOM_SPOUSE	EVENT	EVENTDATE	CITY	COUNTY_PAR	ST	SOURCE
Hi	Johnathan				C 45+	1820		Pike	MS	300001 30010 p26
Ha	Joseph			_Elizabeth	b	1828			GA	MS Scot 1860C p16
He	Joseph		John Luthe	Hester	b	1842		Prentis	MS	
Hi	Joseph			_Palmer Mary	m	16 Nov 1870		Marshall	MS	IGI
He	Joseph			_Boyd Sarah	m Joe	22 Mar 1883		Tallahatch	MS	IGI
He	Joseph	Ca		_ Clark Harriet	b HomesteadCert#2795	1833		Anson?	NC	MS Kemp 1885
He	Joseph	Ca		_Clark Harriet Ann 1	b Joseph Calhoun	07 Dec 1835		Anson?	NC	MS Kemp d1893
He	Joseph	Ca		_ Clark Harriet 1	b	1835		Anson?	NC	MS Kemp 1880C p1288
He	Joseph	Ca		_ Clark Harriet 1	L 160 Acr	12 Jan 1879		Kemper	MS	S24T11R14
He	Joseph	Ca		_ Clark Harriet 1	Homestead Final proo	27 Dec 1884	Pea Ridge	Kemper	MS	Dees Jn wit
He	Joseph	Ca		_Little Mildred 2	L 160 Acr Patented	25 May 1885		Kemper	MS	S24T11R14
He	Joseph	E			War Cvl Union CoH	1863			MS	2ndInf NARS
Hi	Joseph	J	John	Elizabeth	b	1848			MS	MS Tish 1850C p120
He	Josephine		William	McDonald	b	1830			LA	MS Leak 1850C p26
He	Josephine	L		_Henson William D	m	24 Apr 1856		Leake	MS	IGI
He	Joshua		J D	Clarisa	b	1838			AL	MS Tish 1850C p838
He	Joshua	H			War Cvl CoD Pvt	1863			MS	26thInf NARS
He	Joshua	L		_Story Margaret	m	19 Jul 1859		Tippah	MS	IGI
He	Joshua	L			War Cvl CoL&E Capt	1863		Tippah	MS	2nd MS Inf
He	Julia			_Lawrence Randolph	m	10 Jul 1875		Coahoma	MS	IGI
Ha	Julia			_Johnson Major Major	m	29 May 1875		Leake	MS	IGI
Hi	June		Eli M	Biggers_Brown Jim	b Lillia	1851			NC	MS Monr t
Ha	Kate			_Carpenter William	m	08 Oct 1881		Perry	MS	IGI
Ha	Keziah			_Guest Zachiah R	m Kizziah	08 Sep 1868		Yazoo	MS	IGI
He	Laura		Richard	_Clark Hugh	b C under Clark	1826			SC	MS Kemp 1860C p82
Ha	Lawson				Land Ofc	12 Jul 1833		Lowdnes	MS	Williford Lawson?
He	Lazarus			_ Ceny/Carry	b	1786			NC	MS Choc 1850C #148
He	Lazarus			_ Ceny/Carry	b res of R Lawler	1786			NC	MS Choc 1860C #1478
He	Lazarus			_ Cenny/Carry	War 1812 enl	1813		Pendleton	SC	MS Choc Pen 1851
He	Lazarus			_ Cenny/Carry	Pen Appl War 1812	12 Apr 1851		Choctaw	MS	BL rec'd
He	Levi			_ Korntz Martha	b d26Aug1915	27 Jul 1834				MS Overlta? res
He	Levi				b resof Calvin Grist	1836			MS	MS Noxu 1850C p214
Ha	Lewellyn			_Johnson Nancy	m	09 Jan 1881		Yazoo	MS	IGI
He	Lillia		Eli M	_Brown Jim	m June	28 Nov 1872		Monroe	MS	Biggers mom
He	Lizzie	Le			Ward of J M Henson	07 Jan 1870		Tuscaloosa	AL	MS Monr res
He	Lonie		E N	Annie	b d21Jan1887	01 Dec 1886		Kemper	MS	Henson Cem
Ha	Lucendy			_Benson James A	m	20 Dec 1841		Monroe	MS	IGI

LN	FIRSTNAME	IO	FATHER	MOM_SPOUSE	EVENT	EVENTDATE	CITY	COUNTY_PAR	ST	SOURCE
He	Lucy	KY	John Luthe	Kinningham_Young Wm Mar	b	04 Jul 1856		Tishamingo	MS	IGI
He	Lucy	KY	John Luthe	_Young William Marion	m	08 Jan 1878		Prentiss	MS	IGI
Hi	Lucy	M		_Young John	m	27 Nov 1871		Lee	MS	IGI
Hi	M	A		_Cunningham R D	m	14 Dec 1868		Monroe	MS	IGI
Ha	M	C		_McCrary S S	m	27 Dec 1866		Tallahatch	MS	IGI
Hi	M	E		_Lea W J	m	03 Dec 1873		Amite	MS	IGI
He	M	E		_Hanna R F	m	17 Dec 1878		Yalobusha	MS	IGI
He	M	F		_Carpenter J M	m	11 Dec 1873		Tippah	MS	IGI
He	M	K		_Anderson F E	m	12 Dec 1875		Tippah	MS	IGI
He	M	R		_Hopkins J A	m	27 Jan 1869		Tippah	MS	IGI
He	Madie	Al		_Baker W J	m	26 Dec 1882		Tallahatch	MS	IGI
Hi	Malinda		Henry W	_Owens John H	m	01 Jan 1866		Tishamingo	MS	GA Walk f
He	Malinda		Henry W	Pinelope	d	1867		Prentiss	MS	GA Walk f
He	Malissa		E D		b	1857		Kemper	MS	1860C #577
He	Malissa	E	Edward	Mary M	b	1856		Kemper	MS	1870C #251
He	Malissa	E	Edward	Mary M	b	1857		Kemper	MS	1860C #395
Hi	Malissa	F		_Boykin William Jasper	m	03 Jan 1871		Clarke	MS	IGI
Ha	Margaret			_Watsen Elisha	m	16 Nov 1873		Lafayette	MS	IGI
He	Margaret	F		_Harris William F	m	03 Feb 1876		Yazoo	MS	IGI
He	Martha		John Luthe	Hester	b Mattie	1840		Prentis	MS	
He	Martha		Wright	Elizabeth	b	1845			MS	MS Leak 1850C p26
Ha	Martha			_Furguson A M C	m	30 Aug 1865		Leake	MS	IGI
Hi	Martha			_Land William	m	02 Sep 1875		Monroe	MS	IGI
Hi	Martha	A	John	Elizabeth	b	1845			MS	MS Tish 1850C p120
Ha	Martha	E		_Scarbrough Jn W Dr	b d1873	1828			MS	MS Goodspeeds Hist
Ha	Martha	Ja		_Saxon Samuel	m	22 Dec 1842		Leake	MS	Harris? IGI
Ha	Martha	R		_Edwards John	m	02 Aug 1866		Leake	MS	IGI
He	Mary			_Johnson John	m	17 Feb 1777		Leake	MS	IGI
Hi	Mary			_Standard Lowelsa	m	05 Jan 1830		Warren	MS	IGI
He	Mary		J	Lavinia	b	1839			TN	MS Tish 1850C p22
He	Mary			_Grist Calvin	m	10 Sep 1843		Noxubee	MS	Greer? IGI
Hi	Mary			_Austin John B	m	19 May 1858		Sunflower	MS	IGI
He	Mary			_Conklin James E	m	13 Apr 1880		Warren	MS	IGI
He	Mary	An		_Haney Ephraim F	m	12 Sep 1855		Tishamingo	MS	IGI
Ha	Mary	C		_Lammons H A	m	14 Mar 1872		Yazoo	MS	IGI
Hi	Mary	De		_Carter Hanibal	b Mary Delia				MS	MS Fam R Rev Sold p50
Hy	Mary	E		_Muir James G	m	23 Jan 1848		Claiborne	MS	IGI

88

LN	FIRSTNAME	IO	FATHER	MOM_SPOUSE	EVENT	EVENTDATE	CITY	COUNTY_PAR	ST	SOURCE
Hi	Mary	E		_Kelly F	m	07 Mar 1867		Tallahatch	MS	IGI
He	Mary	E		_Stone G W	m	02 Sep 1869		Tallahatch	MS	IGI
Hi	Mary	E		_Monroe Stephen L	m	29 Nov 1882		Hinds	MS	IGI
Ha	Mary	Fr		_Bridges John Patrick	m	19 Apr 1882	Carthage	Leake	MS	IGI
Hi	Mary	Ja		_Bailey W B	m	06 Jan 1881		Tallahatch	MS	IGI
He	Mary	Lo	Joseph Cal	_Hudnall James P	b d1929	02 Jun 1878	Bluff Spri	Kemper	MS	Clark mom
He	Mary	Re	Richard	Francis_Mardis John	b	1835			AL	MS Kemp 1870C
He	Mary	Re	Richard	Francis_Mardis John	b	1835		Bibb?	AL	MS Kemp 1850C #486
He	Mary	Re	Richard	_Mardis John W	b in res J Perkins	1836			AL	MS Kemp 1860C #402
He	Mathew				C	1840		Tippah	MS	p189
He	Mathew				C	1840		Tippah	MS	p208
He	Mathew				Tax	1841		Tippah	MS	AIS#4
He	Mathew				Tax	1845		Tippah	MS	AIS#4
He	Matilda		Lazarus	Ceny/Carry_Lollar Redde	b	1834		Tuscaloosa	AL	MS Choc 1850C #148
He	Matilda		Lazarus	_Lollar Reden Jasper	m	1851		Choctaw	MS	
Ha	Michael			_Kassler Josephine	m	25 Sep 1871		Hinds	MS	IGI
He	Minerva		Wright	Elizabeth	b	1841		Bibb?	AL	MS Leak 1850C p26
He	Minerva		Andrew	Sarah E	b	1841		Kemper	MS	1850C #485
Ha	N			_Braugh Elizabeth	m	11 Feb 1845		Madison	MS	IGI
He	Nancy		Wright	Elizabeth	b	1836			AL	MS Leak 1850C p26
Hi	Nancy		Brooks	_Adams John	m	05 Oct 1837		Anson	NC	MS t
He	Nancy				b C res of C Grist	1838			MS	MS Noxu 1850C p214
He	Nancy		George Wa	Tackett	b	1851	Tupelo	Lee	MS	IGI .
He	Nancy			_Graham Samuel R	m	17 Apr 1860		Tippah	MS	IGI
Ha	Nancy			_Joiner James	m	04 Feb 1872	Tupelo	Lee	MS	IGI
He	Nancy	J	John L	Jane L	b	1843			MS	AR Newt 1850C p11
Ha	Nancy	J		_Smith W C	m Nannie	01 Jun 1867		Tallahatch	MS	IGI
He	Nancy	M	Henry W?	_Owens A F	m	18 Jan 1866		Tishomingo	MS	GA Walk f
He	Nancy	Mi	Andrew	Sarah	b Minerva	1844		Kemper	MS	1860C #401
Hi	Nancy	P		_Harris H J	m	03 Mar 1878		Simpson	MS	Hilton?
He	Nancy	TN	John Luthe	Kinningham_Rogers W F	b Nannie	20 Feb 1858		Tishomingo	MS	
He	Nancy	TN	John Luthe	_Rogers W F	m	27 Mar 1879		Prentiss	MS	IGI
He	Nathan			_Young Charity	m	09 Feb 1874		Monroe	MS	IGI
Ha	Notley			_Watkins Lizzie S	m	31 Dec 1867		Jefferson	MS	IGI
He	P	H		_Westmoreland M A	m	02 Mar 1869		Lee	MS	IGI
He	Parthenia		John G		b	1848		Lauderdale	MS	1850C IGI
Ha	Phillip				C 20-30	1830		Yazoo	• MS	10001 00001

LN	FIRSTNAME	IO	FATHER	MOM_SPOUSE	EVENT	EVENTDATE	CITY	COUNTY_PAR	ST	SOURCE
Ha	Phillip				C	1840		Holmes	MS	p248
Ha	Phillip				Tax	1841		Holmes	MS	AIS#4
Ha	Phillip				Tax	1845		Holmes	MS	AIS#4
Ha	Phillip			_Oldenbruch Augusta	m	03 Aug 1854		Adams	MS	IGI
Ha	Phillip			_Smith Nancy	m	13 May 1877		Leflore	MS	IGI
Hi	R	A		_Brown Martha Ann	m	16 Feb 1860		Tallahatch	MS	IGI
Hi	R	B		_Wilson L L	m	24 Dec 1885		Choctaw	MS	IGI
Hi	R	H		_Stafford Parmelia	m	29 Oct 1874		DeSoto	MS	IGI
He	R	Z		_Wesson Margaret A	m	05 May 1878		Lee	MS	IGI
Hi	R	Z		_Williams J'J	m	15 Aug 1880		Lee	MS	IGI
He	Rachael			_Markum Thomas	m	07 May 1838		Noxubee	MS	IGI
He	Rebecca			Mary_Satefield	b	1837			AL	MS Kemp 1850C #496
He	Rebecca			_Satefield	m	1857		Kemper	MS	1870C #398
He	Reding		Wright	Elizabeth	b	1848			MS	MS Leak 1850C p26
He	Reuben	W			War Cvl CoI Pvt	1863			MS	40thInf NARS
He	Reuben	We	Andrew	Gray_Ross Elizabeth	b Wesley	1846		Kemper	MS	1860C #401
He	Reuben	We	Andrew	_Ross Elizabeth	m R W	02 Nov 1873		Williamson	TX	MS Kemp b
He	Richard			_ Frances	b in res J Perkins	1793			SC	MS Kemp 1860C #402
He	Richard			_ Frances	b bur Kirland Cem	1793			SC	MS Kemp
He	Richard			_Frances	b	1794			SC	MS Kemp 1850C #486
He	Richard			_ Frances	b of son Wm M	1831			SC	MS Kemp 1850C #486
He	Richard			_ Frances	b of son Wm M	1834			AL	MS Kemp 1860C #396
He	Richard			_ Frances	b of dau Mary R	1836			AL	MS Kemp #402
Hi	Richard			_ Frances	C 21-45 State	1837		Kemper	MS	1M-18 3F-16 1F16+
Hi	Richard			_ Frances	C Slaves 19 40-50	1840		Kemper	MS	3121101 011001 p8
Hi	Richard			_ Frances	Tax	1841		Kemper	MS	AIS#4
He	Richard				L 164.57 Acr Patent	11 Sep 1844		Kemper	MS	S294T11R14 NW 1/4
Hi	Richard			_ Frances	Tax	1845		Kemper	MS	AIS#4
He	Richard			_ Frances	L 39.15 Acr	23 Jan 1854		Kemper	MS	S21T11R14 SW1/4SW1/4
He	Richard				L 39.15 Acr Patent	01 Apr 1856		Kemper	MS	S21T11R14 SW1/4SW1/4
He	Richard				L 78.30 Acr	24 Jan 1860		Kemper	MS	S21T11R14 NW1/4SW1/4
He	Richard				L 78.30 Acr	24 Jan 1860		Kemper	MS	S21T11R14 SW1/4NW1/4
He	Richard			_ Frances	Wid res of	1870		Kemper	MS	Mardis Jn 1870C
He	Richard	Sr	Paul Old		War Rev Pen Res bf	1845		DeSoto	MS	#4909
Hi	Right				C Wright?	1840		Bibb	AL	MS t? p128
Ha	Robert			_Whitney Kate	m	03 May 1870		Yalabusha	MS	IGI
He	S			_Jones William	m	17 Aug 1877		Alcorn	MS	IGI

90

LN	FIRSTNAME	IO	FATHER	MOM_SPOUSE	EVENT	EVENTDATE	CITY	COUNTY_PAR	ST	SOURCE
He	S	A		_Storey Thomas	m	12 Jul 1860		Tippah	MS	IGI
Ha	Sallie			_McCauley H S	m	26 Nov 1885		Yazoo	MS	IGI
He	Sallie	E		_Giddings W H	m	25 Sep 1882		Warren	MS	IGI
He	Sally		John Luthe	Hester	b	1839		Prentis	MS	
He	Samuel		Lazarus	_Elondar	b	1833		Tuscaloosa	AL	MS m
Hi	Sarah			_Avery Simeon	m	30 Dec 1828		Amite	MS	IGI
He	Sarah			_Sullivant William	m	30 Aug 1838		Noxubee	MS	IGI
He	Sarah	J		Lavinia	b	1846			MS	MS Tish 1850C p22
Ha	Sarah			_Broach B R	m	15 Feb 1888		Leake	MS	IGI
Ha	Sarah	A		_Goforth T J	m	09 May 1865		Yalobusha	MS	IGI
Ha	Sarah	An		_Wilson John P	m	25 Dec 1854		Yalobusha	MS	IGI
Hi	Sarah	E	John	Elizabeth	b	1843			MS	MS Tish 1850C p120
He	Sarah	E		_Hamilton Jeremiah	m	16 Feb 1860		Itawamba	MS	IGI
Ha	Sarah	E		_Mills John	m	28 Jul 1875		Leake	MS	IGI
Hi	Sarah	F		_Bryan William	m	05 Jun 1861		Yalobusha	MS	IGI
Hi	Sarah	H		_Allen F J	m	13 Dec 1866		Leake	MS	IGI
He	Stephen		John Luthe	Hester	b	1843		Tishomingo	MS	
Hi	Stephen	J	John	Elizabeth	b	1850			MS	MS Tish 1850C p120
Hi	T	F		_Wall Nellie	m	06 Oct 1880		Carroll	MS	IGI
He	T	J		_Clemons Mary A	m	03 Apr 1867		Tishomingo	MS	IGI
He	T	O		_Moore Katie	m	02 Nov 1879		Prentiss	MS	IGI
He	T	O		_Tucker Tennie	m	22 Nov 1883		Prentiss	MS	IGI
Hi	T	R		_McGowan Antonia	m	27 Sep 1876		Hinds	MS	IGI .
He	Thomas			_Mary	Planter b	1806			SC	MS Noxu 1850C p215
Ha	Thomas			_Ryan Mary	b d03Aug1900	12 Aug 1810	Ocean Spri	Jackson	MS	Gen Exch of MS V12
He	Thomas				L Sales Ofc 1837-	1834		Noxubee	MS	BkA
He	Thomas			_ Mary	b of dau Easter	1836			SC	MS Noxu 1850C
He	Thomas				b res Jms Jackson	1837			MS	TX Aust 1850C p93
He	Thomas				C	1840		Noxubee	MS	p97
He	Thomas				Tax	1841		Noxubee	MS	AIS#4
He	Thomas				Tax	1845		Noxubee	MS	AIS#4
He	Thomas				b C res of Jernigin	1849			MS	MS Noxu 1850C p243
He	Thomas		Andrew	Sarah E	b	1854		Kemper	MS	1860C #401
He	Thomas	L	William Ma	Little_Sadie 1	b d03Mar1940				MS	Kemp bur Magnolia
He	Thomas	L	William Ma	_Embry 2	b d03Mar1940				MS	Kemp bur Magnolia
Ha	Thornwald			_Parke Mamie	m	13 Feb 1885		Lauderdale	MS	IGI
Hi	Valley			_Basye Albert	m	07 Jan 1880		Hinds	MS	IGI

LN	FIRSTNAME	IO	FATHER	MOM_SPOUSE	EVENT	EVENTDATE	CITY	COUNTY_PAR	ST	SOURCE
Hi	Virgain	M		_Manning J P	m	26 Feb 1885		Sunflower	MS	IGI
Hi	W	A		_Kennedy Mary J	m	24 Apr 1873		Warren	MS	IGI
He	W	D		_Stubblefield Sallie	m	22 Jan 1882		Yazoo	MS	IGI
Ha	W	H		_Pope Susan	m	27 Oct 1885		Marion	MS	IGI
He	W	J		_Vaughn J E	m	25 Feb 1875		Oktibbeha	MS	IGI
He	W	S		_George Annie	m	04 Nov 1882		DeSoto	MS	IGI
He	Wesley		Andrew	Sarah	b Reuben Wesley	1842		Kemper	MS	1850C #485
Hi	William			_Barefield Polly	m	17 Oct 1826	Vicksburg	Warren	MS	NC f IGI
He	William		Thomas	Mary	b	1832			SC	MS Noxu 1850C p215
He	William				C	1840		Tippah	MS	p182
Ha	William				C	1840		Yazoo	MS	p316
He	William				Tax	1841		Tippah	MS	AIS#4
Ha	William				Tax	1841		Yazoo	MS	AIS#4
Hi	William			_David Mary A	m	14 Feb 1843		Marshall	MS	IGI
He	William				Tax	1845		Tippah	MS	AIS#4
Ha	William				Tax	1845		Yazoo	MS	AIS#4
He	William		John Luthe	Kinningham	b	1847		Prentis	MS	
He	William			_Winn Martha J	m	26 Mar 1854		Noxubee	MS	IGI
Hi	William			_Lemmons Margaret E	m	24 Jan 1872		Yazoo	MS	IGI
He	William				L f state of MS	19 Oct 1887		Kemper	MS	
Hi	William	A	William	_Countryman Margaret	m	24 Jun 1852	Vicksburg	Warren	MS	Barfield mom IGI
He	William	D		_Henson Josephine L	m	24 Apr 1856		Leake	MS	IGI
He	William	D			War Cvl CoH 2nd Lt	1863			MS	40thInf NARS
He	William	J		_ONeal Bertha	m	06 Mar 1855		Lauderdale	MS	IGI
He	William	Jr	William Sr	McDonald	b	1829			LA	MS Leak 1850C p26
Hi	William	K		_Miller Elizabeth	m	07 Nov 1873		Marshall	MS	IGI
He	William	M	Richard	_Margaret	b	1831			SC	MS Kemp 1850C #497
He	William	M	Richard	Frances_Margaret	b	1834			AL	MS Kemp 1860C #396
He	William	Ma	Joseph Cal	Clark_Little Mildred	b Wm Martin	30 Jan 1866			MS	MS Kemp res
He	William	Ma	Joseph Cal	_Little Mildred	m d28Jan1934	18 Jul 1888		Kemper	MS	MS Kemp res
He	William	Ra		_Robinson Susan E	m	14 Mar 1876		Tallahatch	MS	IGI
He	William	Sr		_ McDonald Harriet	b	03 Jul 1791			NC	MS Jeff t
He	William	Sr		_ McDonald Harriet	Wid b	1798			GA	MS Leak 1850C p26
He	William	Sr		_McDonald Harriet	m	08 Nov 1816		Jefferson	MS	MS Fam R Rev Soldier
He	William	Sr		_ McDonald Harriet	C 26-45	1820		Jefferson	MS	100010 01000 p54
He	William	Sr		_ McDonald Harriet	b of son Wm	1829			LA	MS Leake 1850C
He	William	Sr		_ Harriet McDonald	d	10 Feb 1835	Clinton	Hinds	MS	

92

LN	FIRSTNAME	IO	FATHER	MOM_SPOUSE	EVENT	EVENTDATE	CITY	COUNTY_PAR	ST	SOURCE
He	William	Sr		_ McDonald Harriet	C wid	1840		Leake	MS	p28
He	William	Sr		_ McDonald Harriet	Wid Tax	1841		Leake	MS	AIS#4
He	William	Sr		_ McDonald Harriet	Wid Tax	1845		Leake	MS	AIS#4
He	William	Sr		_ McDonald Harriet	Wid d	1873		Copiah	MS	Cem & Bible R of MS
He	William	W		_Grady Martha Ann	m	17 Jan 1866		Monroe	MS	IGI
He	Wright			_Elizabeth	b Right?	1814			NC	MS Leak 1850C p26

INDEX TO ALLIED FAMILY NAMES

Hanson, Henson, Hinson, Hynson are indexed within each state

Birrem J W M	38
Birse, J R	35
Bishop, Sarah Nancy	21
Bizer, Harriet	81
Black, Alexander	58
Black, William W	57
Blackbune, Josephine H	85
Blackney, Mary	3
Blair, Margaret	30, 33, 38, 39, 53, 54, 57
Blanton, Charles	66
Blaylock, Elizabeth	27, 32, 33, 35, 37
Bolen, Thomas	82
Bonds, Mattie	43
Bonner	74
Boon, Rachael	85
Boon, William	38
Boone	54
Booth, Caroline Priscilla	30, 39, 43, 45, 47, 54, 60, 72
Bostick, Abraham J	28
Boston, H	7, 15
Boswell, Sarah	70, 71
Bowers, Daniel	35
Bowl, Ommie M	23
Bowles, Georgia Ann	82
Bowman, Fannie Mae	2
Boyd, Emma L	83
Boyd, Sarah	87
Boykin, William Jasper	88
Boykins, Mary J	3, 8, 20, 81
Bradshaw, William	35
Brady, John N	28
Brand, Mary	52
Brandon, Mary M	36
Branel	52
Brantley, Ann Elizabeth	34, 67, 76
Brantlies Dist	64, 73
Braugh, Elizabeth	89
Brebner, Elizabeth	23
Bridges, John Patrick	89
Brinkley, Missouri	83
Brisco	34
Britton, James H	58
Broach, B R	91
Broadway, Elizabeth	79
Brown,	52, 65
Brown, Althis Ann	23
Brown, Charlie S	81
Brown, Jane	50
Brown, Jim	87
Brown, Louisa	27
Brown, Martha Ann	90
Brown, Maude R	6

Brown, R D	81
Browning	65
Browning, Esther	23
Bruce, Rebecca	50
Bruce, Samuel G	58
Bruce, Sarah	76
Bryan, William	91
Bryant, William J	59
Buckley, B G	82
Buleson, Michael	16
Bumpass, Ethelinda J	83
Bundy, Louisa Ann	21, 23, 24, 70
Burch, John Miles	33
Burchets Dist	45, 46, 49, 68
Burger, Charles	38
Burney, Etta	25
Burris, Allen	56
Burson, Phoebe J	7
Bush, Nancy Ann	3, 21
Buston	9
Butler, Dora Ann	22
Butler, Ellen	21
Butler, George E	67
Butler, M	46
Butts Co	47
Byers	35
Byrd	43
Byrd, Ann	77
Cain, Amanda	37, 55
Caldwell, W	28
Calway	74
Camp, T Pascal	62
Camp, William T	61
Candler, Sam	43
Cannady, Eliza	21, 24, 28, 36, 38, 40, 53, 57, 58, 70
Cannady, Elizabeth	24, 27, 70
Canten, Charles	66
Cardin, John	47
Carpenter, Anna	36
Carpenter, J M	88
Carpenter, William	87
Carroll	49
Carroll, Jesse	35
Carroll, Sallie	70
Carter, Americus	67
Carter, Hanibal	88
Carter, James	34
Carter, John J	63
Cartlidge, Rebecca Ann	50
Cartwright, Martha	27, 30, 53, 58, 59, 61, 76
Cathy, Nancy	6
Cats, John	2, 28

Litchfield, Mary	40	McCrary, Mary J	22
Little, Mildred	82, 87, 91, 92	McCrary, S S	88
Lollar, Redden	15, 89	McCrees Dist	61
Lollar, Riley	3	McDaniel, Frances E	8, 13, 15, 17
Long, Amanda	85	McDonald, Harriet	77, 83, 92, 93
Looney, Abner	58	McDowell, Rebecca	12
Lord, Lillie Mae	76	McDuffie, Nancy	27, 34, 50, 55, 56,
Lott, Mary Jane	34		57, 58, 60, 73, 74,
Lott, Nancy	43, 50		75, 76, 77
Loveless, James	39	McElroy, P	18
Lowe, Martha G	50	McElvy, Clara	22
Lowery, Elizabeth	40	McFall, Dennis	52
Lowry	81	McFarland, Mary	5, 10, 15
Lowry, Lavinia	84	McGowan, Antonia	91
Loyd, Sarah	63	McHan, Arminda	35
Lucas	68	McLauren, Callie	82
Luckett, O A	83	McLeod	30
Lumpkins Dist	32, 37, 45, 46, 50,	McLeroy, Rachael	37
	52, 61, 68, 74	McNeil, James	62
Luter, Mary Ann	85	McSweeny, Sopia	80
Lyles, Fannie	8	Meacham, Lynda Gayle	37
Lyman, Hall Jr	21	Meafre	33
Lynch, Thomas	77	Melton, Frances	53
Lynches Dist	42, 49, 68	Menard, John	23
Mahoney, S	67	Merrill, Franklin	35
Mainer, Pinelope	38	Merritt, Opelia Angeline	11, 86
Manis, Reubin	60	Middlebrook, John Edward	2
Mann	60	Middleton	25
Mann, J H	80	Middleton, Elizabeth	81
Mann, Martha	38, 83	Middletons Dist	46
Manning, J P	92	Miles	49
Manors, John	51	Miles, A R	81
Marbury, Leonard	69	Miller, Arthur	21
Mardis, Ann Eliza	52, 86	Miller, Elizabeth	92
Mardis, John	14, 89, 90	Miller, Frances	83
Markum, Thomas	90	Miller, George	46
Marseys Dist	61	Mills, Frances N	84
Martin, John	45	Mills, John	91
Martin, Mary	12	Mills, Julia	22
Masters, Mary Ann	71	Mitchell, Charles	22
Mathews, W W	56, 68	Mitchell, John	59
Mathews, William	34	Mitchell, Nelson	23
Mathis, William	34, 35, 60	Mobley, Mildred J	60
Matteson, Clarence	24	Monroe, Stephen L	89
Matthison, Ruth	21	Montgomery, H	48
Mattox, Wilma	76	Moody, Daniel	64
Maxwell, Rhoda	27	Moore, Daniel	58
McAfee, Elizabeth	24	Moore, Green	82
McCall	25	Moore, Jane	2, 10, 12, 13, 29,
McCalpin	49		30, 55, 56, 57, 71
McCauley, H S	91	Moore, Katie	91
McCay, Henry K, Genl	31	Moore, Louisa A	77
McCoy	65, 74	Moore, Martha A	21, 22, 23, 24, 39
McCoy, Mary Elizabeth	81		

ALLIED FAMILY NAMES...cont.

Radford, Harry	51	Scoggins, David	75
Rainwater, James	67	Scott, David B	35
Ramsey, Nancy	73, 75	Scovalls Dist	31
Ramsey, Wade Hampton	66	Scrivner, Callie	80
Randle	48, 51	Scroggins, Millinton	64
Randolph	48	Scruggs, Rebecca	35, 53, 54, 77
Ransom, Ed	67	Sealy, Mary Ann	4
Ray, Rufus Sr	80	Sellars, Peter	56
Redus, James C	83	Sellers, William	66
Reece, Jane	60	Sexton, Christopher	3
Reece, Mary	75	Shackley, Elizabeth	2, 5, 6, 9, 12, 13,
Reed, George	67, 71		16, 17, 19
Reed, Martha L	71, 77		
Reeves	41	Shadwick, Jincy A	29
Reeves, Augusta	32, 33	Shannon, Adeline	83
Reeves, Samuel	34	Shelton, Louisa	29
Reynolds, Margaret	72	Shephearde, Martha J	34
Rhodes, Samuel	27	Shipman, Lucinda	72
Rice, Ann	64	Shockley, Elizabeth	50
Richardson, Alice B	84	Short, Elizabeth	38
Rimes, Levinia	83	Short, Mary B	37
Rite, Fanny	86	Shouse, Carrie E	40
Rivere, Mary E	8	Silvey, Jesse	45
Roberson, Martha E	20	Simmons, Charles	81
Roberts, John	10	Simms, James	35
Roberts, Samson W	38	Simms, John D	56
Robertson, Calvin L	67	Sims, Betty Ann	49
Robertson, Elenor	8	Sims, Louisa	38
Robinson, James	60	Sims, Peggy	27, 28, 34, 37, 58,
Robinson, Jesse	36		63, 64, 65
Robinson, Nancy	56	Sims, William	64
Robinson, Susan E	92	Slater, Adeline	83
Rodgers, Chesley	64	Slaughter, Beverly	25
Rogers	46, 70	Slaughter, Malinda	11
Rogers, David	62	Smathers, Louisa	34, 36
Rogers, W F	89	Smith	6, 9, 11, 16, 17,
Rogers, William A	57		33, 40, 61, 73,
Roper, Charles F	62	Smith Wid	43
Rosebells, Cav	5	Smith, Amanda	38
Ross, Elizabeth	90	Smith, Elizabeth F	70
Ruddle	39	Smith, Emily A	86
Rushing, Lucinda	3, 14, 18	Smith, George Blakely	57
Russell, Alice	83	Smith, George W Capt	24
Ryan, Mary	91	Smith, Green Jackson	66
Sanders, Areaney	18	Smith, H P MD	47
Sanders, James	34	Smith, John	36
Sanders, Thomas A	64	Smith, Joshua	67
Sandifer, Peter H	82	Smith, Mary Louise	37
Sanford, Asa	54	Smith, Matilda	55
Sartor, Sarah H	2, 3, 10, 29, 30	Smith, N H	28
Sartor, William C	13	Smith, Nancy	90
Satefield	16, 79, 90	Smith, W C	89
Saxon, Samuel	88	Smith, William	85
Scarbrough, John W Dr	88	Smiths Dist	42, 46, 67
		Smiths Legion	32

ALLIED FAMILY NAMES...cont.

Warren, Martha Ellen	2, 5, 6, 7, 8, 13, 15, 17	Williams, Henry	15
Warrens Dist	50	Williams, J J	90
Warrick, Salena	53	Williams, Johnathan	58
Watkins, Abner	28	Williams, M C	84
Watkins, Lizzie	89	Williams, Nancy	51
Watkins, Mary Ann wid	1	Williams, Rena	72
Watsen, Elisha	88	Williams, Susan F	44
Watsen, Elizabeth	84	Williams, William	34
Watson, Maggie	85	Williams, William S	32
Watson, William M	60	Williamson, Benjamin	23
Watsons Dist	29	Williamson, Macaja	40
Welbourne, P	74	Wilson, A I	45
Weldon, Johnny B	56	Wilson, Alice Mrs	72
Wells	34	Wilson, John P	91
Wesson, Bammie	80	Wilson, L L	90
Wesson, Douglas	80	Wilson, Mary	85
Wesson, Margaret	90	Winborn, Donnie	80
West	11	Winn, Martha J	92
West, Elizabeth	53	Winnes Dist	25
West, John	58	Wisenhunt, Arthur	67
Westbrook	47	Witchers Co	61
Westbrook, Moses	62	Wofford, Louisa	37, 42
Westmoreland, M A	89	Wood, Lucindy	72
Whatley, Wilson	58	Wood, Mahaley	56, 62, 64, 68
Wheeler	52	Wood, Mariah	39
Wheeler, Elizabeth	54	Wood, Polly Ann	59, 76
Wheeler, Robert M	38	Wood, Thomas	35
White	44, 47, 60	Wood, Thomas G	58
White, Nancy C	3, 5, 7, 12, 14, 15, 17, 66	Woodbury, John H	23
		Woodland, Thomas	57
White, Rebecca	45	Woodley, Nancy A	50
White, Robert	56	Woodruff, Mary	86
White, Sarah Ann	85	Woolfork, Jordan	30
White, Susannah	79	Worlix, Sarah	53
White, Thomas	79	Wray, Elizabeth Sophia	31, 63
Whitley, Good	2	Wright, Hallie	84
Whitlow	31	Wrights Dist	41, 49, 51, 68
Whitney, Kate	90	Wyatt, George B	21
Whitten	2, 13, 27, 34, 57, 77	Yancy, Cyrus	51
		Yarbrough, M E	85
Whitton, Mary Ann	67, 77	Yarbrough, Sarah	44
Whitton, William	31	Yates	61
Wigington, Sarah	35	Yather, Dovia	35
Wilcox, Andrew Jackson	36	Yeates, John	61
Wilcox, Jeff Dr	58	Young, Charity	89
Wilder, Nancy	63	Young, John	88
Wiley, A	7, 16	Young, K	75
Wiley, Rebecca Ellen	7, 8, 42	Young, Tony	22
Wiley, Sarah	32, 33, 44, 45	Young, William Marion	88
Wilies	63, 70		
Wilkinson, Malinda	10, 11		
Willard, Catherine	50		
Williams, Edwin J	33		

www.ingramcontent.com/pod-product-compliance
Lightning Source LLC
Chambersburg PA
CBHW080336270326
41927CB00014B/3240